THE DAYS I KNEW

Lillie Langtry

PHOTO BY W. & D. DOWNEY

THE DAYS I KNEW

By
LILLIE LANGTRY
(LADY DE BATHE)

With a Foreword by
RICHARD LE GALLIENNE

Illustrated

Panoply Publications
North Hollywood, California

Copyright 2005 by Panoply Publications.
Published in the United States of America
by Panoply Publications.
All rights reserved.
Printed in the United States of America.

ISBN: 1-886571-13-9

Publishing History:
1925 -- George H. Doran Company, New York, New York
2005 -- Panoply Publications, North Hollywood, California

Table of Contents

Illustrations

PROLOGUE

If Lillie Langtry had put an exclamation point after the title of her autobiography it still wouldn't have done justice to the extraordinary life this beautiful lady led. But, typical of the dignified Mrs. Langtry, she chose not to sensationalize her life story with a title that could have been, deservedly, much more provocative. Instead, she chose to title her book, simply, "The Days I Knew." But what days they were! Filled with enough events and personalities to make Lillie Langtry not only one of the most fascinating women of the Victorian-Edwardian eras, but of all times, her autobiography is as compelling as was her event-filled life.

Lillie had it all. Beauty, brains, charm, business acumen. If she had lived in the 21st century she would easily have qualified as one of the most well-known women of modern times. As it was, she created a sensation from the moment she settled in London as the young bride of Edward Langtry. She was soon the most sought after "professional beauty" of London's top artists and photographers. She became close friends with Oscar Wilde and much of London's literati.. And she soon was the acknowledged mistress of Prince Albert-Edward, Queen Victoria's son and the future King Edward VII of England.

But that's just the beginning. Lillie Langtry's life story is so engrossing that it's hard to believe one woman could have had such a full life, but that she did. A list of Lillie's close friends and acquaintances would read like a who's who. Not only did she know kings and queens and presidents and prime ministers, but such diverse personages as Judge Roy Bean, who claimed to have named a town after her in Texas, to Rudyard Kipling were part of her life story.

Despite having no stage training at all, Lillie decided to become an actress and in no time she was the most popular and successful performer in the world. She owned a theater in London, land in California, and some of the top race horses in England. She was probably the first person to be used in product endorsement advertising and she was the darling of what today is called the tabloid press. She was admired and mobbed by fans all over the world, much like today's rock stars and actors. While Lillie has been portrayed in two motion pictures dealing with Judge Roy Bean, it is understandable why there have never been any movies made entirely about her. There's just too much to tell in the approximately two hours usually allotted to feature films. But, to its credit, Masterpiece Theater produced a series on the fabulous lady in 1978 and needed 13 hours to do her story justice.

Now it's time to let Lillie tell it herself. As Richard Le Gallienne says in his foreword, she does it with aplomb and humor. History owes a big thanks to this enchanting woman for taking the time and effort to tell us about the marvelous days she knew.

FOREWORD

Of all forms of fame that of Beauty is the greatest, in that it is the simplest, for it is not the fame of achievement, of which one can trace the beginnings and follow the development, but it is the fame of a miracle. It is man's wonder at a perfect thing suddenly before his eyes, he knows not how. It is his adoration of a mystery — for beauty belongs to the supernatural. In this way the fame of Helen of Troy is in its essence greater, because stranger, than that of Homer, for the greatest poet is still a man, but a beautiful woman is something more than a woman. She belongs with such marvels as the moon and the sea.

To have been the representative of Beauty in one's own time, its very symbol, is a peculiarly aristocratic form of immortality. It is nearest to the fame of the gods. It is like being some immortal statue, as though one should be the Venus de Milo in real life. Such fame is at once the most ancient and the most romantic, and such fame has been Mrs. Langtry's all her days.

Born into an age of great symbolic personalities, as Tennyson meant poetry, Mr. Gladstone politics, Sarah Bernhardt and Henry Irving the stage, Mrs. Langtry, the "lily" that suddenly flowered in Jersey, meant Beauty personified; and almost instantly she meant that, not only for London draw-ing–rooms, but for the whole world. For backwoodsmen in America, as well as for poets and painters in England, "the Jersey Lily" became immediately the current symbol of the loveliness of woman.

Not since the lily of the valley in Solomon's Songs has any lily in life or literature won so universal a fame. There were other women famous for their beauty when hers came to bloom, women to whom she pays self–forgetful tribute in the following pages, but there was not one whose beauty had that quality of universality which made hers a beauty, not for England alone, but, so to say, Beauty Internationalised. And still her name means just that.

It must be a very strange thing to know oneself the most beautiful woman in the world. Many women, doubtless, think themselves that, but to know it by every form of testimony and tribute, from kings to cowboys, to have been mobbed, almost crushed to death, on account of it, to have seen it written in letters of fire upon the sky, to have had towns named after you because of your beauty: here is evidence that would bring conviction to the least vain of women — and that Mrs. Langtry is as near being that as any woman can humanly be who has thus had the world at her feet her book very attractively reveals.

That she should be conscious of her own significance in the history of her time is to be expected. For her to ignore it would be the most tasteless of affectations. It would be like the British Museum pretending not to know that it is the British Museum. Her book would have no *raison d'etre* otherwise, and indeed one of its great charms is the simple way in which she accepts the fame of her beauty as a fact — but a fact she is able to write of with a remarkable detachment, in the same spirit of wonder that it should be happening to her as overcame her when, a young girl from Jersey, with but one frock, she suddenly found herself the bewildered idol of London fashionable society.

The history of that one frock is one of her most charming chapters, told with that humour which is the salt of her autobiography, a quality rare

10

indeed in modern autobiographies — for it was evident, too, from the beginning, that, in Meredith's phrase,

This golden head has wit in it . . .
. . . she has that rare gift
To beauty, Common Sense.

This endowment of character is seconded by the cleverness of a pen which many professional writers might envy. The lightness of its touch throughout would make any subject–matter attractive, and its skill is particularly notable in the way it conveys the atmosphere and tone of the various worlds Mrs. Langtry has moved in: the romantic charm of her account of her girlhood days in Jersey, with its skilfully woven references to the picturesque history and customs of the Channel Islands, with their pride of Norman blood to this day; the gay devil–me–carishness of London's smart set, with something still as feudal Olympians, with all their modern sophistication; the worlds of politicians and financiers; the worlds of Ascot and Cowes; the world of writers, painters, and wits; the world of the stage; and last, but not least understandingly, the world of America, all its sides from Fifth Avenue to — Langtry, Texas; that little town with its population of devoted cowboys, on the very edge of Mexico, "down there by the Rio Grande."

I venture to say that among all her trophies Mrs. Langtry values none so much as "Roy Bean's revolver," Roy Bean having been the founder of *her* town. Some years before this relic came into her possession Roy Bean had invited her to visit Langtry. This she was unable to do at that time, but in sending her regrets Mrs. Langtry offered to present an ornamental drinking fountain to the town as a token of her appreciation. But came Roy Bean's quick reply that "it would be quite useless, as the only thing the citizens of Langtry did *not* drink was water." Years afterwards, however, when Roy Bean had handed in his checks, she did visit the town, and she gives a charming, and rather touching, account of her reception from its romantic, gallant inhabitants.

It is delightful to think of her "trudging through the sage–brush and cactus" to "the Jersey Lily Saloon," where her dead admirer had administered justice at the point of the revolver which was afterwards presented to her with this inscription: "Presented by W. H. Dodd, of Langtry, Texas, to Mrs. Lillie Langtry, in honour of her visit to our town. This pistol was formerly the property of Judge Roy Bean. It aided him in finding some of his famous decisions and keeping order west of the Pecos River. It also kept order in the Jersey Lily Saloon. Kindly accept this as a small token of our regards."

I am sure that Mrs. Langtry will agree with me that it was thus reserved for America to pay her the most tremendous, romantic, and touching compliment of her career.

To have been painted by Millais and all the great painters of her time must, of course, have been gratifying, but what portrait at the Royal Academy could compare with Roy Bean's revolver!

To have had Judge Roy Bean at her feet, to have had Oscar Wilde sleeping on her doorstep — so that Mr. Langtry, returning home, stumbled over his prostrate form — to have drawn the sting of Whistler's waspish butterfly, and to have had the austere Mr. Gladstone for one of her admiring intimates, sometimes reading Shakespeare to her, sometimes bringing her books, sometimes giving her good advice (as for instance: "In your professional career, you will receive attacks, personal and critical, just and unjust. Bear them. Never reply and, above all, never rush into print to explain or defend yourself") — this surely is an astonishing gamut of fame.

And to tell of it all so gaily, at once with a girlish enjoyment and grati-

tude, and the *aplomb* of a woman of the great world, is a rare achievement indeed. Never was Beauty Enthroned so comradely human, so rip-
pling with fun, and so wittily alert for all the humour of the multicoloured
scene, in which she has been called to play so distinguished a part.

It is such a book as Helen of Troy might have written, with a laughing
eye on Achilles, Agamemnon, and the other heroes of her disastrous face
— if only she had possessed Mrs. Langtry's sense of humour. But if Helen
had possessed humour there might have been no Trojan war. To unite
beauty and humour is the paradox which Mrs. Langtry here so brilliantly
achieves, in a record which is not only her own story, but the vivid picture
of the Victorian Age at the height of its splendid summer.

RICHARD LE GALLIENNE

THE DAYS I KNEW

Chapter
1

My names are really Emilie Charlotte — both dreadful, to my way of thinking — but, happily, perhaps on account of my skin being unusually white, I was nicknamed "Lillie" very early in life, and that sobriquet has clung to me ever since. An only daughter, with six brothers, named respectively Frank, William, Trevor, Maurice, Clement, and Reginald, I ranked the youngest but one, coming between the last two mentioned. My mother was a Miss Martin, whom my father met, fell in love with, and married during his incumbency of St. Olave's, Southwark, London. At the age of thirty-four, my father, William Corbet Le Breton, became Dean of Jersey, which was destined to be my birthplace.

The appointment had been offered him as soon as it became vacant, but he was then only twenty-nine, and, acting on the advice of his father, who thought him too young for so serious a responsibility, he preferred to remain for a further period in the curacy of St. Olave's. When, five years later, the deanship was bestowed on him, he left London for the island of his birth (with his wife and four elder children), and of which he remained dean until his death in 1888. On leaving St. Olave's, his parishioners presented him with a silver salver lengthily inscribed, one portion of the inscription alluding to his zeal and solicitous care for the poor "whereby he has endeared himself to all who knew him."

My father was educated at Winchester, at that time a week's journey from Jersey, yet the nearest Public School of note. There, as a junior, he was fag to Lord Selborne, who, I believe, once rapped him unmercifully over the head with a frying–pan for not cooking his bacon properly, so I imagine the culinary art was not one of his minor accomplishments. His room–mates at Winchester were Cardwell, Lowe, and Roundell Palmer, who afterwards oddly enough became Ministers in the same Cabinet. From Winchester he went to Oxford, where he became scholar of Pembroke and fellow of Exeter. He was a remarkably handsome man, and widely adored for his geniality and charm of disposition.

His hair turned white at a very early age. Indeed, I never remember it otherwise. His eyes very blue, looked one through and through. He was over six feet in height, of rather ruddy complexion and majestic bearing, a characteristic which he retained throughout his life. I feel I cannot close this description of my Very Reverend father without a frivolous reference to his well–modelled limbs, which were vastly admired in the Island and certainly did credit to the silk stocking he wore as a dean. Perhaps the following anecdote will convey a better idea of his appearance than anything I can say.

At one of Queen Victoria's levees attended by my father, General Sir John Pennefather, who, I have heard, was known in military circles as "Sir Damnsetey Curesgy," presumably on account of his frequent strong language, was also present, and, after regarding the dean attentively for some moments, walked up to him and said, "Do you know, sir, that when you joined the Church, there was a deuced fine sergeant–major spoilt!"

Notwithstanding Sir John's words, I am convinced that the Stage suffered a greater loss than the Army, for my father had the true histrionic gift, and his dramatic talent would have undoubtedly made him a fine actor. He had an extraordinarily retentive memory, which he trained so assiduously in learning by heart a certain amount of poetry every day that it became a difficult matter to find any English or Latin verse which he could not recite verbatim on the instant it was suggested.

My mother was petite and lovely, with blue eyes, a perfect skin and complexion, regular features, curling auburn hair, and the most fascinating smile. Her girlhood was passed at Chelsea, of which parish the father of Charles Kingsley, author of *Water Babies* and *Hypatia,* was rector, and she lived with her widowed mother in close vicinity to the rectory. The families were very intimate, and I know that Charles Kingsley, later in life, described her to one of my brothers as the most bewitchingly beautiful creature he had ever seen. One of the Kingsley brothers wanted to marry her, Henry, I think, who was more her own age.

I have in my possession a book of extracts from the works of various poets, selected for her by Charles Kingsley, so she must have liked poetry as well as music. Being also extremely fond of an open–air life, she rode, drove, and walked a great deal, devoting much of her time to gardening, for she had a passion for flowers and unusual taste in grouping them. Probably it was the healthy life she led which enabled her to retain much of her beauty to the end of her long life of eighty–two years. My mother was very fond of animals and birds, and an incident connected with two of her dumb friends occurs to me.

She had a greyhound called "Hawk," and for a year or two a seagull, which she had found on the seashore with a broken pinion, divided favour with him. She brought Jacko, the seagull, home, mended him up, and he became persona grata at the deanery. Finally, presuming on his popularity, he made short work of a brood of tame young partridges. My mother,

17

in a spirit of justice, tapped him with her riding whip, whereupon Jacko arose in his wrath and sailed away. Twelve months later, while picnicking on the rocks, a gull alighted and began disputing a bone with the dog. It was Jacko! The bird remained during the meal, helping himself to tid–bits from my mother's plate as he used to do. He seemed well pleased to be with us again but I suppose he liked his liberty better, for, when we moved, he took wing to rejoin his companions.

And now, having introduced my family, let me say something about my birthplace, an island which lies some sixteen miles distant from the old province of Normandy, and where many quaint customs survive, and a *terra incognita,* I am sure, to a great many people. As a matter of fact, it is surprising to find how little the average Briton knows of Jersey. To him, it is generally no more than an unimportant speck on the map, and even upon its exact location he is very hazy indeed.

He also seems quite uncertain as to whether its inhabitants are English or French, so I may say at once that they are pure Norman, the Channel Islands being all that remain of the old Duchy of Normandy which con-quered England, and to this day we acknowledge only the sovereignty of the Duke of Normandy, as was shown to be the case in the recent visit of King George V, to Jersey. We are not descendants of the English as the Canadians and Australians are, nor can we be considered as a British Colony, seeing that by ancient charter we are a self–governing political unit. Certain duties devolve upon the *seigneurs* in connection with the reception of their Sovereign Duke, one of which consists of riding into the sea up to the horses' saddle girths to meet him.

We have our own jurisdiction as well as our own assembly, or local parliament. This assembly, or States, as it is termed in Jersey, consists of the lieutenant–governor, bailiff (the civil head), the dean (ecclesiastical head), twelve jurats (aldermen), twelve rectors, twelve connectables (constables), and fourteen deputies. It also includes the crown officers, who are allowed to speak, but not to vote.

The official language of the States, and, indeed, of the churches and law courts, is French, and we natives also speak a *patois* which so nearly resembles the Norman *patois* of the present day that, when travelling in Normandy recently, I found little difficulty in making myself intelligible to the peasants.

The law of Jersey still continues full of picturesque and feudal customs. One of the most curious of these sanctioned survivals is the *clameur de Haro* (the outcry of *Haro*). Although long since abolished in Normandy, the *clameur* may still be raised by any Jerseyman who thinks his rights are challenged or his property threatened. If he wishes to avail himself of this ancient form of protection, he falls upon his knees and, in the presence of two witnesses, cries aloud three times: *"Haro! Haro! Haro! A l'aide, mon prince, on me fait tort!"* (Haro! Haro! Haro! Help, help, my prince! I am being wronged!")

This invocation stays any proceedings on the part of the supposed or real oppressor until the case comes before the court, and, as that local body has a tantalising method of pigeon–holing cases *au greffe* (in the registry office) — in other words, of postponing them indefinitely — it is apt to result in no benefit to either of the belligerents. The "Haro" appealed to is Rollo, the first Duke of Normandy, and I once saw the *clameur* put into practice myself.

Viscount Ranelagh, years ago, bought a pretty bungalow overlooking one of the bays and divided by a narrow lane from a Jerseyman's farm. Finding this passage in bad condition, and regarding it as a joint possession, he magnanimously commenced to improve it, but to this the Jerseyman offered violent opposition, claiming the lane as part of his own property. He preferred it with its deep cart–ruts, and, as often as Lord Tanelagh filled them up, the Jerseyman redug them, finally outwitting the Englishman by digging a deep trench across the debated road during the night. In the morning, falling on his knees, he raised the *clameur de Haro,* and thus made reprisals impossible. Probably the chasm remains to this day, though both disputants have long been in their graves.

The Island of Jersey is studded with old, grey–stone manor houses, which carry with them the title of *seigneur.* Many curious rents were exacted by the *seigneurs* in olden days, one being the picturesque payment of a chaplet of roses on St. John's Day. Another still more airy one is chronicled in an old book as having been paid on pain of imprisonment, viz., a dozen butterflies. What a dainty tribute! Many of these singular tithes still exist, and even now Sieur Le Breton has every year to pay four shillings and threepence, the equivalent of a cartload of ashes while another family pays four shillings and sixpence a year in lieu of the presentation of eighty eels.

Jersey enjoys the benefit of the Gulf Stream, and therefore the climate is so mild that ixias, camellias, palms, and geraniums flourish in the open air throughout the winter. The sky is intensely blue and the sea more violet than the Mediterranean. Indeed, with its indented shores fashioned by nature into numberless small and beautiful bays with their stretches of golden sand, its country lanes with their high hedges topped by green aisles of arching trees, its apple orchards, its soft–eyed cattle browsing knee–deep in cool green valleys through which brooklets of clear water wander, and the comely milkmaids in native costume, the little Isle is certainly most attractive.

Of the smaller islands of the group, Guernsey, Alderney, Sark, Herm, and Jethou, I know very little, except for a passing visit. Guernsey is the next most important in point of size, but its scenic features have rather diminished owing to the numerous and prosaic glass–houses erected by the farmers in order to supply the London market with early vegetables and grapes. Alderney is practically a military post. Herm and Jethou, which lie opposite St. Peter Port, the town of Guernsey, belonged until the war to Prince Blucher, and are merely islets, but Sark is ideally romantic and picturesque. Still, as the inhabitants of each are clannish, keeping aloof from each other and very seldom intermarrying, I hope, as a Jersey woman, to be forgiven if I seem prejudiced in favour of my own little "country."

Both Guernsey and Jersey have really unique glass–covered markets. Ours is positively palatial, with a fountain playing in the central hall, about which stalls of flowers and fruit form a tempting display, and where women in their quaint Jersey sunbonnets sit around in the midst of their "cabot" baskets laden with home–made butter and home–grown vegetables. On Saturdays the world and his wife meet here, and no woman, whatever her position, feels it *infra dig.* to do her own marketing and bargaining with the pleasant–mannered, dignified country folk.

The genealogy of many of the Jersey families can be traced back an extraordinarily long way. My remote ancestors were *seigneurs* of Noirmont, a very picturesquely situated manor on the seashore, and one of them was among the Jerseymen who followed William the Conqueror and fought in the Battle of Hastings. He figures in the Bayeux tapestry, and this fact incited me recently to inspect the famous fabric for the purpose of tracing in the features of this distinguished person a resemblance to myself, but the result was not very satisfactory. He also seems to have had some dispute regarding the boundary of the *seigneurie,* and took his grievance to Rouen, Normandy, where the facts were chronicled in the archives of that ancient city.

Another Le Breton was a bishop under Edward I, and in the same king's reign the family contributed a Judge Le Breton, who seems to have run through his money and to have become so hard–up that the king graciously presented him with his robes. I only hope he served His Majesty especially well in consequence.

But my favourite here is Raoul Le Breton, a man after my own heart, an adventurous spirit, who, in King John's reign, fought his way up the Seine, with five hundred retainers, to take Paris. I love Raoul for his pluck and enterprise, and I cordially endorse his taste in desiring to possess so fascinating a city. He pushed his way to the very gates of the citadel, but, needless to say, his ambitious designs were there checked, and he and his bold followers captured. I am bound to add the deplorable fact that Seigneur Raoul is insultingly referred to in French histories as "The Channel Islands Pirate." I think it may have been this same Le Breton who gave a service of communion plate to the Church of St. Brelade's, where, I hope, it is still preserved. Possibly this gift was intended as an atonement for his piratical misdeeds.

These appear to be the more interesting of my progenitors, and the only ones about whom I remember details; though a shameful Le Breton helped to murder Thomas a Becket, and another fought gallantly under Lord Howe and was one of the bearers of the news of victory. The latter died of his wounds, and is buried at Salisbury in the Church of St. Thomas. Yet another ancestor was the first Bishop of Ely.

To come to later days, a great–uncle of mine, Sir Thomas Le Breton, was a distinguished scholar who received the Odyssey and the Iliad of Homer as a prize for the best Latin poem at Oxford. These books always found a place in my father's library at Jersey, and I have heard the latter say that the presentation to Sir Thomas was made by Dr. Johnson, who wrote in them: *"Spartam quam nectus es ornati,"* which I suppose may be freely translated by: "You adorn the country of your adoption." He must have been a handsome man, if Sir Thomas Lawrence's portrait of him does not flatter; and he was, perhaps, the last sitter to the great painter, who had by that time given up work.

It happened thus. As bailiff of the Island, Sir Thomas Le Breton had made the then long and arduous journey to London to defend the threatened rights of the Jersey States. This he was successful in doing, and his grateful country not only subscribed for and presented him with a very finely modelled silver epergne, but begged him in addition to take the opportunity of having his features perpetuated by Sir Thomas Lawrence, the greatest painter of his day. He called for the purpose on the master, only to be told by him that he had retired, but an interested scrutiny of my great–uncle's appearance must have impressed Lawrence, for he exclaimed, "Damme, you are such a handsome fellow I'll paint your portrait, nevertheless!"

The old rectory of St. Saviour's (familiarly known during my father's incumbency as the "deanery") snuggled comfortably at the bottom of a hilly lane leading from the parish main road. It was built of the grey granite quarried in the Island, and occupied three sides of a square; two sides were covered by the dwelling; the third, forming the large courtyard, being given over to a row of buildings used in olden days for the home–manufacture of cider. The making of this mild beverage had long been discontinued, but the great stone wheel for the crushing of the apples, together with the huge stone troughs, vats, and other primitive appliances, still remained, while a dovecote, symbolical of the rector's calling, stood in the courtyard.

A portion of the house proper bore the date of 1100, cut in a coping–stone, but the original building had evidently been added to from time to time. Its fact was almost entirely covered with climbing roses — red, white, pink, blush, and (to me most beautiful of all) the single damask. Underlying these were cherry and pear trees of great age, the blossoms of which in spring–time mingled with the roses in delicious disorder. Climbing to my own bedroom window, and gracefully framing it, was an immense white jessamine, warring for existence with a vigorous climbing deep–red rose.

The large, high–walled garden to the east was given equally to flowers and fruit, and here a fig tree — rich, in season, with its purple yield — reared its fertile head. To the south, a long terrace with a gently sloping lawn beyond comprised the remainder of the pleasure grounds, with evidences on all sides of my mother's wonderful love of flowers. There was also a large portion of the glebe fields stocked with vegetables to satisfy our healthy appetites, and which at times we all helped to weed.

There were two main entrances to the rectory, the door consecrated to my mother's use being dignified with a glass portico, always well filled with flowering plants in sharp contrast to the severely business–like entrance to my father's study and our schoolroom. The first floor was a labyrinth of small, low rooms, with deep window–seats and many–paned casements; these rooms were divided into groups approached by separate and winding stairs. A drawing–room and dining–room, which had been added by my father, seemed almost palatial in comparison with the rest of the house.

Looking out on the slanting lawn at the rear, these rooms commanded a view of the beautiful undulating lands that are known in Jersey as "cotils."

One wing in the deanery was set apart for the children, and there the younger of us romped, unhindered, to our heart's content, in charge of an old, white–haired nurse named Madama Bisson, resplendent in frilled caps decorated with mauve ribbons; and I add parenthetically that I never see a certain piece of sculpture advertising a more or less familiar brand of soap without recalling instantly the dear old soul's vigorous and wholesome methods in the discharge of her duties.

A born story–teller, she used to fill our easily excited minds with narratives of daring French invasions and bold smugglers. An especially fascinating tale had to do with one Baron de Rullecourt, who, with a handful of followers, had landed on the Island some eighty years previously with conquest in his mind, and had been ignominiously defeated by Major Pierson at the head of the military. Madame Bisson's father had witnessed the thrilling event, and had seen my great–grandmother flee with her youthful family from the scene of conflict in the Royal Square, the skirmish having been later immortalised by the Bostonian painter, David Copley, in his picture of "The Battle of Jersey," now in the National Gallery, London.

As may be imagined, our nurse's stories had a very disquieting effect on childish minds, and any unusual noises at night brought us bolt upright in bed, terrified at the possible return of our French enemies. There was, of course, no danger of such a happening, but smuggling still continued, and Madame Bisson could give such real accurate accounts of the smugglers' doings as to eventually create a suspicion that one of her sailor sons followed this particular calling.

It may be thought that, an only girl surrounded by six brothers, I was utterly spoilt. Quite the contrary, my brothers lost no opportunity during my earliest youth of impressing on me what a miserable handicap it was to be a girl, a silly creature, given to weeping on the slightest provocation, easily scared and full of qualms. So I was quick to perceive that, in order to be allowed to take part in their sports and not to be left out in the cold, I must steady my nerves, control my tears, and look at things from a boy's point of view. Following this course, I conquered their prejudices, becoming a partner in all their games and numerous escapades, and sharing, though always in a mitigated form, the punishment meted out to the transgressors.

We kept rabbits, guinea–pigs, canaries, ferrets, and every kind of chicken. Once, forgetting to feed a pet canary, it died of starvation. Filled with the deepest remorse, as I had every reason to be, I enclosed the unfortunate bird in a night–light box and buried it with full funeral honours in a corner of the garden, inscribing on a wooden headstone over the grave, "Alas, poor Dick!" — the quotation, I think, having been cribbed from Goldsmith. I found on a recent visit to Jersey that the grave was still carefully preserved by the present occupant of St. Saviour's. He had also thought it worth while to remove from a window a pane of glass on which I had engraved my name with my engagement ring, and to have it framed and hung in one of the rooms. How proud I felt!

Living the life of my brothers transformed me into an incorrigible tomboy. I could climb trees and vault fences with the best of them, and I entered with infinite relish into their practical jokes. I have a lively recollection of my youngest brother and myself patrolling the old tree–shaded churchyard at midnight (when we were supposed to be in bed) mounted on stilts and draped in sheets, disquieting late passers–by very effectually. This prank continued until someone wrote to the Jersey papers, promising the ghosts of St. Saviour's graveyard a dose of cold lead if they appeared again. We had a veritable passion for annexing door–knockers, and scarcely a door in the parish was allowed to retain one. We braved threats, dogs, enraged householders, even shotguns to obtain these trophies.

One of our chief targets was an old man named Wilkins, a retired tradesman, who lived, with his two spinster daughters, at the head of the Deanery Lane. He was patient and long–suffering, but occasionally we exasperated him beyond endurance, and he would reluctantly descend on my father with a formal complaint.

Having relieved him of his door–knocker one evening, we tied a long, strong cord to his bell, making the other end fast to a stone, which we threw over a wall opposite, with the result that everyone who passed by, either afoot, or on horseback, struck the cord, causing the old man's bell to ring furiously. At each fresh clanging, Wilkins emerged with the promptitude of a cuckoo clock striking the hour, and hurled the most violent language at the innocent wayfarers. Finally, our audible chuckles behind the wall located the real culprits, and Wilkins preceded us to the deanery, where, after an interview with my father, fitting chastisement was inflicted on us.

About the last escapade which I remember was one in which my sex prevented me from taking an active part. A time–honoured status of an anonymous personage, wearing a wreath of laurels and a medley of garments, was salved by the Jerseyites from a Spanish ship wrecked on our shores during the reign of George II. As it seemed a pity to waste it, the Islanders labelled it "George Rex," after the Hanoverian king, and erected it in the Royal Square of St. Heliers, where it had stood unmolested ever since, until my brothers conceived the appalling idea of tarring and feathering this royal and stony individual.

I shall never forget the tremendous and wrathful outburst which ensued when the townspeople discovered the outrage. It is an ill wind, however, which does not blow profit to some quarter, and an enterprising photographer coined money by snapping his spurious Majesty for souvenir purposes before scourers and painters had made him presentable again. Not infrequently, through our reputation for all manner of pranks, my brothers and I got the name without the game, everything mischievous that was done being attributed off–hand to the "dean's family."

While the tomboy element was conspicuous in me, I had my serious side as well, and would read for hours; longer sometimes than my parents thought good for me. I never went to school, and for that reason had few

27

girl friends. A French governess laboured faithfully to impart knowledge to me, but I am afraid I was rather a handful. My brothers were all educated at Victory College (the Jersey public school), and the only real work I did was with their tutor when he came each evening to overlook the preparation of their work for the following day. He gave me a fairly good education in the classics and mathematics, which was supplemented by lessons from German, French, music and drawing masters. My father, being a remarkably clever and progressive man, believed firmly in the higher education of women.

At the age of thirteen I developed, with two girl friends, a taste for spiritualism and table–turning, and gradually, through our interesting experiences, became engrossed in it. One particular table which we used in our seances displayed such extraordinary agility, cut so many capers, and answered some of our questions so intelligently, that I began to regard myself as a medium, and to feel that I really was, as the spirits we evoked assured me, the cause of these manifestations. Even to this day table–turning fascinates and mystifies me.

Some years subsequent to my youthful experiments I discussed the subject with Victorien Sardou, the famous French dramatist, himself an ardent spiritualist, and asked him why the spirits never really enlightened me, although they were quite ready to rap our answers after I had sat for a few moments at the table. He replied that I had not pursued the matter far enough, and that I was as yet in touch only with the *cuisiniers* (by which I presume, he meant the underlings of the occult world). He asserted, an assertion which I did not and do not credit, that spooks may reveal themselves by showering flowers about the room and performing other seemingly impossible acts, and wound up with the sweeping statement that only fools did not believe in the supernatural.

Perhaps it was Sardou who interested Sarah Bernhardt in spiritualism, for, happening to call on her one day in Paris, I found them both sitting about a table in a darkened room in company with three or four old women, but the spirits had not been in the right mood that afternoon and nothing had occurred. In any case, there was no trickery in *our* table–turning, and we three girls were deadly frightened on one moonlight night to feel ourselves being dragged on a large sofa from one end of the drawing–room to the other, amid a weird rustling like the whirring of huge wings.

I grew up, my brothers also; and the boys nearly all elected to serve their Queen by land or water. (To–day of the once merry group that frolicked about St. Saviour's, only two remain, Clement and myself.)

With my girlhood, new interests came into my life. Not a few of the parochial duties devolved upon me. Frequently, when my mother, owing to indisposition, could not accompany my father on his visits, or if, for some equally good reason, she was unable to present prizes at school and other Island functions, I served as her substitute, and also did my share in visiting the sick and distressed.

I dare say thus being put forward a little prominently had the effect of making me rather precocious. At all events, when I approached my four-teenth year, I began to think that I should be included in invitations to the pleasant picnics and small informal dances which are a feature of Jersey social life. My mother agreed with me, and, in spite of my youth, I be-came her companion on these occasions. Going about as I did, it was impossible not to meet people older than myself, and, before I knew it, and to my bewilderment (I was scarcely over fourteen), I received my first proposal, a very serious one, from an officer whose regiment was quartered in the Island.

He was the son of the then Archbishop of Canterbury, but he failed to find favour in my eyes. Subsequently, one or two other suitors appeared, these also without making any impression on me. Such experiences, however, had set my thoughts drifting into a new channel, and, like other girls, I began to dream of the real Prince Charming who would one day appear. In a short time he came, in the person of Edward Langtry, an Irishman, about 30 years old, a widower, hailing from Belfast. His father, I might mention, was the first man to run a line of steamers from Belfast to Stranraer, and his public–spiritedness and practical interest in the welfare of the former city gained him the title of "The Father of Belfast." His portrait, the first ever painted on commission by Millais, still hangs on the wall of the Public Library there.

At this time my brother Willie returned from India to be married. Mr. Langtry, who was well known in the Islands, and who had a large and luxurious yacht called the *Red Gauntlet,* gave a ball at the Jersey Yacht Club as part of the wedding festivities. It was a far more elaborate and extravagant affair than anything I had hitherto witnessed, and it electrified me. The walls were hung with quantities of flags; the supper was less sketchy than I had been accustomed to, and, to crown all, the hall and staircase were lined with sailors in their spotless white suites. To me, it was simply dazzling, and Arabian Nights' Entertainment, and its donor instantly became in my eyes a wonder!

Then followed various cruises in the *Red Gauntlet,* my father accompanying me. One took us to the French coast and back. The sequel may be surmised. I thought myself desperately in love, and at the end of six weeks accepted Mr. Langtry's proposal of marriage. Being the only daughter, my elation was not shared warmly by my father and mother. The former desired me to see more of life before I married, and the latter had set her heart on my having a London season previous to the settling of such an important matter. But the stronger the opposition, the more determinedly did I cling to my engagement, the result being that I had my way. Very early one morning I was married in St. Saviour's Church, within whose walls many of my ancestors are commemorated by tombstones.

I elected to be married in my travelling gown, as I hated the idea of a big wedding and the conventional bridal array. My husband and I sailed away the same day in the *Red Gauntlet* to his yachting *pied a terre,* Cliffe Lodge, situated on Southampton Water. I entered eagerly with him into the sport of yachting, and we lived all that summer on board an 80–ton racing yawl called the *Gertrude,* going from one regatta to another to compete in sailing matches, of which we won several, the most important of these being the International Yacht Race at Havre, which the *Gertrude* carried off in a gale. How I enjoyed the excitement of that race, crowding on sail to the verge of danger, with a swirling spray drenching us to the skin.

Occasionally, however, yacht racing could be dull in the extreme. To roll about becalmed for hours, whistling for a breath of wind, was deadly. Once, in a big race up the Thames from the Nore to Erith, we drifted along so sluggishly that I went to bed in disgust, and though we floated past the winning post in the small hours, Mr. Langtry refrained, out of consideration of my slumbers, from firing the announcing cannon, and discovered to his consternation the next day that he had lost the prize by not doing so. The two leading vessels, of which one was the *Cetonia,* had become imbedded in some shoals, and the yacht arriving long after us was awarded the cup.

I need dwell no further on my life at this period. It was uneventful until I was prostrated by a severe attack of typhoid fever, which naturally laid me up for some time at Cliffe Lodge, Southampton. When I became convalescent my physician ordered a change of air, and we decided on London, a decision which later events proved to be a most momentous one. I have no idea what led us to select the great, smoky city as a sanatorium, but we arrived at Waterloo Station one murky morning in January, and, after stopping at an hotel for a day or two, took what we considered suitable apartments in a thoroughfare now known as Eaton Place.

How strange and confusing the bustle and turmoil of the greatest city in the world was to me can only be realised by those few who, like myself, had lived to the age of sixteen without ever having seen a railway train. As for my husband, an extremely shy man, who had spent his life since leaving Oxford in outdoor country sports, he felt quite like a fish out of water.

Chapter
2

Soon after my arrival in London my first deep grief assailed me. By telegram I heard of my youngest brother's death. Crushed by the young mare he was riding, he fought against his injuries for three days, only to succumb at last. And I didn't even know of the accident. The dreadful news, so cruelly sudden; my speechless sorrow; the interminable journey to Jersey, during which I lay weeping all night; the agonist grief of my mother when we met — all these things made me feel that life was over. I returned to London in a state of deep depression, caring little for anything.

I knew only a few English families, who, for economic or climatic reasons, had sometimes wintered in our sunny Island. Among these hibernating visitors were Lord and Lady Suffield and their children, with whom I rode after about the country lanes and knew fairly well. Perhaps the first compliment paid to a girl in her teens lingers longer in her memory than the subsequent pretty speeches that may be showered on her. Anyhow, it was Lord Suffield who, at one of those informal picnics in which

Jerseyites delight, made the following remark: "Do you know, Miss Le Breton, that you are very, very beautiful? You ought to have a season in London." I am sure no one ever so alluded to my appearance before.

Since Lord Suffield's flattering remark had broached the subject, I may say that it is a matter of fact that Jersey has always possessed more beautiful girls than Nature usually apportions to the square mile; and, among the many I call to mind, two at least have become famous for brains as well as for good looks. Their maiden name was Sutherland, now they are respectively Elinor Glyn and Lady Duff Gordon (Lucile). They were my juniors and still in the schoolroom when I married.

After our first experience of London life we paid a visit to the Island in the yacht *Hildegarde,* and incidentally dined at Government House. As I deposited my cloak, and took a last survey of myself in the glass, I observed two pretty, red–headed girls named above peeping from under the muslin–covered dressing– table. How they got there I don't know, but someone contrived this ambush to satisfy their curiosity.

Other visitors who came to avoid the English winter were the Rendleshams — still, it seemed unlikely that the "long arm of coincidence" would bring us into contact with any of these. Indeed, neither my husband nor I remembered that we had any acquaintances in the vast city. On our return to London we passed our time as country cousins do — walking in the Park watching for royalty to pass, for I had never set eyes on even a minor one, and in going to museums and picture galleries, seeing many interesting things that were new to me, and which, although I still felt very sad, made me feel a little more contented with life.

It must, therefore, have been the finger of Fate that, one afternoon a fortnight after my return, pointed the way to the Aquarium at Westminster. It had been newly opened, and was a popular resort at the moment, and there in the crowd we came across Lord Ranelagh, the hero of the "Haro!

Haro!" episode, and his two daughters, with whom I had become friends in Jersey. They seemed very pleased to see us again, and we went down to spend a few days with them at their Fulham house, which was a convenient drive from town in those days of no motors. The suburb was still quite countrified, and Lord Ranelagh's Sunday afternoon parties were very popular. His delightful creeper– covered mansion boasted a large fruit and vegetable garden, where grew strawberries galore.

Everyone enjoyed having tea on the mossy, tree–shaded lawn, sloping down to the Thames, and interesting people were always to be found there. Our meeting with Lord Ranelagh completely changed the current of my life, for, shortly after, through him and quite unexpectedly, we received our first invitation in London, a card for a Sunday evening at–home from Lady Sebright, a very enthusiastic amateur actress, fond of literature and art, and who loved to gather at these Sunday evening receptions men and women conspicuous on both callings, besides a purely social element.

The evening came and we rattled up to Lady Sebright's house in Lowndes Square in a humble four–wheeler. Being, of course, in deep mourning, I wore a very simple black, square–cut gown (designed by my Jersey modiste), with no jewels — I had none — or ornaments of any kind, and with my hair twisted carelessly on the nape of my neck in a knot, which later became known as the "Langtry." Very meekly I glided into the drawing–room, which was filled with a typical London crush, was presented to my hostess, and then retired shyly to a chair in a remote corner, feeling very un–smart and countrified. Fancy my surprise when I immediately became the centre of attraction, and, after a few moments, I found that quite half the people in the room seemed bent on making my acquaintance. One distinguished person after another was led up to my corner by my hostess, they in turn bringing others, till my shyness and confusion gave way to utter astonishment at finding myself singled out for such marked attention.

One of the first to be introduced was John Everett Millais, probably the most eminent English painter of the day, a native of the Island in which I was born, and who beamed in friendly enthusiasm while he claimed me as his countrywoman. He was tall and broad–shouldered; his handsome, ruddy, mobile countenance was strong rather than sensitive in character, and his swinging walk suggested the moors and the sportsman. Manly is the only word which will accurately describe the impression he made. Later, when I came to know him better, I discovered that he affected none of the eccentricities, either of dress or manner, usually ascribed to artists, that he was quite sane, and that in his working hours he did not wear a velvet jacket, but a well–worn, home–spun, belted coat, which, I am sure, had done yeoman service on his beloved Scotch moors. In a word, he was as natural as if he were not a genius.

Among other notabilities whom I met on that, to me, memorable occasion, and who afterwards became my firm friends, were James McNeill Whistler, the famous American artist (with wonderful speaking hands); Henry Irving, approaching the zenith of his fame, his star blazing brilliantly at the Lyceum; Lord Wharncliffe, made rich by finding coal on his Sheffield property and wisely spending the surplus on art collection and art encouragement; Abraham Hayward, the well–known essayist; Frank Miles, the artist; and William Yardley, an amateur actor and leading cricketer of the day.

There was a rush of cavaliers to take me down to supper, but Millais won the day, of which I was glad, for I was fearfully shy, and his gay assumption of kinsmanship made me feel more at ease with him than with others I had met that evening. He asked me to sit to him, and his compelling personality made me readily consent that he should be the first painter to reproduce on canvas, what he called, the "classic features" of his countrywoman. And so ended my first night in London society.

This wonderful experience was still fresh in my mind the next morning, and I felt nothing could eclipse it, but, in the afternoon, on returning to our rooms in Eaton Place after a walk, Mr. Langtry and I found the table heaped with cards and notes of invitation, to dine, to lunch, to dance, from people whose distinguished names were familiar, but who, themselves, were personally unknown to us. A complete transformation seemed to have taken place in my life overnight. It was quite staggering, and thenceforward visitors and invitations continued to pour in daily, until they became a source of grievance to our landlady, who was obliged to engage an extra servant to respond to the battering of powdered footmen on her humble and somewhat flimsy door.

Our first dinner, I think, was with the Earl and Countess of Wharncliffe, at their beautiful home in Curzon Street, which stood in a garden and was long and low like a country house. Brilliantly clever and artistic, it would have been difficult to find a more perfect example of the *grande dame* than was the tall, handsome Lady Wharncliffe. I am not sure whether she was more beautiful that night, sitting at the head of her table, which glowed with golden tulips that matched her golden hair, or as I saw her later at Wortley, near Sheffield, bending her graceful head over her embroidery frame, at which she seemed to work as perpetually as Penelope. But, oh! after that first dinner at Wharncliffe House, she smoked cigarette after cigarette, and my country soul was shocked!

Among her guests was Madge Robertson (Mrs. Kendall) — accompanied by her husband — not only the most accomplished actress of the day, but a model of all the virtues, and the only actress at that time received in the "inner circle" of Society. Sir Edward Poynter, afterwards President of the Royal Academy, was also present. He had just commenced work on four enormous canvases, a commission from his host which occupied the painter's time for four years. It was arranged that very evening that I was to pose for the central figure, Nausicaa, in one of these pictures. In another, Lady Wharncliffe was portrayed as some other Greek "celebrity," for the friezes were all devoted to classical subjects. The artist's wife and Miss Violet Lindsay were also included in the paintings, which I subsequently saw fulfilling their destiny in the great hall at Wortley.

Invitations to receptions and balls were so numerous that we were mostly obliged to attend two or three of each in an evening in order to keep our engagements. Whatever my husband said and felt, I absolutely revelled in the novelty of it all, and, though at this distance of time I cannot call to mind details, there was scarcely a great house in London that I did not visit during my first season.

Devonshire House, with its renowned marble stair–case, was certainly one of the most attractive. We went to one of the Marquis of Harrington's political receptions there. On our arrival he left his place at the head of the stairs and conducted me round the magnificent rooms, pointing out a few treasures, and, on my admiring the lovely coloured water–lilies reposing in marble pools, he drenched his clothes pulling them out as an offering, as also the gorgeous liveries of the footmen, into whose arms he flung them and who strewed our brougham with such quantities of the dripping blossoms as to make the latter conveyance rather moister than was convenient; but I think "Harty–Tarty." as he was familiarly called, did nothing by halves.

At these various gatherings I met practically all the well–born and well–known men and women of the day, and the point most apparent in connection with them was their entire lack of self– assertion. While I carried away with me from these functions a general sense of pomp and grandeur, there was a simplicity about the people which one finds only in those born to greatness, or who have achieved it. Probably the security of their station enabled them to be charming and gracious. Certain it is that they were absolutely free from the affectation and "smallness" which, sooner or later, make their appearance in many who merely buy a position with money.

Through all this procession of opera, dinners, and balls I wore, extraordinary as it may sound to members of my sex, my one black evening gown, the creation of Madame Nicolle, the fashionable dressmaker of St. Heliers, Jersey; still, the meagreness of my wardrobe did not seem to be noticed by others, and it was not even realised by me. The gown, needless to say, had grown considerably the worse for wear as the season wore on, and my maid, I am sure, disapproved of it heartily. It had its end like all things earthly.

One afternoon Mrs. Cornwallis–West, mother of the Princess of Pless and Constance Duchess of Westminster, rushed into my drawing–room in a fever of excitement. She had come up from Ruthyn Castle, her husband's country place in Wales, without an evening dress, and suddenly she wished to attend the opera. We had become great friends, almost sisters, and she implored me to lend her my well–known garment. She carried it off, and, being absolutely reckless of my property. not only wore it to the opera, but went on to a ball afterwards, danced all night, and the next day my maid (with a beaming face) exhibited the gown to me practically in rags. So another frock was ordered from my Jersey *costumiere,* who still had the distinction of dressing me, but with the order went a suggestion for much stouter material, in case I might again be asked for the loan of it, and madame's artistry found expression this time in a black satin of such substance that it was a menace to the community when I danced.

Photography was now making great strides, and pictures of well–known people had begun to be exhibited for sale. The photographers, one and all, besought me to sit. Presently, my portraits were in every shop–window, with trying results, for they made the public so familiar with my features that wherever I went — to theatres, picture–galleries, shops — I was actually mobbed. Thus the photographs gave fresh stimulus to a condition which I had unconsciously created. One night, shortly after their appearance, at a large reception at Lady Jersey's, many of the guests stood on chairs to obtain a better view of me, and I could not help but hear their audible comments on my appearance as I passed down the drawing–room. Itinerant vendors sold cards about the streets with my portrait ingeniously concealed, shouting "The Jersey Lily, the puzzle is to find her."

One morning I twisted a piece of black velvet into a toque, stuck a quill through it, and went to Sandown Park. A few days later this turban appeared in every milliner's window labelled "The Langtry Hat." "Langtry" shoes, which are still worn, were launched, and so on and so on. It was very embarrassing, and it had all come about so suddenly that I was bewildered. If I went for a stroll in the Park and stopped a moment to admire the flowers, people ran after me in droves, staring me out of countenance, and even lifting my sunshade to satisfy fully their curiosity. To venture out for a little shopping was positively hazardous, for the instant I entered an establishment to make a purchase, the news that I was within spread with the proverbial rapidity of wildfire, and the crowd about the door grew so dense that departure by the legitimate exit was rendered impossible, the obliging proprietors being forced, with many apologies, to escort me around to the back door.

Instead of the excitement abating, it increased to such an extent that it became risky for me to indulge in a walk, on account of the crushing that would follow my appearance. To better illustrate my predicament I may state as a fact that, one Sunday afternoon, a young girl, with an aureole of

40

fair hair and wearing a black gown, was seated in the Park near the Achilles statue. Someone raised the cry that it was I, people rushed towards her and, before the police could interfere, she was mobbed to such an extent that an ambulance finally conveyed her, suffocating and unconscious, to St. George's Hospital.

It would be difficult for me to analyse my feelings at this time. To pass in a few weeks from being an absolute "nobody" to what the Scotch so aptly describe as a "person"; to find myself not only invited to, but watched for at all the great balls and parties; to hear the murmur as I entered the room; to be compelled to close the yard gates in order to avoid the curious, waiting crowd outside, before I could mount my horse for my daily canter in the Row; and to see my portrait roped round for protection at the Royal Academy — surely, I thought, London has gone mad, for there can be nothing about me to warrant this extraordinary excitement. I felt apologetic, and inclined to disclaim aloud any hand in bringing about the strange attitude of all classes in London towards me.

While this overwhelming public attention may have been amusing and flattering at first, it soon began to have its unpleasant features, as I have demonstrated, and I was debarred from many little pleasures in consequence. For instance, Lord Rosslyn had bought a wonderful–stepping horse for her ladyship's victoria, of which she was justly proud. Always a lover of horses, I was counting on an airing behind this particular one, but when she called to fetch me one morning to drive in the Park, I was disappointed to see a very ordinary animal. She explained the fact by saying that she had been afraid to bring out the high– stepper, as the combination of him in the shafts and myself in the carriage, might create a sensation too great for comfort.

Indeed, there were many simple amusements I was now forced to forego that I had enjoyed in my "nobody" days. My husband greatly disliked all this publicity, sometimes losing his temper and blaming *me!* As can be readily understood, his position was an onerous one, for, aside from the vexation of seeing his wife stared at as a species of phenomenon, we never went out but that he was kept busy hurrying me from one place to another as he saw the familiar crowds beginning to assemble. Still, it is easy to imagine the marvel of it all to a country girl like me, who had not been allowed by my band of brothers to think much of myself in any way.

I had occasionally stood and studied photographs of the recognised beauty, Lady Dudley, which had found their way into the little stationer's shop of St. Heliers in my quiet Island, and I sometimes wondered what it must be like to be such a great and fashionable beauty. And so, when I realised that people were even acquiring the habit of standing on chairs in crowded drawing–rooms for a glimpse of *me,* is it surprising that I thought it uncanny?

In my day London society was very different to what it is now. Actors and actresses were not then generally received. Rank was more highly considered, and the line more finely drawn between the social grades, the inner circle being, consequently, comparatively small and rigorously exclusive, and the world was more hypocritical and narrow–minded. America and the Colonies had not the enormous accumulated wealth which they boast at present; South Africa had not yet yielded her crop of millionaires, and the leisured classes which now fluctuate between the mother country and their own land scarcely existed.

Travel was less easy and much less luxurious, and very few Americans were to be found in London. In the vastly enlarged society of to–day, the excitement caused by my advent could never be repeated. It was likened at the time to the furore created by the famous Gunning sisters a century previous, and, although I feel an embarrassment in chronicling the curious whim of the public which eventually led to my being treated like a lion at the Zoo (without the compensating bun), it seems inevitable that the unusual conditions which caused the brooklet of my life to deviate in its course should be explained.

An interesting feature of my first London season was a magnificent ball given at Dudley House for some visiting royalty. Lady Dudley wrote me saying how earnestly she and Lord Dudley desired my presence, then very tactfully and gracefully intimated that she hoped I would put off my mourning for that evening, as Lord Dudley had so inherent a dislike for black as to taboo her wearing it, and, moreover, it depressed him so strangely that he could not bear the idea of anyone appearing at his house in that sombre hue.

The letter was so kindly expressed that I could not feel offended, and as I had met her very often, and I liked her as much as I admired her, I immediately began to consider the question of indulging Lord Dudley's weakness for colours. I may remark, *en parenthese*, that the poverty of my wardrobe was not due to motives of economy, but rather to my dislike of the "fitting" process, and, frankly, also the result of my absolute indifference at the time to elaborate frocks, though my views regarding finery changed completely later on.

Having decided that the function at Dudley House was worth the harassing ordeal of being "fitted," I gave an order to a fashionable London dressmaker, and appeared at the ball in a white velvet, classically severe in line, and embroidered with pearls. Looking back, and judging from the sensation it caused, it must have been a striking creation. As I entered the ballroom the dancers stopped and crowded round me, and as I pursued my way to greet my hostess they opened out to allow me to pass.

Speaking of Lady Dudley brings me again to the photograph craze. Like every other fashionable rage, it had its comic side, and, after the shopkeepers had exhibited my pictures in their windows alongside royalties and distinguished statesmen, all the pretty women in society rushed pell–mell to be photographed, that they, too, might be placed on view. They were portrayed in every imaginable pose. Anything the ingenuity of the camera–man could devise to produce an original or startling effect was utilised with more or less happy results. Some smothered themselves in furs to brave photographic snowstorms; some sat in swings; some lolled dreamily in hammocks; others carried huge bunches of flowers (indigenous to the dusty studio and looking painfully artificial), and one was actually reproduced gazing at a dead fish!

I myself, on one occasion only, foolishly gave his head to the photographer, who represented me with a dead bird in my hand and an expression of grief on my face (an inspiration of his own) which, I suppose, was designed to touch the heart of the sentimental public.

The fad reached such lengths that it finally gave rise to a popular music–hall ditty, the refrain of which ran something as follows,

> I have been photographed like this,
> I have been photographed like that,
> But I never have been photoed
> As a raving Maniac.

The lines offered capital opportunities for "clowning," and the song proved mo small factor in helping to kill a craze which was one of the silliest that ever attacked Englishwomen. Still, though the collecting of photographs representing unknown people has never appealed to me, some of the elaborate pictures of the society belles, or professional beauties, as they came to be called, were without doubt so prepossessing that the public might well be excused for buying them to decorate their rooms.

44

One of the most photographed subjects during the mania was Mrs. Cornwallis–West, already the mother of three beautiful children. She was petite, with a vivid complexion, golden hair worn short in the manner of to–day, and flashing hazel eyes; and equally attractive whether walking, on horseback, or in a ball gown. She was high–spirited, vivacious, and extremely witty, sometimes audaciously so, and the possessor of a fine singing voice.

Mrs. Lake Wheeler, another of the "professionals," was tall and slender, with a very small head and face, and regular features. Her beauty was of line and expression rather than colour, and, while disappointing to some people when first seen, its charm grew on acquaintance. Then there was the Duchess of Leinster, of the commanding Juno–like type; Miss Violet Lindsay, now the Duchess of Rutland, whose clear–cut cameo–like face has been immortalised by Watts, Shannon, Poynter, and other celebrated painters, and who is herself a fine artist and an intellectual.

Lovely women from other lands flashed upon the view during the London season. One, very much admired in Paris, was Madame Bernadaki, a Russian, but she was rather of the bovine type. I first saw her at a reception at the Russian Embassy, where she was pointed out to me. She had a dead–white skin, accentuated by her black hair and eyes. She was, however, as the American so delicately puts it, too "ample" for the English taste. In slim contrast was Madame K— noted for her willowy figure, and especially for her graceful neck and shoulders, and the superb poise of her head. She was invited to a house party at Chatsworth to meet the Prince of Wales, and he told me that she appeared at breakfast in a most transparent blouse which, in those prudish Victorian days, scandalised the entire party, including the famous hostess. If a young woman had sat at that table in the present fashionable gossamer attire I suppose they would all have fainted.

An American of remarkable popularity, besides being very attractive and good–looking, was Miss Minnie Stevens, afterwards Lady Paget. A Mrs. Schlesinger, American also I think, and whom I saw but once, had a lovely face, which I have never forgotten – fair and delicate, framed in beautiful golden hair, swept high in classic coils. And there were many others, more or less celebrated for their looks, who besieged the photographers.

Apropos of the beauties, a weird story has pursued me through life to the effect that I once, at a supper party in those days, so far forgot my manners as to drop a piece of ice down the Prince of Wales' back. The tale has become so generally believed that I may be excused for not only alluding to it and emphatically denying it *in toto,* but for relating at the same time the true story of the incident which gave rise to this silly false one. One of the most admired women among those I have just mentioned was at a ball. It was the small hours, and her waiting husband was getting bored. He hunted for his wife and found her, very wide awake, surrounded by a bevy of admirers, thoroughly enjoying herself. His suggestion that they should go home was, therefore, not received with enthusiasm. As he persisted, and waxed rather warm in argument, she, when his back was turned, deftly popped a spoonful of strawberry–ice down his spine to settle the question. This defiance of marital authority was seen by many, and, being repeated as a good story, found its way into the society papers with no names attached, and later became the foundation for the vulgar fabrication which I have seen in print over and over again, and in which, I repeat, there is not a grain of truth.

Nor was this the only occasion by many on which this audacious Irish beauty bested her devoted husband, for, going one evening to dine at their house with five or six congenial spirits, I noticed that his place at the table was unoccupied. No apology was offered nor allusion made to the circumstance until later in the meal, when the wine came to an end, and our hostess thereupon gaily informed as that we could not have any more as, having had a difference of opinion with our absent host, she had watched her opportunity and locked the poor man up in the wine cellar!

Chapter 3

A great deal of my time, and perhaps the most interesting part of it, was now taken up in sitting to painters. J. E. Millais had fixed an early date to begin my portrait on our first meeting at Lady Sebright's reception, but when I arrived at his studio on the appointed day I was surprised, and certainly disappointed, to find that it was his intention to paint me in my plain black gown, precisely as I was at the moment. I had hoped to be draped in classic robes or sumptuous mediaeval garments, in which I should be beautiful and quite transformed. As the sittings progressed, however, and I grew to understand the master's art better, I realized that he loved only the actual and the truth, and that, in his portraits, he dissimulated nothing, rather emphasising the individuality of the sitter than deviating from nature to embellish his subject.

I am venturing to express an opinion that, while the sentimental canvases of "The Black Brunswicker" and "The Huguenot Lovers" were among the most popular of his pictures in his youth, the artist's lasting fame will come from his portraits and his landscapes. Of the latter, who that has seen that great work "Chill October" could forget it? This masterpiece of dreariness — a pond with wind–swept sedges — was the most admired landscape of its year at the Burlington House exhibition.

Millais had just moved into his new home at Palace Gate, which was directly opposite the Broad Walk, Kensington Gardens, and had so planned his house that the windows of his favourite rooms commanded the long vista of arching elms. It was a veritable palace that he had built. The decorations, extremely simple, were light in tone, which was then unusual, the hall and broad staircase being lined with Italian marble, and on the landing of the first floor, where his studio and reception rooms were situated, a fountain plashed into a huge marble basin.

My portrait was all but finished before there had been a word of discussion regarding a title. Then, one day, he said, "Isn't there a lily that is grown in the Island called the Jersey lily?" On my replying affirmatively, he asked me to send for one. It is a fragile little flower, neither decorative nor imposing, and I think my countryman was rather disconcerted when it arrived. Still, he painted it held in my hand, and, in calling the portrait "The Jersey Lily," gave at the same time a title to the picture and a sobriquet to me, by which I was for ever afterwards known. The work is three–quarter length, showing me in a black, clinging gown, fastened with innumerable black bows. At the throat a white lace collar with a gardenia — immortalised at someone's special request — tucked in one side; the crimson lily, *Nerine sarniensis,* providing the only touch of colour in the scheme.

The progenitors of this lily, and of many other varieties of the South African amaryllis, which are now common in my native Island, found their way to its shores in a romantic manner. About a hundred and fifty years ago, a sailing vessel from the Cape of Good Hope, laden with the bulbs, was driven by a gale to the rocky Jersey coast and totally wrecked. The following spring myriads of exquisite blossoms from the marooned lilies made their unexpected appearance, springing from the sand above high–water mark. The Islanders, bless them, love flowers, so they dug up and transplanted them to the gardens around their cottages, and they thrived so well in their adopted country that to–day there are wide hedges of pink belladonnas, while nerines, vallotas, arums, and so forth, that flourish in the open air. Whither the ship was bound no on knows; but it was a windfall for us.

In addition to his important picture of me, Millais painted a full–face kit–cat portrait, which in a moment of generosity I gave to an American friend. He died, and I think his sister took possession of it; anyhow, it is somewhere in the States. The artist presented me with it, and, before doing so, wrote on the back "Millais thinks this isn't good." But it was a very distinctive and natural piece of work, and I trust that it may some day find its way into the Metropolitan Museum of Art in New York, and thus help to keep my memory green in the hearts of the hospitable American people.

"The Jersey Lily" was duly exhibited at the Royal Academy, hung in a favoured place, and created so much interest that it had to be roped around to preserve the portrait from injury by the crowd which constantly surged about it. The painting was afterwards purchased by one Martin Kennard, a total stranger to me. I believe it has since become the property of Cora Countess of Strafford.

I spent a delightful month one summer in Scotland with Sir John and Lady Millais. Both the painter and my husband were ardent fishermen, and spent most of the day beguiling salmon. The Millais shooting–box which Sir John rented from the Duke of Rutland, was only a few miles from Perth. Quite close to it was Birnam Wood, made famous by

Shakespeare in *Macbeth,* and under its ancient trees I spent many happy hours, picnicking and rambling with Lady Millais and the family.

At tea–time on the lawn, when the fishing was done with, Sir John would settle himself in a chair and make sketches of me in every position and on any scrap of paper that was handy, evidently for the pure pleasure of using his pencil, for when the drawings were finished he would care- lessly throw them down anywhere, but his wife, shrewd Scotchwoman that she was, went about carefully gathering them up, and saying, "These will be verra valuable one day." When I last saw the little sketches re- ferred to, they had been framed and were hanging in a prominent position in Lady Millais's boudoir.

An amusing incident which happened at one of the numerous dinner– parties at their house in Kensington comes back to me. We were talking about our birthplace, and a guest inquired casually, "Let me see, when did we take Jersey?" At which Millais shouted in his great boyish voice, "Take Jersey, eh? You mean, when did we Normans conquer England!'" Then continuing to me, "And, I say, Mrs. Langtry, when did *we* subjugate London?"

Millais was an energetic but spasmodic worker, always stood while he painted, and would apply himself like one inspired for about twenty minutes, after which he would throw down his brush and palette, re–light his pipe, which was never out of his mouth, contemplate me for a quarter of an hour, and then start again in a fresh frenzy.

He told me that I was the most exasperating subject he had ever painted, that I looked just beautiful for about fifty–five out of sixty min- utes, but for five in every hour I was amazing. I do not think he ever worked on my portrait in my absence, as did some other artists to whom I sat. One day I was walking with Millais in Knightsbridge when we met Lord Wolseley. He had just returned from one of his successful expeditions, and was looking rather self–satisfied. We stopped to speak to him, and the artists, with a sly glance at me, said, "We have just been admiring a first–rate portrait of you!" Lord Wolseley, who was very pleased, asked, "Where?" "My dear fellow," replied Millais, "you will find it on the pavement a little farther on, sandwiched between the Eddystone Lighthouse and a flitch of bacon!"

The same year, Edward J. Poynter painted me in a gorgeous golden gown. The picture was shown at Burlington House and afterwards most kindly presented to me by the artist, and is the only original painting of myself that I possess to–day. I think Sir Edward did not catch my colouring so accurately as did Millais or Watts, but, nevertheless, it is a fine portrait.

Watts, in *The Dean's Daughter*, chose, like Millais, to picture me in black, wearing a quaint little poke bonnet from which he ruthlessly tore the opulent ostrich feather which I regarded at that time as the glory of my head–gear. But, on seeing the picture exhibited in later years, I realised that he was quite right in his somewhat arbitrary ideas, for the portrait was not dated, and might have been painted yesterday or to– morrow, a quality which — Watts thought — works of all great artists should possess.

In imaginative art I think no painter of the day could vie with George Frederick Watts. I can see now, as distinctly as if I had studied it only yesterday, a huge canvas in his studio, named "Love Fighting Death." Love — tiny and impotent — is struggling vainly to prevent the stalwart, grey–clad figure of Death from entering an English rose–wreathed cottage door.

Watts was an enthusiastic lover of early Italian art. He adored colour, and constantly lamented its absence in the streets of London, insisting that our sense of it was being lost, and claiming it to be of distinct educational value to the multitude. He lived absolutely alone, rather hermit–like, in a reposeful, artistic, Queen Anne house off Holland Park. While sitting to him I noticed how strikingly his pointed white beard, flowing gown, and black skull–cap, made him resemble the master he worshipped — Titian. And nothing pleased him so much as to be told of this resemblance. It produced in him the ingenuous pleasure of a child. How simple are the great! And such a charming simplicity!

Quite as interesting as Millais, he was of a markedly different temperament. One always felt at rest with him. I spent hours and hours posing without experiencing strain or fatigue. For one portrait alone I gave him forty sittings, and it still remains unfinished. It was to be called "Summer," and represented me full–face, in purple and gold drapery, holding a large basket of roses in my arms, and with a background of bluest sky.

Sometimes scarcely a stroke of work was done in the studio. Watts would ring for tea, ignore the sitting, and, instead, entertain me with lengthy dissertations on art. They were really absorbing lectures, and through him I learned in some measure to appreciate the mysteries and splendours of his favourite Italian school. Subsequently, when I visited the famous galleries of Europe, I realised what a debt I owed to him. He had an extremely sympathetic nature, and interested himself in the smallest details of my life; some of my happiest hours were spent in the company of this soft–voiced, gentle–mannered artist, whom I shall always regard as the greatest poetical painter of his time.

As for Sir Edward Burne–Jones, he was strongly impressed by my "healthy appearance," to quote his exact expression. I spent a good deal of time in his studio, by way of antidote to his "greenery gallery" models, as they were irreverently termed by the philistines of the art world. Occasionally I sat for studies, and sometimes for more important works. Twice I contributed my face for studies in his well–known picture called "The Golden Stair," in which I may be detected, both full–face and in profile, on two of the lower steps.

An imposing symbolical painting he did of me was named "Dame Fortune," which was bought by Arthur Balfour and placed over the mantelpiece in his dining–room in Carlton House Terrace, London. Clad in grey draperies, a tall, very tall figure, I am depicted with resolute and pitiless face, turning a huge wheel on which kings, princes, statesmen, millionaires, and others rise, reach the top, and then fall, to be crushed by the ever–revolving wheel of Fate — a cruel picture, but horribly true. Fine in conception and execution though it is, I always disliked it, and it seems a strange work to be signed by Burne–Jones, whom I so often met socially at the house of our mutual friends, George Lewis and his wife. He was a poet and a dreamer, by nature so sweet and simple that the association of a bitter thought with him seemed utterly incongruous. I remember no other picture of his so implacable in character as "Dame Fortune."

A young artist who was attracting much attention at this period through his drawings of beautiful women was Frank Miles, to whom I sat for a pencil portrait, which was bought as soon as finished by Prince Leopold, who came there very often while I was posing. It was a head in profile, my name being delicately suggested by a background of faintly pencilled lilies. Prince Leopold hung it over his bed in Buckingham Palace, where it remained, until, one day when he was ill, the Queen went to see him. She evidently did not approve, for I was told she then and there took it down, standing on a chair to do so.

Frank lives in a curious old–world house looking over the Thames, at the corner of Salisbury Street, Strand, London. It was a very ghostly mansion, with antique staircases, twisting passages, broken down furniture, and dim corners. In the late afternoon interesting people, artistic, social, and literary, of both sexes, found their way to his dusty old studio; among those I met there being Her Royal Highness Princess Louise, Duchess of Argyll, handsome and artistic, and a clever sculptor; the poetess,

Violet Fane, who wrote ardent love poems, which in those hypocritical days were considered highly improper; Forbes–Robertson; Ellen Terry; and, of course, our mutual friends, Whistler and Oscar Wilde. Many purely social lights dropped in for a cup of tea, thoroughly enjoying the Bohemian atmosphere. Among those I later came to know very well, and to stop with in the country from time to time, were the Duchess of Westminster, a frequent visitor; the Duchess of Beaufort; Lord and Lady Dorchester; and Lord and Lady Rosslyn.

Poets also came to Miles' studio: Rossetti, Swinburne, and William Morris, the latter not only a poet, but the great "uplifter" of home decoration, sorely needed in the Victorian era — the man who made dados, friezes, and subdued greens popular. Sometimes Walter Pater put in an appearance, and there also I met apparently frivolous scions of great families who have now become pillars of their country, and many Oxford undergraduates, of whom not a few have since become famous.

Franks Miles was a gardener first and an artist afterwards, and every time I sat to him there would be some new flower awaiting me. He was the pioneer in the revival of the abandoned herbaceous border and also in bringing flowers within the means of the general public. Through him Oscar Wilde became a flower worshipper and popularised the daffodil and the daisy, but Frank had won reputation as a cultivator and hybridiser of beautiful lilies and narcissi before Oscar ever thought of pinning his love to them.

Their combined influence certainly created a desire among flower lovers to plant beautiful bulbs and perennials in their gardens and to eschew geraniums and the detestable ribbon border which had hitherto been the main decoration of pleasure grounds. The artist originated a naive scheme for planting the London parks with bulbs, and obtaining permission from the authorities to allow the children to pick the blooms, but the idea was never carried out. While alluring, I doubt if it would have been found practical.

Miles had a knack of conveying the sense of colour in his simple pencil drawings, which was the more extraordinary, as he confessed to me one day that he was almost colour–blind. But this ability made him well adapted to depict the beautiful fair colouring of Miss Maynard, now Countess of Warwick, and a world–renowned beauty. She told me only recently that Miles had especially invited her stepfather to "gaze" on his "latest model," and the introduction resulted in an immediate dinner being arranged by her mother, Lady Rosslyn, who asked many of her friends to meet my husband and myself. She also said that I appeared at this large dinner–party in the same black gown I had worn at the studio, having simply turned the collar in at the throat as a concession to the occasion. Lady Warwick was still in the schoolroom at the time, but, with her younger sister, Blanche, watched my arrival from the stairs; and I dare add, as it happened to so long ago, her final statement that my gown made no difference in the effect I created.

James McNeill Whistler did a portrait of me, and the numerous sittings were, I think enjoyed by both of us. By the way, I wonder what became of that unfinished picture and the yellow robe in which he was painting me? Both are still in existence I fancy.

In personal appearance — and the individuality of few modern painters has had wider exploitation — Whistler reached the high point of eccentricity. He was a small, thin man. His face, deep lined (the skin resembling parchment in colour and texture), was lit by alert, beady, black eyes, and oddly emphasised by oily, curly hair, wholly of midnight blackness with the exception of the one famous, carefully trained, snow–white lock on the forehead, which added a final weird touch. His expressive hands, with their delicate, tapering fingers, were thin almost to transparency, and he wore his nails so extraordinarily long that they produced a sense of discomfort. To estimate his age was impossible, but from his wrinkled face he might have been positively antiquated. Not an Adonis by any means, but of so unusual a type that his appearance was oddly arresting.

His unquestionable genius was, I think, not sufficiently esteemed by English art critics in general, and some of them scored his work savagely. Not being the kind of man to suffer in silence, he counter–attacked in the newspapers, criticising his detractors in letters of bitter irony and scorn, but permeated with such dry humour that he captured the public and silenced the enemy.

Original always, Jimmy, in lieu of his name, elected to sign his correspondence with a weird Japanese butterfly, which, in defiance of the law of insectology, he provided with a baneful, arrow–like sting, more or less long and pronounced according to the nature and destination of his letter. But when he wished to emphasise his friendship, he drew the little insect as seen at the end of this note to me, in which the quaint butterfly is depicted in stingless and inoffensive guise.

"Most Beautiful Lilly, — You must come to the Suffolk Street Galleries on this very next Sunday, say at about five o'clock or so. If you stay but awhile, and show the people that it is your happiness to be there, *voila!* You were most lovable the other morning, and I wonder how the other chaps would *sauter* at all anywhere away from you.

"Do send the enclosed to Mrs. Cornwallis–West; I don't know where she is staying.

"You have your own card, of course, though equally of course the place is yours."

Whistler's studio in Tite Street, Chelsea, was called "The White House," and had been built for him according to ideas of his own. It has left an indistinct mark in my memory of a jumble of narrow stairs and

57

passages, quaintly–shaped rooms, low ceilings, mustard–yellow walls, matted floors, and blue and white china, the whole creating an effect of studied eccentricity quite in keeping with its owner's whimsical personality.

The artist's American cuisine was celebrated, and it was in his house that I first tasted the delicious buckwheat cakes, pop– overs, corn muffins, and other cereals that make breakfast such a tempting meal in the most hospitable country in the world. In the dining–room were further evidences of the host's *penchant* for Japanese art — the blue and white plates, coffee–cups, and other accessories being of Oriental design. Scattered over the table were queer little dishes containing mysterious relishes and compounds prepared by the painter himself, while in the centre stood a bowl (Japanese, of course) filled with water, on which a single blossom floated, perhaps a eucharist lily.

The first time I breakfasted at his house I met George W. Smalley, a potent force in London both politically and socially, knowing everyone worth his trouble, and having the *entree* everywhere. He was a *litterateur* of a very high order, and such a good conversationalist that he commanded attention without raising his low, steady voice. He was an art critic, and correspondent of the *New York Tribune*, and, I think, wrote political articles for *The Times.* In addition to all these intellectual attainments, he was a hearty gossip. I reprint here portions of an article written by him years after that first meeting.

"It was in Whistler's house in Tite Street, in Chelsea, that I first saw the woman whose beauty was, I suppose, more famous than any other of her time. I had gone to breakfast — a twelve o'clock breakfast, such as Whistler liked giving in those days, with such American delicacies as corn bread and buckwheat cakes to astonish the dull palate of his British friends. When the door into the parlour opened, this lady was sitting in a low chair

58

in the corner by the fire, and the light of the fire shone on her face. A vision never to be forgotten; the colouring brilliant and at the same time delicate; the attitude all grace. There was a harmony and a contrast all in one; the harmony such as Whistler loved; the contrast such as it pleased her Maker to arrange; between softness and strength; the lines of the woman's full body flowing gently into each other, but the whole impression was one of vital force. There was no one else in the room. As her renown, presently to be world–wide, had just begun in London, I knew who it must be. When Whistler a moment later came in, he said: "Of course, you and Mrs. Langtry know each other?" That was all the introduction we ever had.

"I supposed Whistler was going to do her portrait, but I cannot remember that he ever did. The one which London admired next May in the Royal Academy came from a heavier brush than his, and was signed 'Millais.' But Mrs. Langtry was the despair of all the portrait painters. Other beautiful women have been, and still are. Whistler himself was of an uncompromising nature in the presence of beauty. The story of Lady Eden's portrait needs no re–telling. The portrait of Miss Connie Gilchrist was not to the taste of that young lady's many admirers. It hung in the studio that morning. Whistler was not a man who asked for an opinion on his work, nor expected you to give it unasked as many artists do. If they do not, for what was the institution Show Sunday invented? But Mrs. Langtry, who, even in those early days passed Acts of Parliament for her private use, took command of the situation. 'Oh! Mr. Whistler, what a lovely portrait. I have seen Connie Gilchrist but once, but I am sure it is hers. Nobody but you could have done it so beautifully.'

"As guests we could have no other opinion. As critics we might think it a flimsy piece of work, as Whistler in his heart probably did. But before this he had said: 'A work of art is complete when it expresses the idea in the mind of the artist.' He varied this formula, but he held to his opinion and painted on it, though not always. Miss Connie Gilchrist, with all her celebrity, never, I think, forced her way into the never–crowded ranks of the professional beauties, of whom Mrs. Langtry was the acknowledged queen.

"I stayed on after the company had drifted away, and Whistler began at once with his explosive questions: 'Of course, you knew Mrs. Langtry?' 'I had never seen her.' 'Then you had never seen the loveliest thing that ever was. Don't tell me that you don't think her perfect. It doesn't matter what you think. She *is* perfect. Her beauty is simply exquisite, but her manner is more exquisite still. She is kindness itself.' I was in no mood to dispute any of these propositions, but as I saw much of Mrs. Langtry afterwards, Whistler's account of her did not seem to me quite complete. But with or without Mrs. Langtry, Whistler's breakfasts were like no other ever given. In social life, as in art, conventions were to him so many objects of content. He, too, like Mrs. Langtry, passed private Acts of Parliament for this private use. The Acts of Parliament of these two were for our use too, we were to obey them. None of us minded, only it was sometimes difficult to know when they were passed and what they were, and when they were repealed and when a new act came into force."

After my appearance on the stage I met at Whistler's that remarkable architect, E. S. Godwin, and, there being a vacant plot of ground right opposite our mutual friend in Tite Street, he set about drawing for me plans for an inexpensive house, but my triumvirate of counsellors, Oscar Wilde, Frank Miles and Whistler, insisted on offering so many suggestions regarding the building, which Godwin good–naturedly assented to, that when the rough sketches were inspected, it was discovered that there was no possibility of a staircase, and before the architect had time to remedy the oversight, my engagement to tour the United States put an end to the project.

I might mention that a number of studies of me were made by Lord Leighton in his characteristically finished style, and that I sat for a shepherdess in his picture "Arcadia," which I have never seen since. Some years later, when I was about to appear in New York as Galatea in W. S. Gilbert's fantastic play, Frederick Leighton designed my garment, making the draperies of flesh tint, with blue and gold touches, as he said that all Greek statues had originally been coloured.

Lord Houghton gave a commission for a portrait of me to be painted by his *protege* and friend, Henry Weigall. It was not considered very successful, however, and the only person I ever heard admire it was General U. S. Grant, and he was too splendidly bluff and sincere not to have meant what he said.

A feature of the London season was a series of tableaux, planned for charitable purposes by Lady Freke, and given at her enormous house in Cromwell Road, South Kensington. They are still remembered as being exceptional. Each tableau was directed by a great painter, and represented one of his best know works. Millais selected his poetic picture "Effie Deane," choosing me to represent the heroine. The young girl leans over a stile, taking leave of her betrayer, her maiden snood, to which she has forfeited the right, held in her hand — a very pathetic portrayal of what Mr. Gladstone thought Scott's greatest novel, *The Heart of Midlothian.* One Godfrey Pearse, who sat for the lover in the original picture, posed with me for the tableau.

It was while I was sitting for Millais, by the by, that I made Gladstone's acquaintance, the artist being engaged at the same time in painting the familiar, speaking likeness of the great statesman which is now in the National Portrait Gallery, London.

Chapter
4

The first of the royalties I met was Prince Leopold, the youngest son of Queen Victoria, the meeting happening at a dinner–party given by the Marchioness of Ely, and after this we often met at her house, as well as at Alick York's, and other of his intimate friends who planned small dinners and theatre–parties for him; but he was rather delicate and often ill.

The Prince was a tall, transparent–skinned young man, of gentle manners and extreme simplicity, artistic and of marked intellectuality; at our little London house he was a frequent visitor, and we occasionally went cruising with him in the Queen's yacht *Alberta* during our sojourn at Cowes. Among his few guests on some of these cruises were two little American girls, twins, whose keenness and American vivacity made them amusing and at that time original, but as H.R.H. was to a certain extent kept in leading strings by his august mother, we used to hide below on these trips till we got out of range of the Osborne House telescopes.

Apropos of Prince Leopold there is rather an amusing story, for the truth of which I cannot vouch, told in connection with a personal friend of his, who was one of Queen Victoria's equerries. This young man was constantly mimicking his friends, but the imitation which he considered his cleverest, and which he took special delight in airing, was one of "Her Most Gracious." The Queen heard of it, and one night at Buckingham Palace as dinner was about finished, she turned suddenly to the young equerry and said:

"Mr. So–and–So, I understand that you give a very good imitation of me. Will you do it now?"

A dismayed silence ensued, for the miserable young man, scarlet with confusion, was incapable of speech. The Queen then repeated more peremptorily:

"Mr. So–and–So, I wish you to do as I ask."

Forced to obey, the trembling victim proceeded to give a greatly modified and extremely bad imitation. When he had finished, the Queen gave the signal to rise, and, saying in a freezing tone to the now almost fainting equerry, "*We* are not amused," left the dining–room with her ladies. If the story be true, it would seem very merciful to Her Majesty to let the young man off so lightly.

It was one evening late in June, during my first season, at a supper given by Sir Allen Young, the arctic explorer, at the London house after the opera, that I met His Majesty King Edward, then Prince of Wales. Sir Allen, a wealthy bachelor, had spent a great deal of his time in searching for the North–west Passage. He had made two or three expeditions hunting for the Pole, one of them in his own yacht, the *Pandora*, which he had had specially fitted out for the purpose.

He was a fidgety creature, already in the forties, and had in his grey eyes the curious, far–away look which one associates with an explorer. He had very little small talk, replying mostly in monosyllables when addressed, but he was chivalrously devoted to his friends, hospitable, popular, and one of His Royal Highness' frequent hosts. By all who knew him he was familiarly called "Alleno."

There were about ten of us at this party, and we were all waiting about for supper to be announced. *I*, at all events, quite unaware that so illustrious a guest was expected, was wondering at the delay. Suddenly there was a stir, followed by an expectant hush, a hurried exit of Sir Allen, then a slight commotion outside, and presently I heard a deep and cheery voice say: "I am afraid I am a little late." Sir Allen murmured something courtier–like in reply, and the Prince of Wales, whose face had been previously unfamiliar to me except through photographs, appeared in the doorway of Stratford Palace drawing–room.

Evidently he had been attending an important function, for some glittering orders and the blue ribbon of the Garter added to his regal appearance. He glanced around the room, shook hands with the bobbing women and bowing men, with all of whom he was acquainted. My husband and I were the only newcomers. I happened to be standing by the fireplace when Sir Allen advanced to present me to His Royal Highness.

For various reasons I was panic–stricken at the prospect, and for one bewildered moment really considered the advisability of climbing the chimney to escape, but, my presence of mind returning, I stood my ground and made my curtsey, after which, again for various reasons, I greatly enjoyed watching my husband go rather stammeringly through a similar ordeal.

At the supper–table I found myself seated next to the Prince, who, however, extracted only monosyllabic replies either from myself or my husband, the latter being even more dumb than I was. But, though silent, I was immensely interested in watching the Prince, and soon realised that, while good–natured and pleasant to everyone, he preserved his dignity admirably, in fact I decided that he would have been a brave man who, even at this little *intime* supper–party, attempted a familiarity with him. He displayed a sincere fondness for Sir Allen Young, praised his cook, and seemed bent on making the evening a jolly one; but this remarkable consideration for his host and hostess, I discovered subsequently, was always apparent. He really worked to make one's dinners and parties successful — an easy task with his magnetic personality.

His affability to servants was well known to all who entertained him, for he seldom passed one without a word or a kind look, and I think he was equally good–natured to his own entourage, for I remember that one year H.R.H. returned from Marienbad very proud of his lost inches. It was suggested that the improvement would be more apparent if his waist-coat was also reduced, and he said: "I want to, but my servant says I shall soon fill it out again. Saucy fellows, these valets!"

Another of the Prince of Wales' coterie, and another of his informal hosts, was Christopher Sykes, a Yorkshire squire and, like Sir Allen Young, a rich bachelor. He was a very tall, solemn man with pale eyes, bushy eyebrows, and a tawny beard, still more tongue–tied than Sir Allen, and given to bowing (with preternatural gravity) almost too impressively to the Prince in sole response to any remark addressed to him. A friend quite the reverse of Sir Allen Young and Christopher Sykes, and in wide con-trast to them, was the Earl of Clonmell, known to his intimates as "Earlie." His was a strong Irish individuality, and he really rippled with fun.

These and other friends joined His Royal Highness in the morning or evening rides in the Row, where he took exercise daily, often accompa-nied by the Princess of Wales, the royal red brow–bands of their and the equerry's horses never failing to occasion a certain commotion. The fash-ionable hours to ride during the London season were either very early, before breakfast, when what was termed the "Liver Brigade" made its appearance, or, preferably, at seven in the evening. The latter hour caused dinner to be a very late meal, seldom commencing before nine o'clock.

I remember that, on one occasion, when riding with the Prince, it was past that hour when I left the Row, as etiquette demanded that I should ride on so long as His Royal Highness elected to do so. Mr. Langtry and I were, as usual, dining out, and when I arrived home I found him impatiently waiting on the doorstep, watch in hand, and in all the paraphernalia of evening dress. After a scrambling toilette we eventually arrived at the Clark–Thornhills', in Eaton Square, where we were due, to find it was nearly ten o'clock. Everyone was waiting, of course, but, before I could apologise, my hostess greeted me pleasantly, saying: "So and So on his way here saw you riding in the Park, and, as we knew you couldn't get away, we postponed dinner indefinitely." After the very natural grumbling of my husband, these words served as balm to any troubled soul. It is so difficult to please everyone.

Probably the most entertaining of the Prince's set were the Beresfords — Lords Marcus, William, and Charles. They were all as handsome as paint, and as merry as the traditional Irishman or sandboys. Full of native wit, charm, and *bonhomie*, the positively radiated high spirits, their ready *bon–mots* and amusing doings causing constant mirth.

The first summer we spent at Cowes, H.M.S. *Thunderer*, of which Lord Charles Beresford was Commander, was in the Roads, and several impromptu dances were given on board. All the cabins being below the water line, it was necessary to supply them with oxygen artificially, through air–shafts. One afternoon, while Lord Charles' small cabin was being inspected by royalty and others, his love of mischief caused him to switch off the supply of air and to watch the effect of his practical joke with great delight. Very soon our faces became scarlet, our breathing grew difficult, and we began to go through the uncomfortable sensation which must be experienced by a fish out of water. Fortunately, Lord Charles did not go beyond the frightening–limit, or the Beresford joke might have developed into a Beresford tragedy.

The Prince of Wales loved music, and could discuss it critically. Almost every night he might be seen at the opera in the omnibus box, surrounded by his chosen intimates. But the real musician of the family was the Duke of Edinburgh (the handsome sailor Prince), who was a very fine violinist, and played frequently in public. London was then the affluent possessor of two Opera Houses, Covent Garden and Her Majesty's, and, with Patti in one house and Christine Nilsson at the other (both at their zenith), and Trebelli and Scalchi, the contraltos, there was a plethora of good music, which the Royal Family evidently appreciated from their constant attendance at one or other of the Opera Houses. I thought Her Majesty's the more beautiful house of the two, with its amber satin hangings, but it has long since ceased to exist.

The appearance of the Princess of Wales, now Queen Alexandria, in the royal box, wonderfully lovely and faultlessly dressed, seemed almost to dim the beauty of every other woman in the house, and her grace and fascination were such that one could not take one's eyes from her.

Anglo–American matrimonial alliances, which have since grown plentiful, were comparatively few at that time. The two prominent American wives of the day were Lady Randolph Churchill and Consuela, Viscountess Mandeville and later Duchess of Manchester. Lord Randolph Churchill was the Chief Secretary for Ireland, and, as he and Lady Randolph were much in residence there, I did not see her until a subsequent London season. Then, one night, at a ball given by Sir George Wombwell, my attention was attracted by a radiant, black–eyed, black–haired beauty in a cloud of white tulle, with a large diamond star gleaming on her exquisite forehead. Hers was indeed a handsome face, aglow with intellectuality.

Lady Mandeville, fair and ethereal, was of so merry and witty a disposition that she was a general favourite, and was *person grata* at Marlborough House, where their Royal Highnesses entertained constantly. It was at one of their Sunday dinners, which were usually small and of a rather *intime* character, that I made the acquaintance of this cheery American, and I believe that it was that same evening which was also the occasion of a great kindness shown to me by the Princess of Wales.

I had become suddenly ill after dinner, and was suffering excruciating pain, until the sympathetic Miss Knollys found an opportunity to ask if I might be excused. The Princess, so considerate and compassionate always, immediately told me to hurry home to bed, which I thankfully did. Half an hour later the Household Physician, Francis Laking, was ushered into my room, having been sent by command of the Princess of Wales to see me and report to her on my condition. By the next afternoon I was feeling better, and was lying on the sofa in my little drawing–room about tea–time, when the butler suddenly announced Her Royal Highness, who entered, followed by her inseparable secretary, Miss Charlotte Knollys.

The honour of the unexpected visit brought me at once to my feet, ill though I felt, but the Princess insisted on my lying down again, while she made herself tea, chatting kindly and graciously. She always used a specially manufactured violet scent, and I recall exclaiming on the delicious perfume, and her solicitous answer that she feared possibly it was too strong for me. I have always heard that Her Royal Highness never permitted scandal or gossip in her presence. Certain it is that, whenever I found myself in the magic circle, the discussion invariably turned on *things*, not people.

A much–beloved American in London, whom I must not overlook, was Mrs. Fanny Ronalds of Boston. Her attractive appearance and fine, perfectly–trained voice, made her welcome everywhere, and she was good–nature personified.

Lillie Langtry

Lady Gladys Herbert, later Countess of Lonsdale and ultimately Marchioness of Ripon, was superbly beautiful, with brilliant colouring, and the features and carriage of an ideal Roman Empress. We were great friends, and at one time almost inseparable. I spent part of one summer with her at Lowther Castle, soon after her first marriage, and she met me at Carlisle Station with her pony car to drive me to the Castle. As we whisked through the Park, and the impressive walls of Lowther loomed before us, she intimated that the one thing she was most anxious for me to see was the emu strutting about on the grass. Splendour was her birthright, but the emu was a novelty.

After the rush and fatigue of a London season, it was a heavenly relief to find oneself under the beautiful trees of Goodwood Park, at the end of July, for the final fashionable race–meeting of the season. Baron Ferdinand de Rothschild always rented a house as near the course as possible for the week's racing, and each year invited the same small party, which included Lord and Lady Gerard, Harry Tyrwhitt, ourselves, and one or two more. He was very fussy over details, and dragged us all to Singleton by an unnecessarily early train, marshalling us to a saloon, where a greedy Rothschild lunch was served *en route*. When we arrived he went straight off to the kitchen, with as many of us as cared to follow him, to see that all was going on well. Yet whenever he ate a meal a tray of medicine bottles appeared as an antidote. In the train he contented himself with specially prepared uninviting cold toast sandwiches. Once Bill Gerard maliciously threw them out of the window, saying he could not bear to look at them, so Ferdy sulked and ate nothing.

One evening my maid's dress caught fire when I was dressing for dinner, and our united screams were disregarded. When I got down the baron was raging because he thought the owners had left children in the house. So, had I not put out the flames, we might have burned to death.

Goodwood over, everyone who owned a yacht, or who could, by hook or crook, manage to get on board one, went to Cowes, that little village in the Isle of Wight, celebrated through having been chosen by Queen Victoria for her summer residence for many years. During nine months out of twelve Cowes was empty, forlorn and forgotten, but immediately Her Majesty was in residence the hotels and boarding–houses filled with such rapidity that by the 1st of August it was crammed and jammed with royalty and well– known people from all quarters of the globe and it was impossible to find the tiniest place to lay one's head.

One of the interesting sights to see was the "great and near– great" rubbing shoulders on the lawn of the Royal Yacht Squadron, while outside a crowd waited in the hope of catching a glimpse of Queen Victoria as she drove along the short sea–front, accompanied by the devoted Princess Beatrice.

The "Cowes Week," with the daily sailing competitions for every size and class of yacht (culminating in the struggle for the Cup), the cruises in floating palaces by day, and the dances on shore by night, was a whirl-wind of gaiety. After that the principal yachts flitted on to other regattas, and soon only a small flotilla remained in the Solent. At the period to which my memory has taken me, Mr. Langtry had sold his last remaining yacht, and we were the guests of Sir Allen Young on his comfortable schooner *Helen*. During the yachting season the Prince and Princess of Wales, accompanied by their sons and daughters, lived entirely on the royal yacht *Osborne*, for the reason that Osborne Cottage, I do not know why, was considered unhealthy. Their guests in the month of August of this particular year were the King and Queen of Denmark, with their then unmarried daughter, Princess Thyra (afterwards Duchess of Cumberland), sister of the Princess of Wales; the Crown Prince of Denmark, who later became King, and Prince Wilhelm of Glucksberg. Dinner–parties were

70

given on board the *Osborne* nightly, to which a favoured few were invited, and, after dinner, weather permitting, we danced on the deck. Sir Allen Young on several occasions also had the honour of entertaining the Royal Party on the *Helen* for tea and a sail.

The King and Queen of Denmark were remarkable for their simple manners and their affability to everyone who had the honour of meeting them or serving them, which accounts for the sincere affection in which they were held by all classes in the Isle of Wight. They much enjoyed being rowed about the bay by Mr. Langtry in the *Helen's* dinghy.

Prince Wilhelm of Glucksberg, who was very sprightly and amusing, gave me a photograph of himself in uniform, having written under his signature "with cap on head." I also had photographs of the Danish King and Queen, but I regret to say that they have been lost or appropriated, as were many other photographs and letters I received from celebrities from time to time. Perhaps owing to my busy life, I have not superintended the packing and storing of my treasures as carefully as I should have done. But no one can steal from my memory the affectionate embraces of their Majesties of Denmark when that happy season in the Isle of Wight came to an end.

There was a jeweller's shop in the High Street called Benson's, where we used to buy each other inexpensive presents. Being in Cowes when the two Princes set off in the *Bacchante* for a voyage round the world, I gave a small trinket as a souvenir to the Duke of Clarence. The next day he showed it to me on his watch–chain saying: "I had to take off my grandmother's (Queen Victoria) locket to make room for it."

The Royal Yacht Squadron, which has its headquarters at Cowes, is, I believe, the most exclusive club in the kingdom. It is the only Yacht Club which flies the white ensign of the Navy with its white red–crossed burgee, and, in consequence of this proud distinction, it has power to accord special privileges to yachts entering the various ports at home or aboard, as I discovered when we were yachting with one of the members, Sir Allen Young, and again when we were cruising in the Prince of Wales' schooner *Hildegarde*, graciously lent by him to my husband and myself one summer. The Squadron Club is a castle on the sea–front (there are many castles in the Isle of Wight).

The world at Cowes lived generally on yachts or in apartments, although some few people have houses and cottages. Lord Harrington and Mrs. Cust were two of these fortunate ones, and Lord Hardwicke, whose lovely house called "Egypt" was occupied that year by the Empress Eugenie and the Prince Imperial, was another. It was there that I was presented to the Empress of the French, who took part in the life of Cowes. Her beauty and charm were still very evident, but she had been, naturally, much saddened by the trying events through which she had passed. The Prince Imperial, on the contrary, bubbled with youthful spirits and was a ready originator of practical jokes, then very much in fashion, and of one of which I was, as well as others, a victim.

Being still greatly interested in "spirit rapping" (familiarly termed "table–turning"), a "serious" investigation was arranged at Mrs. Cust's hospitable and popular cottage on the sea–front for the purpose of convincing sceptical friends. Even royalty waxed curious.

At the appointed hour we assembled, and sat with joined hands round the table, but *immediately* after the lights had been extinguished there were such violent upheavals that they seemed too good to be true, and on someone's striking a light, Prince Louis Napoleon was discovered hard at work throwing the furniture about. Perhaps I was not so surprised as the rest of the investigators, for I felt him let go of my hand, and thus break the "chain." After this philistine interrupter had been respectfully put out of the room, the door carefully locked, and calm restored, we again waited expectantly in absolute darkness and silence for something to happen, and in about ten minutes it did. Once more a "manifestation" occurred, uncanny but tangible. Then matches were struck again suddenly, disclosing the undefeated Prince Imperial, who had climbed the side of the house with the aid of a wistaria growing thereon and re–entered the room through the window! There he stood with several empty paper bags in his hand, while most of the "investigators," and especially the Prince of Wales, were literally snowed over with flour.

Poor young Prince! Not long after he fell in the Zulu War, ambushed and cruelly assegaied. Oscar Wilde commemorated the sad event in some verses entitled "Louis Napoleon," the first of which I remember:

> Eagle of Austerlitz! Where were thy wings
> When, far away, upon a barbarous strand,
> In fight unequal, by an obscure hand,
> Fell the last scion of thy brood of kings?

Everyone relaxed at Cowes, and Mrs. Cust's cottage was the scene of many more ebullitions of high spirits and mischief. One night a donkey was hoisted to the bedroom of the son of the house as a surprise for him — a proceeding in which both the aforesaid Prince took part. I believe they dressed him up and put him in bed, though how to keep him there must have puzzled them.

A little story connected with Napoleon III and the Empress Eugenie, which was told to me at Cowes, seems to have a special significance, following those years of terrible world–conflict.

The incident occurred at the breaking–out of hostilities in the Franco–Prussian War. One day, Napoleon, passing the apartments of Eugenie, noticed with her a well–known jeweller and designer from one of the big houses of the Rue de la Paix, who had brought to the Palace a collection of gems which the empress had expressed a desire to see. Napoleon entered the room, gazed admiringly at the jewels for a few minutes, and then said to the man:

"They tell me you are one of the most famous designers in the world."

"You honour me, sire," was the reply.

"I have heard," continued Napoleon, "that you can transform the most insignificant object into a thing of artistic beauty."

"Again you honour me, sire," returned the man.

"Let me see," went on Napoleon, plucking a single hair from his head and offering it to the tradesman, "what you can do with that."

"It shall have my best attention, sir," replied the jeweller, placing the hair carefully in his wallet."

A month later, when the clash of war had come, a small package was delivered at the Tuilereis for the Emperor. He opened it and found a jewel case. Inside was the hair, with a tiny gold disc attached to each end, one bore the word "Alsace" and the other "Lorraine." Underneath was written: "You hold them by a hair."

Chapter
5

Vividly I recall the first meeting with Oscar Wilde in the studio of Frank Miles, and how astonished I was at his strange appearance. Then he must have been not more than twenty–two. He had a profusion of brown hair, brushed back from his forehead, and worn rather longer than was conventional, though not with the exaggeration which he afterwards affected. His face was large, and so colourless that a few pale freckles of good size were oddly conspicuous. He had a well–shaped mouth, with somewhat coarse lips and greenish–hued teeth. The plainness of his face, however, was redeemed by the splendour of his great, eager eyes.

In height he was about six feet, and broad in proportion. His hands were large and indolent, with pointed fingers and perfectly–shaped filbert nails, indicative of his artistic disposition. The nails, I regretfully record, rarely received the attention they deserved. To me he was always grotesque in appearance, although I have seen him described by a French writer as "beautiful" and "apollo–like." That he possessed a remarkably fascinating and compelling personality, and what in an actor would be termed wonderful "stage presence," is beyond question, and there was about him an enthusiasm singularly captivating. He had one of the most alluring voices that I have ever listened to, round and soft, and full of variety and expression, and the cleverness of his remarks received added value from his manner of delivering them.

His customary apparel consisted of light–coloured trousers, a black frock coat, only the lower button fastened, a brightly flowered waistcoat blossoming underneath, and a white silk cravat, held together by an old intaglio amethyst set as a pin. I do not think I ever met him wearing gloves, but he always carried a pale lavender pair, using them to give point to his gestures, which were many and varied. Apropos of his dress, I recall seeing him (after he had become celebrated and prosperous), at the first night of one of his plays, come before the curtain, in response to the applause of the audience, wearing a black velvet jacket, lavender trousers, and a variegated waistcoat, a white straw hat in one hand and a lighted cigarette in the other.

In the early part of our acquaintance Wilde was *really* ingenuous. His mannerisms and eccentricities were then but the natural outcome of a young fellow bubbling over with temperament, and were not at all assumed. Later, when he began to rise as a figure in the life of London, and his unconscious peculiarities had become a target for the humorous columns of the newspapers, he was quick to realise that they could be turned to advantage, and he proceeded forthwith to develop them so audaciously that it became impossible to ignore them.

He was ridiculed and he was imitated. When he wore a daisy in his buttonhole, thousands of young men did likewise. When he proclaimed the sunflower "adorable," it was to be found adorning every drawing–

room. His edict that severely plain and flowing garments were the only becoming covering for the female form sent every young woman, and manly elderly ones, scampering off to their *modistes* with delirious suggestions for Grecian draperies.

In the queer jargon of the day, he was the "Apostle of the Lily," the "Apostle of the Transcendental," and, among the revilers, the "Apostle of the Utterly–Utter and Too–Too." His affectations, I may say, were mainly for the benefit of the general public. To his friends he always remained the same, and both friends and enemies were forced to confess his brilliancy in spite of his shams. His vogue spread rapidly, and soon he was lionised by both artistic and social sets of London. It seemed to me, however, that he gradually grew less spontaneous and more laboured in his conversation as he became the fashion, which was not to be wondered at when he was counted on to be the life of every afternoon tea, and was expected to supply a *bon mot* between every mouthful at dinner.

His mother, Lady Wilde, lived a retired life in Onslow Square, sometimes emerging from her seclusion to give an afternoon at–home to guests invited by her two sons. On these occasions she used to pull down the blinds and light the lamps, even on summer days. She was a poetess, and wrote verses under the *nom de plume* of Esperanza, so perhaps her son partly inherited his poetic gift from his mother. Some said his elder brother, Willie, was as clever in his way, but I found him quite uninteresting.

When I met Oscar he had come down from Oxford fresh from winning the prize for the best poem of the year, called "Ravenna," but he was very modest about his success, and I heard the fact only from others. Presently, other and beautiful verses from his pen began to attract unusual attention and admiration, and it was then that I became the inspiration for one of his happiest efforts. The poem, which with a dedication to me, originally appeared in *The World* (a society paper edited by Edmund

Yates), is included in Oscar's first volume. He presented me with a white vellum–bound copy bearing the following charming inscription:

"To Helen, formerly of Troy, now of London."

I append this poem:

THE NEW HELEN

Where hast thou been since round the walls of Troy
    The sons of God fought in the great emprise?
        Why dost thou walk our common earth again?
        Hast thou forgotten that impassioned boy,
    His purple galley and his Tyrian men,
        And treacherous Aphrodite's mocking eyes?
For surely it was thou, who, like a star
    Hung in the silver silence of the night,
        Didst bear the Old World's chivalry and might
Into the clamorous crimson waves of war!

Or didst thou rule the fire–laden moon?
    In amorous Sidon was thy temple built,
        Over the light and laughter of the sea?
Where behind lattice, scarlet–wrought and gilt,
    Some brown–limbed girl did weave thee tapestry,
All through the waste and wearied hours of noon;
    Till her wan cheek with flame of passion burned,
And she rose up the sea–washed lips to kiss
    Of some glad Cyprian sailor, safe returned
From Calpe and the cliffs of Herakles?

Lillie Langtry

No! thou art Helen and none other one!
    It was for thee that young Sarpedon died,
And Memnon's manhood was untimely spent;
    It was for thee gold–crested Hector tried
With Thetis' child that evil race to run,
    In the last year of thy beleaguerment;
Ay, even now the glory of thy fame
    Burns in those fields of trampled asphodel,
Where the high lords whom Ilion knew so well
    Clash ghostly shields, and call upon thy name.

Where hast thou been? In that enchanted land
Whose slumbering vales forlorn Calypso knew,
Where never mower rose at break of day,
But all unswathed the tramelling grasses grew,
    And the sad shepherd saw the tall corn strand
Till summer's red had changed to withered grey?
    Didst thou lie there by some Lethean stream
Deep brooding on this ancient memory,
    The crash of broken spears, the fiery gleam
From shivered helm, the Grecian battle–cry?

Nay, thou wert hidden in that hollow hill
    With one who is forgotten utterly,
The discrowned Queen men call the Erycine;
    Hidden away that never mightst thou see
The face of Her, before whose mouldering shrine
    To–day at Rome the silent nations kneel;
Who gat from Love no joyous gladdening,

79

The Days I Knew

But only Love's intolerable pain,
Only a sword to pierce her heart in twain,
    Only the bitterness of child–bearing.

The lotus leaves which heal the wounds of Death
    Lie in thy hand; O, be thou kind to me,
While yet I know the summer of my days;
    For hardly can my tremulous lips draw breath
To fill the silver trumpet with thy praise,
    So bowed am I before thy mystery,
So bowed and broken on Love's terrible wheel,
    That I have lost all hope and heart to sing,
Yet care I not what ruin Time may bring,
    If in thy temple thou wilt let me kneel.

Alas, alas, thou wilt not tarry here,
    But, like that bird, the servant of the sun,
Who flies before the north wind and the night,
    So wilt thou fly our evil land and drear,
Back to the sower of thine old delight,
    And the red lips of young Euphorion;
Nor shall I ever see thy face again,
    But in this poisoned garden–close must stay,
Crowning my brows with the thorn–crown of pain,
    Till all my loveless life shall pass away.

Oh Helen! Helen! Helen! yet a while,
    Yet for a little while, O tarry here,
Till the dawn cometh and the shadows flee!

Lillie Langtry

For in the gladsome sunlight of thy smile
Of heaven or hell I have no thought or fear,
    Seeing I know no other God but thee;
No other God save him before whose feet
    In nets of gold the tired planets move;
The incarnate spirit of spiritual love,
    Who in thy body holds his joyous seat.

Thou wert not born as common women are!
    But, girt with splendour of the foam,
Didst from depths of sapphire seas arise!
    And at thy coming some immortal star,
Bearded with flame, blazed in the Eastern skies
    And waked the shepherds on thine island home,
Thou shalt not die: no asps of Egypt creep
    Close at thy heels to taint the delicate air;
No sullen poppies stain thy hair
    Those scarlet heralds of eternal sleep.

Lily of love, pure and inviolate!
    Tower of ivory! Red rose of fire!
Thou hast come down our darkness to illume,
For we, close caught in the wide nets of Fate,
    Wearied with waiting for the World's Desire,
Aimlessly wandered in this House of Gloom,
    Aimlessly sought some slumberous anodyne
For wasted lives, for lingering wretchedness,
    Till we beheld thy re–arisen shrine,
And the white glory of thy loveliness.

In the heyday of his popularity Oscar and his fads were utilised by Gilbert and Sullivan as their motive of *Patience*, and one of the former's best lyrics ended with these lines:

Though the Philistines may jostle
You will rank as an apostle
    In the high aesthetic band,
As you walk down Piccadilly
With a poppy or a lily
    In your mediaeval hand.

Before Oscar had achieved celebrity, and was unconsciously on the verge of it, he always made a point of bringing me flowers, but he was not in circumstances to afford great posies, so, in coming to call, he would drop into Covent Garden flower market, buy me a single gorgeous amaryllis (all his slender purse would allow), and stroll down Piccadilly carefully carrying the solitary flower. The scribblers construed his act of homage as a pose, and thus I innocently conferred on him the title "Apostle of the Lily."

On my first visit to America he was likewise touring under Henry Abbey's management, and I was amused to find him "dressed for the part." He was wearing a black velvet suit with knickerbockers, silk stocking, and black shoes with silver buckles, his neck embellished by a Byronic collar, and was lecturing on Greek art. Being asked by the U.S. Customs on his arrival the usual question: "Have you anything contraband?" he replied superbly, "No, I have nothing to declare but my genius." His success was only moderate, probably due to the fact that the Press agent sought to impress the public with Oscar's personal eccentricities rather than with his genuine culture.

He was lecturing and I was playing at Buffalo at the same time that season, so we visited Niagara in a party, and in an interview he gave a reporter on his impressions of these mighty waters, he announced, that Mrs. Langtry was photographed with Niagara Falls as an unpretentious background!" A year later, when I was presenting the play (adapted from Sardou's *Nos Intimes*) called *Peril* in the States, Oscar became engaged to a beautiful Irish girl, and sent me the following letter announcing the fact:

"I am really delighted at your immense success; the most brilliant telegrams have appeared in the papers here on your performance in *Peril*. You have done what no other artist of your day has done, invaded America a second time and carried off new victories. But then, you are made for victory. It has always flashed in your eyes and run in your voice.

"And so I write to tell you how glad I am at your triumphs — you, – – Venus Victrix of our age — and the other half to tell you that I am going to be married to a beautiful girl called Constance Lloyd — a grave, slight, violet–eyed little Artemis, with great coils of heavy brown hair which makes her flower–like head droop like a blossom, and wonderful ivory hands which draw music from the piano so sweet that the birds stop singing to listen to her. We are to be married in April. I hope so much that you will be over then. I am so anxious for you to know and to like her.

"I am hard at work lecturing and getting rich, though it is horrid being so much away from her, but we telegraph to each other twice a day, and I rush back suddenly from the uttermost parts of the earth to see her for an hour, and do all the foolish things that wise lovers do.

"Will you write me and wish me all happiness, and

"Believe me,

"Ever your devoted and affectionate,

"Oscar Wilde."

Oscar's contemplated marriage did not surprise me, as I knew that he had for some time admitted the girl who afterwards became his wife, and of whom he had often talked rapturously to me. I did not see him again for several years, as I remained in the States, and when we next met in London he had become a successful dramatist.

When his play *The Importance of Being Earnest* was in rehearsal at the St. James's everyone concerned was bound to secrecy by George Alexander. Oscar was adamant, and rather irritating one afternoon when I tried to worm the plot out of him. Next day he come to tea, and I thought I would get my own back, so I said: "Arthur Bourchier lunched here and told me all about it!" (He was playing an important part.) "Who else was there?" gasped Oscar. I said casually, "Only Smalley." (Exit the author hurriedly, moaning.) Two hours later, enter A. B., almost crying with annoyance: "What's all this?" "Only my joke. I'll write to Alexander." I did, and got a freezing reply saying he "did not understand jokes in business." In the evening Tree heard the story at the Garrick. "I am sure the Lily did that," he said.

Oscar was a great student, and even during the whirl of my first season he induced me to improve my mind by attending Newton's lectures on Greek art at the British Museum, to the manifest delight of the students, who used to gather outside the door to receive us with cheers.

Oscar's wild worship of beauty, animate and inanimate, made him dreadfully intolerant of ugliness in any form, and he instinctively disliked and avoided unattractive people, using the most exaggerated language to express this repugnance, and being sometimes merciless in his attitude towards them, while, on the other hand, idealising those he admired, and placing some on pinnacles of his imagination who were unworthy, for his likes were as strong as his dislikes. Except in the case of a sacred few, he made fun of friend and foe alike, and he could be bitter as well. He was annoyed with old Lady C. on account of an ill– natured remark she was supposed to have made about me, and I heard him allude to her thus: "Oh! that old woman who keeps the artificial roses in place on her bald head with tin tacks."

When he was writing *The New Helen* he became so obsessed with the subject that he would walk round and round the streets in which our little house was situated for hours at a time, probably investing me with every quality I never possessed, and, although Wilde had a keen sense of the ridiculous, he sometimes unconsciously bordered thereon himself. For instance, one night he curled up to sleep on my doorstep, and Mr. Langtry, returning unusually late, put an end to his poetic dreams by tripping over him.

There were times when I found him too persistent in hanging round the house or running about after me elsewhere, and I am afraid that often I said things which hurt his feelings in order to get rid of him. After a frank remark I made on one occasion, I happened to go to the theatre, and, as I sat in my box, I noticed a commotion in the stalls — it was Oscar, who, having perceived me suddenly, was being led away in tears by his friend Frank Miles.

It was for me that he wrote *Lady Windermere's Fan*. Why he ever supposed that it would have been at the time a suitable play for me, I cannot imagine, and I had never contemplated him as a possible dramatist. Besides, knowing him as well as I did, and listening by the hour to his rather affected, amusing chatter, was not an effective prelude to taking him seriously, nor had he even hinted that he was engaged on any work. He called one afternoon, with an important air and a roll of manuscript, placed it on the table, pointed to it with a sweeping gesture, and said:

"There is a play which I have written for you."

"What is my part?" I asked, not at all sure if he was joking or not.

"A woman," he replied, "with a grown-up illegitimate daughter."

"My dear Oscar," I remonstrated, "am I old enough to have a grown–up daughter of any description? Don't open the manuscript — don't attempt to read it. Put it away for twenty years." And, in spite of his entreaties, I refused to hear the play.

In some of his many epigrams people declared they recognised clever inversions of the maxims of La Rochefoucauld, La Bruyere, and other French writers. Perhaps so; it is difficult even for a genius to be constantly original.

Wilde was genuinely romantic, and always poetic in thought and speech. As Sir Herbert Tree remarked to me one day: "Oscar turned his words into gems and flung them to the moon!"

As far asunder as the poles and the antithesis of Oscar Wilde was the next poet to dedicate a verse to me. He was Joaquin Miller, the poet of the Sierras, a child of nature and perhaps the most picturesque personality of the literary world. It was at Lord Houghton's house in Arlington Street, London, that I happened upon the famous Californian. The former was the most delightful host of his time in all London. I was always so pleased when he invited us, and he did very often, to lunch, to dine, and to receptions. A widower, with a son — now the famous diplomatist, Lord Crewe — and two charming daughters who did the honours of the establishment. His mode of entertaining seemed so easy and so comprehending, and, although dignified, far removed from the stiffness which is so often dignity's component part.

Literary himself, and the author, as Monkton Milnes, of books of excellent poetry, he was quick to perceive merit in others, and loved to give budding genius a lift along the road of fame. His acquaintance with the literature and men of the New World was also probably vaster than that of most of his countrymen, for no American of note, or colonial cousin, passed through London without being welcome and feted in that large, yet cosy Arlington Street house.

One evening during my first London season I was dining there, and chanced to pick up a volume of Lord Houghton's poems, in which I found a great many sonnets. I laughingly asked my host if I couldn't inspire him sufficiently to write *me* one. He looked at me very whimsically, a wee bit pathetically, and said, "My dear, I am too old."

After dinner, there was the usual reception, and presently he led up to me a very tall, lean man, with a pale intellectual face, yellow hair so long that it lay in curls about his shoulders, a closely cropped beard, and a dreamy expression in his light eyes. I don't remember what he wore, except that it was unconventional. He was so new and strange, that his apparel, whatever it was, seemed to complete the picture. After a while he disappeared from the group surrounding me, and at the end of the evening he returned and read me from a torn sheet of paper the following verse:

To the Jersey Lily:
It all God's world a garden were,
And women were but flowers,
If men were bees that busied there
Through endless summer hours,
O! I would hum God's garden through
For honey till I came to you.

When he had finished it, he added with a dramatic gesture; "Let this verse stand; it's the only one I ever wrote to a living woman."

And it *is* the only verse I believe. Two or three evenings later I went to a concert at Lady Brassey's, who had not long returned from a world's tour with Lord Brassey in the *Sunbeam*, and at the foot of the broad staircase of the house stood Joaquin Miller. He seemed to be waiting for me, and, as I walked upstairs to greet my hostess, he backed before me, scattering rose leaves, which he had concealed in his broad sombrero, upon the white marble steps, and saying with fervour: "Thus be your path in life!"

Often after this we met. He became a lion of the literary world; his poems were on every table. Rossetti, Swinburne, Tennyson, were among his admirers. He had lived a life of adventure, too, beginning to run away from school to mine for gold. He had been adopted by Indians, been imprisoned for some imaginary offence, had escaped from jail through the aid of an Indian girl, swam a river with her to freedom, and married her – – all before he was twenty! At least, that was the story which was circulated in London, and which added piquancy to the interest created by his virile personality.

Ten years ago, and within a week of his death, I was so anxious to see him again that I motored over with some mutual friends to his home in the Piedmont Hills at the back of Oakland, California, where I was playing at the time. After a lovely drive, we gradually ascended the foot–hills of the Sierras until we reached a simple gate and entered his property, "The Heights." Winding up the beautifully wooded slopes — every tree planted by his own hand, he told me — we came abruptly upon his house, a wooden bungalow overgrown with vines. Although he knew I was coming, my visit was conditional on his being well enough to receive visitors, and I felt suddenly reluctant to intrude on the sick man, and afraid I might be unwelcome!

However, as the car stopped at the foot of an impossibly steep incline some yards below the hut, the door was thrown open and Mrs. Miller and her daughter came forward to meet us. We were at once taken into the living–room, which was large and occupied the centre of the ground floor, and there lay the great nature poet. His gaunt, thin form reposed in a tent–like bed, covered with a patchwork quilt, and with buffalo robes thrown over that. His white hair flowed on to the pillow, and his beard, grown very long, gave him a truly patriarchal appearance. A small uncurtained window on the farther side of the bed allowed the strong sunlight to out–line Miller's fine features. He clasped my hand, looked in my face for what seemed to be an age before he spoke, and at last he said:

"The same yes, the same blue eyes! Where did you get those big blue eyes?"

Then he motioned me to sit near him. I told him how glad I was to be allowed to see him, and he answered:

"Who would refuse to see Lillie Langtry? When you reach heaven St. Peter will open the gates wide." (I am not so optimistic.)

The walls of the room were literally papers with photographs and woodcuts of famous people he had known, many of which he requested Mrs. Miller to take down to show me at close quarters. Among these a little faded picture of his friend Tennyson.

In due time his wife arranged a tea–table in the room of the dying man. The daughter, Juanita, soft–footed in moccasins, presided, and tempted me with epicurean and original dishes. There were pickled peaches, hot cakes, fresh goose livers, salted fish, and many other excellent things. The poet sipped a little honey.

The afternoon meal over, we went out and strolled through the property until, farther up the mountain side, we came upon a lane embowered in greenery, consecrated by a ship, and through which Joaquin Miller de-sired his body to be carried to the funeral pyre, built with his own hands on a rocky promontory, and intended for his cremation. It is gruesome to describe, but, in reality, it was a beautiful idea to wish to sink into nothingness in view of the mighty Pacific, and to have his ashes float on the winds that blow through the Golden Gate.

It was at Lord Houghton's also that I met General Grant and his wife, during their tour in Europe. That night they had dined in Arlington Street with him, and Mr. Langtry and I came to the reception. General Grant was, of course, what is called in the States the guest of honour. We arrived rather late, just before supper, and Lord Houghton, making a gallant remark on the *rencontre* of "Mars and Venus," introduced the illustrious personage, and we went in together.

I am sorry that I cannot remember details of our conversation. The only recollection I have is of a rather abrupt, soldier–like man, who had seen great happenings, done great things, and to whom social functions must, perforce, seem small. A man, I thought, young as I was, whose authority was great and whose word could be trusted — a man to give one a sense of security. Like many others in England at the time, I knew little of the history of the United States, and I am not sure that even occurred to me that he had been its President. A great general he was, that I knew, and he looked it.

I naturally met Mrs. Grant also; in fact, he introduced me to his wife across the supper–table, but, as I had little or no conversation with her, I retain her in my memory only as a rather stout figure, in a black gown, with very fat arms.

Chapter
6

With the second season came my presentation to Queen Victoria. I made my curtsey at a May drawing–room. The Marchioness Conyngham was my "presenter," and was introducing also her tall, beautiful daughter, Lady Jane Conyngham, at the same Court. We had arranged it during one of my visits to their country house called "Bifrons" near Canterbury. Having an official position in the Queen's Household, Lady Conyngham had the privilege of the entree (private entrance to the Palace), but this she could not, of course, extend to anyone outside her own family. Therefore, my actual companion on that day was Lady Romney, a charming, cheery woman.

At that time, the Courts were held at three o'clock in the afternoon, and it was certainly anything but agreeable to sit in full costume, with low neck and bare arms, in bright sunlight, for the edification of the surging crowd. Therefore Lady Romney wisely decided that we should time ourselves to be at the palace as late as possible, and so escape the delay in the Mall, warning me, however, that Her Majesty never remained to the end of the drawing–room, owing to the fatigue of standing so long, and that the Princess of Wales would be receiving in place of the Sovereign. Of this I was glad, as I was rather afraid of the Queen. We rather miscalculated, however, for I passed last but two — which certainly was a little overdoing it.

Although one may gown oneself with equal gorgeousness for any other entertainment (with the exception of the official Court– train and head–gear), the preparation for a drawing–room at Buckingham Palace is regarded as an important function by most women, and while I have attended several drawing–rooms since, I have always been impressed with the same necessity of being at my "very best."

I was dressed on the momentous day by the united efforts of my mother and my aunt — no mere maid was to be trusted. I wore an ivory brocade gown, the Court–train, which hung from the shoulders in the style of Josephine, being of the same material. Both were garlanded with Marechal Niel roses, the train being lined with the same pale yellow as the flowers. The Queen had recently expressed her disapproval of the tiny feathers which women had taken to wearing on these occasions, and an edict from the Lord Chamberlain had insisted on the feathers being at least visible to the naked eye. And so, in order to be on the safe side, I had obtained three of the longest white ostrich plumes I could find, and it was with great difficulty that I kept these in position on my head, for I still wore my hair coiled low on the neck.

My aunt thought I ought to have lunch before I started, or I should surely faint, but my mother affirmed that if I ate anything I should certainly have a red nose, and as my aunt had never been to Court and my mother *had*, the latter gained the day, and I starved accordingly.

They rehearsed me in the catching of my train as it would be thrown to me by the pages after my presentation, and also made me practice the royal curtsey until my knees ached. They warned me on no account to glance over my shoulder to see if my train was being properly spread by the pages in attendance, for that would be a sign that I was a country cousin, and so on and so on.

At last the great moment arrived. I handed my train to the pages in my grandest manner, and tried to appear thoroughly composed. Trembling, I approached the royal presence, and, as I did so, I heard the Lord Chamberlain say, "Mrs. Langtry comes next, your Majesty," at which I wondered, as he, the Lord Chamberlain, had not yet received my card.

Enormous posies of flowers were then in fashion, so, steadying myself with an immense bouquet of real Marechal Niel roses, thoughtfully sent to me by the Prince of Wales, I curtsied and kissed the hand of Her Majesty without committing any of the indiscretions against which my mother had warned me. But, at the supreme moment of my presentation, I could not help recalling an incident which I had often heard my father relate. When the Queen was young, she and the Prince Consort and the Prince of Wales paid an official visit to Jersey, and my father, in his capacity of Dean of the Island, had to offer a pen to the Queen to sign some document at Victoria College. He was so overcome with nervousness that he presented her with an old quill that wouldn't write, and he described the extreme *hauteur* with which she let the pen fall from her hand and waited for another.

It seemed to me an amazing thing to be shown into the presence of a sovereign one had heard of an prayed for all one's life, and to approach near enough to bend forward and kiss her hand, and, though the experience lasted but a second, I thrilled with emotion, loyalty, and pride. The Queen's wonderful dignity made me unable to realise that she was a petite woman, and she appeared to me to be the very embodiment of majesty.

She was dressed quite simply, in black, of course, with low neck and short sleeves, and her train was of velvet. Across her bodice was the blue ribbon of the Garter, and diamond orders and jewels studded her corsage. She wore many strings of beautiful pearls round her neck, a small diamond crown, tulle veil, and black feathers forming her head–dress. Queen Victoria looked straight in front of her, and, I thought, extended her hand in rather a perfunctory manner. There was not even the flicker of a smile on her face, and she looked grave and tired.

My ordeal was not yet finished, for I had to curtsey to a long row of royalties, though, having met them all elsewhere previously, they smiled and shook hands as I passed.

My curtseys began with the Prince and Princess of Wales, but they grew less and less profound and more slurred as I remembered I had one more vital moment to face before I was finally "out of the wood." It was the second in which the page, gathering up my train, would throw it to me, etiquette requiring that I should catch it on my left arm and make a dignified exit backwards. Fortunately, this somewhat intricate finale was executed with perfect precision both on my part and on that of the page, and so my first visit to court ended without a misadventure. As my mind had been filled with misgivings consequent on stories I had been told of stout ladies overbalancing themselves in the act of making their obeisance and having to be raised up quickly, still facing the Queen, of others tripping over their trains or hanging on to the royal hand for support, and experiencing other unfortunate happenings, I departed immensely relieved from the throne–room.

Yet after hours of waiting in the crush–room of the palace, penned like sheep, with a heavy train folded on one's arm, and a constant dragging at one's white tulle veil, to be seen only for a moment as one was hurried in and out of the presence, made it seem a great deal of labour lost.

The drawing–rooms are now held at night, and made much pleasanter and less formal. Still, in the Victorian reign, the superbly–gowned women, wearing magnificent tiaras and shining with jewels, sitting waiting their turn in St. James's Park in state coaches that were brought out only on these full–dress occasions, were a joy to behold. The bewigged coachmen, sitting in solitary glory on the resplendent hammercloths, and the powdered footmen in liveries heavy with silver or gold, standing on ledges at the back of these historic carriages, clinging to embroidered straps, were also part of the show. The entrance court of the palace, with the guard of honour of Household Cavalry and its braying band, and the beefeaters in their quaint Elizabethan costumes, showed more conspicuously in the daylight. But the motor–car has removed so much of the picturesqueness and pageantry of the scene in the Mall that the spectators do not, after all, miss much through the change to evening Courts.

On the way home from the palace, Lady Romney expressed some surprise at the presence of Her Majesty till the very end of the particularly long drawing–room but that evening, while dancing in the Royal Quadrille at a ball at Marlborouogh House, I was enlightened as to the cause of the Queen remaining. It seems that she had a great desire to see me, and had stayed on in order to satisfy herself as to my appearance. It was even added that she was annoyed because I was so late in passing. As to my appearance, I wondered what Her Majesty thought of my head–gear. I am afraid the waving ostrich plumes may have looked overdone, as the Prince of Wales that evening chaffed me good–humouredly on my conscientious observance of the Lord Chamberlain's order. At all events, I *meant* well.

Mr. Langtry had been presented by the Prince of Wales himself to the Queen at a levee earlier in the season, and that brings me to a rather amusing incident which occurred years later. My sister–in–law, myself, at H.R.H., after riding in the Park, were coming home down Constitutional

Hill, when we saw signs of preparation for a levee he was to hold. The band, guard of honour, etc., were on the way to take up their stand before the palace. This interested us, and we all three sat quietly on our horses at the corner of the Mall watching the people arrive. The Prince was, strange to say, quite unrecognised by the waiting crowd, and remained so long that he had a great scramble to get to the levee in time.

I know little of England and nothing of the beauty of English homes, coming, as I did, from the tiny Island in which I was born, and were I lived until I was married. My only glimpse of the possibilities and fascination thereof had been at Whitsuntide, which we spent with the Earl of Malmesbury, at Heron Court, in Hampshire. It was an old and beautiful place. I cannot recall the architecture, but the imposing sculptured herons on the entrance gates of the park are still pictured in my memory.

The hall, very large and low, with great oak rafters, had a paved stone floor bestrewn with deerskins, and was filled with armour and trophies of the chase. The whole house seemed crammed with beautiful things. How much Lord Malmesbury had personally added to its treasures, I don't know, but he had been a collector all his life. At all events, the drawing–rooms, Louis XIV, Louis XV and Louis XVI, had evidently been redecorated and refurnished by him after his residence as Ambassador in Paris.

It was in these rooms that I learned to distinguish the different periods of French furniture, china, etc., for they contained quantities of beautiful examples, including some lovely signed buhl tables. It was, moreover, a pleasure to their owner to explain the most minute characteristics of each chair, cabinet, table, or vase. The library was a vast one, and among its treasures were many portfolios filled with rare engravings and cartoons by Raphael, Bartolozzi, Angelica Kauffmann, and others.

One of the features of the grounds was a rhododendron drive some miles long, which wound through an extensive tract of land entirely planted with various coloured choice hybrids. These had grown into huge masses, and were, at Whitsuntide, in full glory. My interest in the old–world plea-sure–grounds was a joy to the gardener, who told me that his master have never permitted a flower to decorate his rooms since Lady Malmesbury's death, and certainly the dinner–table on the night of our arrival did look rather like a mausoleum, bestrewn as it was with statuettes of white–biscuit china, without a solitary blossom to cheer them up, but a little coaxing on my part altered all that; and, ever after, during my visits, there was a profusion of flowers about, though Lord Malmesbury persistently maintained that they spoiled the flavour of the viands.

He was over seventy, but still an enthusiastic sportsman, shooting and fishing with the zeal of youth. The River Avon, which flowed through his property, was plentifully stocked with salmon, and Mr. Langtry, always a keen and crafty fisherman, spent his days battling with them. There is a horrible custom called "crimping," which consists of chopping up the fish while alive with a view to making the flesh more firm. I was out fishing with Lord Malmesbury once, when he landed a beauty after a prolonged tussle. He was delighted, and literally screamed to the keeper to come and crimp it. But I stood over the floundering salmon with my sunshade, and successfully protected it from such a cruel end.

He was remarkably entertaining, and so young in mind that one was apt to forget the reverence due to age, and I must excuse the following practical joke on that score. One night at dinner he looked up compla-cently, after studying the menu, and said:

"Gratin a la Grammont — named after my relative the *duchesse.* You will like that."

When it came, in due course, I was helped first, and found it to be a compound resembling a mixture of chicken mince and *choux–fleur au gratin.* It was scalding hot, as I realised to my cost, for a little taste of it burned my tongue severely. When my host eagerly asked me how I liked it, I concealed my feelings and said:

"Excellent, if it were not cold!"

The poor man, furious with his chef, hurriedly gulped a large mouthful to convince himself, and was such a pitiable object for five minutes that I was really frightened and very much ashamed of my silly joke. But he was *so* fond of good things to eat.

After this visit, we often went to Heron Court, and spent happy weeks there from time to time. As everyone knows, Lord Malmesbury was a great diplomatist, had been Ambassador, Foreign Minister, etc., and the following anecdote shows how the wariness inseparable from diplomacy becomes a habit. One day he discovered me in tears, and I confided to him that I had written a harmless but indiscreet letter at the writing–table in my room, that Mr. Langtry had found it reproduced on the blotting paper, and that it had made him — to put it mildly — cross. The diplomatist expressed sympathy with me, but stormed at his servants who, he said, had strict orders to renew the blotting paper throughout the house *every day to prevent just such a contretemps!*

He treated me rather like a child, and my indignation was great to find, when I went out riding with Lord Manners, one of the guests staying in the house, that a groom was following us. With scorn I dismissed the man as being unnecessary, and when I got back I found Lord Malmesbury stalking about the stable–yard in high dudgeon and much perturbed at what he called my *"disregard of conventionalities,"* although it seems to me to be a natural thing to ride about the park with one of his own relatives unchaperoned. I afterwards came to the conclusion that his wide experience had made him distrustful of human nature. Still I think he was inclined to exaggerate the dangers that beset youth.

Among the many diverting stories he told me was one of (I think)

Lord and Lady Sidney, who were both so hot–tempered that everyone prophesied a separation within a month of their marriage. They went to the bridegroom's cottage on the Thames for the honeymoon, and within twenty–four hours had such a violent quarrel that they wrecked every bit of furniture in the place. After which, they respected each other's temper and lived happily together for the rest of their lives.

My first visit to Scotland, which took place a year later, was a revelation. Once over the border, one realises so strangely a subtle difference from England, the difference becoming more and more pronounced as the Highlands are reached, with their misty blue mountains, firs, heather–clad moors, and wild grandeur of scenery.

Glen Tanar, a beautiful deer–forest owned by Cunliffe Brooks, a commercial magnate, was our objective. It is in Aberdeenshire, and lies between the royal residence, Balmoral, and Aboyne, the historic seat of the "Gay Gordons," of whom the head of the family, the Marquis of Huntly, was married to Cunliffe Brooks' elder daughter. Glen Tanar Lodge was a modern, large two–storey house with no architectural pretensions, but just roomy and comfortable, plainly furnished with chintzes, and adorned with numberless antlers.

There was a large house–party assembled — the men eager for the massacre of grouse and the stalking of deer. They, no doubt, enjoyed themselves hugely killing things, but there is nothing much for women to do, unless they also shoulder a weapon, which is becoming more and more the fashion with them. But this never appealed to me. I have always felt it to be a woman's mission to *give* life rather than take it. I was once persuaded to see a stag stalked, but I felt so sick and sorry for the fine beast that I have never forgotten it.

However, there is no place like Scotland to bring roses to a woman's cheeks. Probably the excess of moisture is good for the skin, and it *does* rain there continually. One day, in a determined drizzle, a gillie observed casually, "It's a fine dee." Another day, when it poured cats and dogs, he said, "It's a saft morning," and that is the utmost a Scot will admit about his humid climate. But with the sensible tweed costume and deer– stalking cap which women affect while in the Highlands, one can defy even a "saft morning."

Still, time may hang heavy on one's hands on wet days, as we found once or twice, so I invented what I thought a very engrossing sport while at Glen Tanar. Procuring a large tea– tray, I sat in it and tobogganed from the top of the stairs to the bottom! The sport was so enthusiastically taken up by the girls staying in the house that Cunliffe Brooks quietly ordered his butler to lock up all the good–looking or silver trays during my visit.

The evening brought compensation for the rather dull days, for there was always dancing in the ball–room, Highland reels schottisches, and usually a sword–dance as a solo, Lord Huntly, or one of his brothers Lords Esme and Granville Gordon, generally contributing the latter. Oh, but they were handsome in their Highland garb, and a man has to be handsome to wear it! And the Gordons knew how! Their tartan is a beautifully blended one of green and blue, which, of course, is only worn as full dress with the black–velvet jacket, bejewelled sporran, black pumps with immense cairn–gorm buckles, tartan stockings, and with jewelled dirks and brooches galore. Truly, these three tall, handsome, blue–eyed Northerners were reminiscent of more romantic times. But, of course, when in bonnie Scotland everyone with the slightest excuse to do so sports a kilt, though not always to his advantage, and I think mine host's rotund figure would have looked better more discreetly clad.

The Highland games, which took place at Aboyne Balmoral, Inverness, and other places, demonstrated that the Scotch costume really only becomes those who have worn it all their lives. Their Royal Highnesses the

Prince and Princess of Wales usually attended these meetings, the Prince in his Stuart tartan, and the Princess looking as lovely in her blue serge workman–like costume, with its scarlet–lined hood, as she did in the splendour of her Court–gown. She generally wore a little deer–stalking cap to complete her costume, and carried a long ebony stick.

General Lord Strathnairn and Lady Erroll, one of Queen Victoria's ladies–in–waiting, were of the party at Glen Tanar, and we all drove over to Balmoral one afternoon and wrote our names in Her Majesty's book. I was not going to write ours, but Lady Erroll said I should get a black mark if I did not, as we had been presented that spring. My friend, Lady Ely, who was in waiting, said the Queen came in twenty minutes later, and the only remark she made on looking over the visitors' book was, "I should like to have seen Mrs. Langtry," and a horseman was sent off to try to overtake us, but in vain. That was the first and only time I ever saw the castle. It seemed to me bleak and uninteresting, and I thought Aboyne far more picturesque.

I was told rather a curious story connected with a statue of Queen Victoria which, during the Prince Consort's life, had been erected, by local subscription I believe, at the entrance to the castle. It appears to have been a mammoth work, and the figure of the Queen, classically robed, was perched on a plinth many feet high. Round the base were grouped cupids and nymphs holding garlands of flowers, and other emblems of youth and love. The statue was placed in position in the early 'sixties, just prior to Her Majesty's annual visit to Balmoral. As she drove up in her carriage she and Prince Albert inspected it, but evidently it did not meet with the royal approval, for next day the whole thing disappeared, my informant telling me that it now lies buried beneath the floor of the guard–house. I believe an engraving of the statue appeared at the time in the *Illustrated London News*.

After a series of visit, which took us as far north as Inverness, we joined Sir Allen Young in his yacht, and traversed Scotland by means of the Caledonian Canal, returning by the west coast of Glasgow, which I found a most enjoyable trip. The banks of the Canal are lined with beautiful country seats along the entire route, and, when we had rounded the dreadful Mull of Cantyre, we entered Loch Fyne to find ourselves in the most fascinating waters of the kingdom. Thence we steamed through the Kyles of Bute, studded with lovely villas, and up the picturesque Clyde to smoky, historic Glasgow.

In November we visited the Lord and Lady Romney at their place in Norfolk, in order to go to a ball given on the Prince of Wales' birthday at Sandringham, which was adjacent to Lord Romney's estate. While a very spacious house, Sandringham is not palatial, but, what is far better, it gives one the idea of being thoroughly liveable and comfortable, even when turned partially upside–down for a dance. The big central hall was used as a ball–room, and I seem to remember an organ in the over–hanging gallery. Then there were drawing–room, library and billiard– room, leading from one to the other, through which we wandered at will.

I do not intend to write details of all the houses we stopped at, but I may remark that the hospitality extended to us made the autumn months of each year pass too quickly. Among these visits, those paid from time to time to Lord and Lady Rosslyn at Easton Lodge, Dunmow, stand out in my memory, and I think I felt more at home there than anywhere else, galloping about the park with their nice daughters, and enjoying myself thoroughly.

One winter later, I tried hunting, and went to stay at Quenby, Lord Manners' hunting box in Leicestershire, for that purpose. But perhaps not having had a chance of beginning as a child, as Englishwomen do, may have been the reason I didn't care for it and I contented myself on future occasions, when bidden to houses like Badminton, where chasing the fox is the all–absorbing sport, with trotting about the roads on a hack in an ignominious fashion.

We stayed with the Reuben Sassoons at Brighton from time to time, where they had a large house in Brunswick Gardens. They had numberless horses and carriages of every description, and it was rare not to see some of the large family driving up and down the sea–front. Reuben Sassoon had a special victoria with a high– stepping horse, and I often drove about with him. The result was that the papers thought it funny to call us "Othello and Desdemona," he being of a very swarthy complexion.

He must have a wonderful faculty for bearing pain, for, at a Christmas family dance given by Sir Albert Sassoon at Brighton, he slipped on the polished floor and broke his arm. A doctor was summoned and set the bone, but the victim insisted on dancing the rest of the evening, which made everyone but himself miserable. Later, he became a great friend of the Prince of Wales, who entrusted his racing commissions to him. When Reuben Sassoon died, he left a gap in his clique not easy to fill.

Chapter
7

The illustrious company of the Theatre Francais, Paris, with its *societaires* and others, for some reason which I cannot recall, once found itself temporarily without a home. Then it was that they decided to brave the unknown perils of the Channel, for the Parisian at that time hated to travel far from his beautiful city, in order to visit England. This artistic invasion of London had been suggested to the Director of the Comedie Francaise by Sir Algernon Borthwick, editor of the *Morning Post*, a great patron and lover of the drama, and especially appreciative of the French State.

The advent of the famous French players caused unwonted excitement, and boxes and seats were taken for the season as for the opera. Among the shining lights of that brilliant bevy were the two Coquelins, Mounet–Sully, Febvre, Fargueil, Sophie Croizette, and Sarah Bernhardt. It is of the last–named that I wish to record my impressions. I met her first at a breakfast given by Sir Algernon Borthwick as a welcome to the principal members of the company, to which many of the fashionable world were invited. It was among the latter that I assisted, as I had no idea then of ever being more than a butterfly. I sat on one side of our host, Sarah on the other.

As my readers are doubtless aware, there are no recognised "stars" in the Theatre Francais, but Croizette had just appeared in *The Sphinx* in Paris, and, as she had made a sensational success in the death scene, in which she took poison and turned to a grey–green complexion in view of the audience, everyone was on the *qui vive* to see her. She disappointed me both on and off the stage, for she was extremely large and fat, with a round uninteresting face, and I found her art conventional. Naturally I write from a lay standpoint, for at that time nothing was farther from my thoughts than the idea of going on the stage. But perhaps acting is often better judged by those who, instead of dissecting and analysing the technique of the actor, allow themselves to appreciate the sincerity of the emotion portrayed according to the temperament of the player.

But let me return to the "Divine Sarah," a title she earned from the subjugated Londoners on her first appearance as the Queen in Victor Hugo's *Ruy Blas*. This great and overwhelming artist was almost too individual, too exotic, to be completely understood or properly estimated *all at once*. Her superb diction, her lovely silken voice, her natural acting, her passionate temperament, her fire — in a word, transcendent genius — caused amazement in a day when British acting (with a few notable exceptions) was of the stagey, posturing description.

She was hailed as the fitting successor to Rachel, was extolled with justice by the critics, and crowned Queen of the Drama of the whole world by the London public and so, *nolens volens*, the Comedie Francaise was provided with a star who, without dimming the lustre of its other members, was the lodestone that drew the public during their sojourn in our midst. Bernhardt's personality was so striking, so singular that, to everyday people, she seemed eccentric; she filled the imagination as a great poet might do.

Her beauty, frankly, was not understood by the masses. It was a period of tiny waists, large shoulders, larger hips; and this remarkable woman, who possessed the beautiful, supple uncorseted figure — the long lines we all admire to–day — was called a skeleton. She gowned herself beautifully, wearing mostly long, trailing, white garments, richly embroidered and beaded, as was the fashion of the time. Around her throat she tied the large bow of tulle made familiar in George Clairin's painting, in which she reclines on a couch, all in white, with a Russian wolf–hound at her feet. In fact, the engraving of that picture, which she later gave me, represents her as she appeared at Sir A. Borthwick's luncheon.

Painters and poets admired her. Oscar Wilde enthused over her likeness to coins of the ancient Romans, and carried me off to the British Museum to hunt for her profile in coins, intaglios, and vases of the period, in some of which we found almost exact replicas of her symmetrical Latin features. Like all great beauty, however, it did not blaze upon one's vision, but grew upon acquaintance. And hers, being a combination of intelligence, of feature and of soul, remained with her until the end of her life.

After their first successful venture, the French players returned to London each year. During one visit, Sarah took a small house in Chester Square, where she spent all her spare time in modelling. I can see her now, her auburn hair in a fluffy tuft, and her slender body clothed in a white working suit of *pantalon* and jacket. When, in two years or so, financial reasons compelled me to go on the stage, the great actress was much interested, and her remark made to George Smalley was repeated to me by him: *Avec ce menton, elle ira loin.*" ("With that chin she will succeed.")

It was not, however, until some years later, when we were both touring the United States, that I saw a great deal of her. Then, in New York, I really came to know her. I had made the city my home, and was living in a charming detached house in West Twenty–third Street. (It is still there, by the by, for a wonder.) Sarah, while playing in New York and the adjacent cities, had settled herself at the Hoffman House. Her son, Maurice, was in attendance, young, good–looking, and with much of his mother's charm.

She dined with me several times, and I noticed that the attention of the guests was concentrated on her, for, even though they did not understand her language, her magnetism held them in its spell. Then there were breakfasts with her at her hotel, sometimes alone with her and her son. The latter was crazy about *la boxe*, and Sarah and I were once beguiled by him into trying a "bout." We entered into it with a great gusto, Maurice giving timely aid to one or other as it was needed, and we were both much the worse for wear at the finish.

I had sold, for a very large sum, the monopoly of my photographs to Napoleon Sarong, then the principal publicity photographer in New York, and I gave him innumerable sittings. One Sunday, Madame Sarah and I went to him together, and Sarong provided a picnic lunch for us in the studio. We were to pose alternately, to lighten the strain, and the little man hoped for great results, which, unfortunately for him, were not realised. Madame Sarah was in one of her merriest moods, and it was impossible for anyone but Sarong to take the sittings seriously. At the crucial moment she invariably gave utterance to some comical remark of witticism that ruined the chances of the camera. Even in the photograph of us taken together one can see the mischievous expression in her face as she pinched my arm at the critical moment.

The second year of the war we were again both playing in New York, and stayed at the same hotel. One day, having occasion to give a decision regarding the destination of some curios I had collected, I went to the store–room, and thereby discovered a curious whim of Sarah Bernhardt's. Every basket of flowers or other floral tribute she had received during her tour was carefully preserved intact in enormous cases and boxes that more than half filled the immense room.

In private life she seemed as natural as a child, and was quite un-spoiled by the adulation of the world. She had an enormous sense of humour, and a quickness of perception which enabled her to grasp a speaker's meaning and reply before he was half–way through his sentence.

The flamboyant advertising methods adopted for Madame Bernhardt's first American tour were possibly necessary when the country was forty–odd years younger, but they really were overdone and incredible, though I did see a satin–lined coffin standing on end in the hall of her Paris house in the Boulevard Pereire, a place filled with souvenirs of her triumphs and treasures collected on her tours. I have heard her speak enthusiastically of the people of the United States, and of the luxury and bohemianism of travelling in America. She was as large–minded as she was wise, and very kind and tolerant to budding talent, having helped many young ac-tresses to success. To have known this great artist and unique woman well and intimately is one of my interesting experiences.

Sooner or later I made the acquaintance of most of the principal art-ists of the Theatre Francais. Coquelin *aine* was the one I knew and liked the best, and the acquaintanceship, begun on that visit to London, ripened into a firm friendship which lasted till his death. His appearance was not an ideal one for an actor, his rather bullet–shaped head, with its close–cropped hair, his snub nose and keen eyes, seeming more indicative of business capacity than artistic imagination, while his short, thick–set figure was certainly wanting in dignity. But his genius overcame these draw-backs and made him a great character– actor. His manner gave one the impression of conceit, but, as conceit is the over–valuation of one's knowl-edge or talent, and he could hardly overrate his, I think it *was* only his manner.

He was an excellent conversationalist. When in Paris, I frequently breakfasted or lunched with him, either at his artistic and comfortable apartment, with his well–filled bookshelves, or at his favourite restaurant — Voisin's. He did all the talking, and did it so well that I was quite content to listen. If I went to the Theatre Francais, Coquelin usually in-vited me to pay him a visit in his *loge* behind the scenes. It was one of the most beautifully furnished of all the artists' dressing–rooms in the house of Moliere. The walls were hung with old Flemish sixteenth–century tapes-tries, and fine Persian carpets covered the floor. There were pictures and rare engravings, statuettes, bronzes, Louis XIII furniture — all combining to make it a very luxurious rest–room.

His art was flawless, and whatever role his physique permitted him to undertake he played to perfection. A master of technique, but without much temperament or charm, he believed that each and every gesture, inflection, and pose, should be the result of deliberate study and rehearsal, and that the mood of the actor should not be allowed to vary the imper-sonation thereafter. So, although his acting was always absolutely true and highly natural, it was never illuminated by those flashes of spontaneity which reveal the soul of the artist, and consequently it did not thrill me as Mounet–Sully's temperamental and picturesque impersonations frequently did. Coquelin intentionally acted emotion without feeling it, and could play the most exacting role after eating a hearty meal, and indeed, he told me it was his habit to dine just before his evening work.

I think the following letters, selected haphazardly from the many in my possession, show Coquelin's friendly nature.

"My dear Mrs. Langtry, — Alas, I am engaged all Sunday! I break-fast with Sir Charles Darling and dine with the F____s, have been engaged for two months, otherwise I would have been happy, very happy. to spend the day with you. *But* I should have found it very long to wait till then for the pleasure of meeting you. Therefore, while you are in town, I hope I may be permitted to profit by it a little.

"Would you care to see *Cyrano* any evening, and will you let me come and see you to–morrow (Tuesday) about three o'clock? If so, it will be very kind of you to send me word to the Walsingham House Hotel, Piccadilly. I shall be so delighted to see you, and even though it will only be as a fellow artist and friend, I shall be very curious to see how you 'embrace with all your heart.' I will do it, if you permit me, with much greater satisfaction than you.

"With all my heart,

"I am,

"Yours,

"Coquelin."

"Thank you, dear Mrs. Langtry, for your charming telegram, but will you remember this favour? I want to see and speak to you. I think I have something very interesting for you, and it makes me happy to do things for you and to be artistically useful. I play twice to–morrow, but Thursday will be at your orders, and the earlier the better. Not having seen you for two years! I feel something missing. Thank you again.

"Your friend,

"Coquelin."

"Dear Madame and Friend, — I think the *premiere* of the *Pompa-*

dour will take place the 10th or 12th of November. I will beg Bergerat to do nothing without letting me know. I want above everything to give you good advice, and for that must wait the result of the first performance. I shall also get him to wait till you come to decide, and if you take the play, we will do our best to arrange with the Porte St. Martin, because I intend to be on your side. That's all I can tell you of my love for Mrs. P., with whom I have somewhat quarrelled. I will tell you how when we meet, for it can be told without the slightest indiscretion, which also attests my innocence.

"I hope you are well. The papers say so. You are causing duels [the duel alluded to was a "set to" with sticks between Lord L. and Sir G. C. in Rotten Row one Sunday morning]; you are playing Marie Antoinette, etc. I hope you are pleased with it all. And if you would make me happy, send me a little photo of yourself in fencing costume. I think I shall like it, because I like you so much.

"Your friend,

"Coquelin."

"Dear Mrs. Langtry, — Have you decided you can do nothing with *Plus que Reine*? Bergerat is ready to do any revisions, and make it possible for you in England. Here is the complete manuscript of *Mms. Pompadour*. I think the play admirable and the part marvellous. Could you read it at once and return me the manuscript, unless you ask me to come and see you and talk it over? I could come to–morrow (Thursday), because Friday I play twice. I leave Saturday morning, I should deeply regret to leave without seeing you again, but I didn't like to bother you.

"Believe me, dear Madame,

"In my best thoughts,

"Coquelin."

Mounet–Sully, the romantic actor, the Ruy Blas, etc., of the company, I never knew very well. I admired his rather mannered art, visited him in his thoroughly untidy dressing–room at the "Francais," and thought him rather weird and quite unlike any human being I had hitherto met, which, of course, made him all the more fascinating to my youthful imagination.

Coquelin's *camarade*, Frederick Febvre, I happened on in the sacred cause of charity. The frequent visits of French artists to London, increasing as years went on, made the accommodation for sick actors inadequate at the French Hospital in Leicester Square, London, and Monsieur Johnson, for many years the English correspondent of the Paris *Figaro*, realising the deficiency, put himself in touch with Febvre, then *doyen* of the Comedie Francaise, and they conceived the excellent idea of endowing a bed for the exclusive use of suffering artists of the Theatre Francais — the necessary sum to be raised by a matinee.

At this time I had been for some years on the stage and was lessee and manager of the Princes' Theatre, Coventry Street. Monsieur Johnson called on me, and explained his charitable errand, to which I at once responded by lending my theatre for the occasion. As a matter of fact, no one ever refused Monsieur Johnson anything.

The benefit was arranged, and on the day the performance was attended by royalty and crammed with notable people. As a novel item on the programme, Febvre had suggested that I should play (in French) with him in a one–act comedy called *Les Brebis de Panurge*, by Meilhac and Halevy, the only obstacle being that, as he was playing in Paris and I in London, rehearsals seemed out of the question. Still, we *had* to rehearse, and we overcame the difficulty by meeting at Boulogne the two Sundays preceding the performance and going over and over the little play for hours, after my sea journey, and with another in prospect. You will see by

112

the following letters that it was a matter of life and death artistically.

"Dear Madame and Illustrious Artiste, — Time is flying. I have sent you through our mutual friend, M. Johnson, the prompt–book of *Les Brebis*, which I am going to have the honour of playing with you on the stage at the Princes Theatre in the performance given to found a bed in the French Hospital [bed for the artists of the Comedie Francaise]. I have told all my honourable colleagues here of the part you are taking in this charitable work, and they are all profoundly grateful.

"Have you begun to work? Remember we shall only have two re-hearsals. I would not worry you for the world, and beg you to accept kindly (until I can tell you in person) my grateful thanks and sincere admiration.

"Frederick Febvre."

"Oh, if Her Majesty (Queen Victoria) would come! It would put plenty of wool in the Comedie Francaise Bed, and what an honour!"

"Dear Madame and Illustrious Artiste, — I have got my liberty for Sunday, May 16th *We must rehearse all day*. M. Cauvet says you have a young woman to play Gabrielle in *Les Brebis*. She ought to come to Boulogne also. As for you, I answer for your success. What time do you arrive at Boulogne, and what hotel do you stay at? Send me word by Cauvet.

"Till I have the pleasure of seeing you, accept my best wishes, and I kiss the tips of your pretty fingers.

"Frederick Febvre."

"Don't forget to sit for the portrait for the little book. Otherwise it will have no chance of success."

The benefit programme was full of good things. Scovel sang Tosti's

"Good–bye," accompanied by the dear, kind–hearted composer. Sarasate played. Saint–Saens assisted, and by what my father, who was an interested spectator, called my "happy audacity" *Les Brebis de Panurge* also proved successful, though there *was* a *contretemps*. Febvre, accustomed throughout his stage life to a prompt–box, suddenly realised its absence, and was so taken aback that he skipped a most important explanatory portion of the plot, and I, playing in French for the first time, had to transpose the lines in order to start the scene anew, after two rehearsals only. Febvre whispered, *Merci. Quel aplomb!*"

In the evening, Monsieur Johnson, radiant at the amount of "stuffing" provided for the French bed, invited me to dine at his little house. Besides Madame Johnson, the party consisted at Chevalier Scovel, handsome and blond, Saint–Saens, and the swashbuckling General Boulanger, the latter, and Henri Rochefort, being just fresh from the failure of their attempted *coup d'etat*. Rochefort did the talking for both. Boulanger, that night, was silent and taciturn, but a striking figure, with his piercing blue eyes and pointed red beard.

He had distinguished himself in the Franco–Prussian War, and had gradually climbed to the position of War Minister, and it was while he held that office that his fire–eating attitude towards Germany in the crisis of 1887 made him a popular idol. The citizens acclaimed him as the right and only man to avenge the nation for their unforgettable reverses at the hands of the Prussians. Odes were written, and songs were composed in his honour and sung all over the boulevards and in the various places of amusement. A ditty entitled *"C'est Boulanger qu'il nous faut"* seemed the most popular.

"Le brave general" and his black horse, "The Man on Horseback," as he was called, dominated French politics for a time by his marvellous personality, and fear was even aroused for the security of the Republic.

Indeed, it was common talk that if he had taken advantage of the hour, and immediately placed himself at the head of the malcontents, he might have made himself master of France, but he let the golden opportunity slip, and failed when he made his belated effort. He fled from Paris to London to escape arrest. Thencefoward, he was exiled, and spent the remainder of his life between Brussels and Jersey, building in the latter place a pretentious stucco Italian castle with turquoise and yellow embellishments, exactly what I should have expected of him. It looked oddly out of harmony with its surroundings in St. Brelade's Bay, where it was located, for the granite manor houses and thatched farms seem the proper style of architecture for the Channel Isles.

He had an ardent love affair with a Madame de Bonnemain, whom, I think, he eventually married. There were several echoes of the Boulangist movement, but the psychological moment had passed, and soon his dramatic effort was forgotten, and he dropped out of the public eye. A few years later the world was startled by the news of his tragic death. He had blown out his brains in the cemetery at Brussels, on the grave of the woman he had worshipped with more devotion than he was generally deemed capable of, she having died in Belgium a few months before. I think he might almost be regarded as the "D'Artagnan" of French history.

Till that evening at Monsieur Johnson's I had never met Henri Rochefort, but, like everyone, knew of him as a man bitterly opposed to those in power, always "agin the government," as the Irishman said, and airing his views so energetically in the French Press that at last he was forced to start and edit a journal of his own — *L'Intransigeant* — in order to give vent to his views. His cruel eyes, pale scarred face, and disagreeable harsh voice, repelled me instantly. He was a habitual duellist, but duelling seemed the natural sequel to any difference of opinion at that time in France. Boulanger had also figured in an "affair of honour" after some explosive utterances while he was *depute*, but what French-man who, even to this day, indulges in great liberty of speech has not?

Rochefort's lovely niece was at the dinner–party, I remember. He seemed sincerely fond of her, so I supposed he had a tender side to his nature. He laid down the law incessantly throughout dinner unchallenged by other guests, which perhaps accounts for his being a comparative dove that evening, and sucking the eternal lozenges, with which he tried to soften his grating voice, instead of cracking them, as someone whispered to me he did when on the war–path. I dare say he crunched a whole box of lozenges over the failure of General Boulanger's attempted *coup d'etat* – – for Henri Rochefort was his guide, counseller, and friend.

Chapter
8

Each successful season brought with it the same orgy of convivial gatherings, balls, dinners, receptions, concerts, opera, etc., which at first seemed to me a dream, a delight, a wild excitement, and I concentrated on the pursuit of amusement with the whole–heartedness that is characteristic of me, flying from one diversion to another from dawn to dawn, with Mr. Langtry in vigilant attendance. I included the round of the clock in recording my social gambols, for there *were* times when, after dancing until sunshine confounded me, I felt wide–awake instead of sleepy, and consequently, changing directly from ball–gown to riding–habit, would mount my hack Redskin, and take him for a breather in the Row, to find it already filled with the hard–working "Liver Brigade," as well as a sprinkling of early–rising *equistriennes*, and indeed, from cock–crow till dusk, this exercise ground seems never entirely deserted.

What a vital part Hyde Park plays in the outdoor life of London! It is

117

not vast and wild like the Bois de Boulogne, Paris, or the Prater in Vienna, nor has it those cunningly contrived hillocks and lakes which add to the picturesqueness of Central Park, New York, but it lies so invitingly at our very doors, a friendly neighbour, beckoning one and all, rich and poor, on wheels, on horseback, or on foot, to share its attractions.

The Park is a flower–garden, too, from the time that its sward is studded with early crocuses and daffodils, until the frost lays its cruel hand on the late autumn blossoms. Londoners know every inch of their playground, and spend so much time there that they regard it with proprietary affection. Among Hyde Park's daylight functions I preferred the meets of the coaching and four–in–hand clubs that took place in the late spring, when the blatant rhododendrons were in full bloom. To sit on the box–seat of one of these perfectly appointed coaches, the Duke of Beaufort's, or some other, to bowl along past the expectant crowd that, in carriages or on foot, awaited the wonderful display of horseflesh, and recognised each coach and its occupants, was a delightful prelude to a spin down to Hurlingham or Ranelagh for lunch.

Now, alas! with the advent of the motor, the coaches are less numerous. It needed a plucky American, the late Alfred G. Vanderbilt, to show us, with his road coach, that we had lost in picturesqueness what we may have gained in speed.

After my presentation at Court, I attended a drawing–room each spring, was duly commanded to a ball at the palace each season, and, gradually becoming acclimatised to my surroundings, wondered why I felt such trepidation when I first mounted the palace steps. Since the death of the Prince Consort, Her Majesty no longer cared to endure the fatigue of these crushes, and had detailed the Prince and Princess of Wales to preside in her stead, and at these State balls the latter was an especially radiant figure.

In those days, waltzes, gallops, and — what was even then old–fashioned — the polka, formed the usual programme, with an occasional Highland schottische after supper as an extra ebullition of hilarity. But at the palace there was a preponderance of stately square measures, nor do I ever recall seeing the royal ladies "pirouetting" on any occasion. Uniform or Court costume was, of course, *de rigueur* among the men, while the women who attended wore their most resplendent raiment and displayed their historic jewels, thus making the gathering a brilliant scene and a carnival of colour. Masses of scarlet– coated footmen scurried about the supper–table, which was gorgeous with the famous service of gold plate, the tazzas thereof being laden with fruits and flowers from the Royal Gardens at Frogmore, and, through the old and greedy sometimes complained of the food provided, these balls at Buckingham Palace completely realised my girlish dreams of fairyland.

Constantly mingling with bejewelled and beautifully clad women, who changed their gowns as a kaleidoscope changes its patterns, created in me a growing desire to do likewise. For the first time in my life I became intoxicated with the idea of arraying myself as gorgeously as the Queen of Sheba, and, being accorded unlimited credit by the dressmakers, who enjoyed designing original "creations" for me, I began to pile up bills at all their establishments, heedless of the day of reckoning that must eventually come.

The period of mourning for my brother being past, the simple black or white that had made dressing economically and becomingly an easy matter was henceforward thrust aside, and I indulged unrestrainedly in a riot of coloured garments. Indeed, the question of clothes become of paramount importance, and temporarily filled my mind to the exclusion of most things. Greek lessons, art, etc., were forgotten, while I spent every possible moment planning bizarre hats and ordering and trying–on elaborate frocks.

I shuddered when I remembered that two morning costumes and one evening gown had seemed ample in my unsophisticated days, and that when I was suddenly, so to speak, assimilated by London society I had been quite unaware of the fact that dress mattered at all. Now I required a new outfit for every occasion, and my husband aiding and abetting me by his approval, I became more and more reckless, allowing insidious saleswomen to line negligees with ermine or border gowns with silver fox without inquiring the cost, until the Christmas bills poured in, laying bear my colossal extravagance.

I felt rather unusual with my plainly dressed hair and unadorned neck, for I still had no jewels of any description, but, appreciating the fact that these coveted ornaments were hopelessly beyond my reach, I tried to comfort myself (after the manner of the fox and the grapes) by the feeble theory that gems dim the brilliancy of the eyes.

Of my many attempts at originality I remember a yellow tulle gown, draped with a wide–meshed gold fish–net, in which preserved butterflies of ever hue and size were held in glittering captivity. This eccentric costume I wore at a Marlborough House ball, but it could scarcely be considered as a very serviceable garment, for the Prince of Wales told me that, the morning after, he picked up many of the insects, which were lying about the ball–room floor.

All this extra dressing made the straw–strewn four wheeler of the period an impossible conveyance, so a chestnut horse and brougham were bought, and lodged in the mews at the back of our doll's house. Then someone presented me with a thoroughbred hack named Redskin (a perfect gentleman in appearance and manners), and he, too, became a member of the family, both of these eagerly desired luxuries adding a drop more to our pigmy ocean of debt.

Mr. Langtry had maintained a strict reticence regarding money matters ever since our marriage, so that I knew little about his income except that what remained of it was mainly derived from inherited Irish land. Still, I gathered from ominous signs that the tenants thereon paid less rent and demanded more outlay every year. Indeed, the tales of woe wafted from Ireland to the absent landlord were so staggering that they made me wonder how these unhappy tenants existed at all. Roofs fell in; pigs died; farms were inundated, and cottages became uninhabitable with such stubborn persistency that, at last, my husband buckled on his armour and went to the Green Isle to investigate the cause in person. But, money, seeming scarcer than ever after that rash expedition, I suspected the good–natured happy–go–lucky Irishman of refilling the pigsties and rebuilding the entire village of Parkgate.

Looking back on this period, I find a difficulty in placing the exact moment when I felt a changed attitude toward the undreamed– of social maelstrom into which I had been swept. Most of the people with whom I associated were either persons of importance in the land, with duties and responsibilities towards their country, or they were artists working hard to become rich and great, while I was absolutely idle, *my* only purpose in life being to look nice and make myself agreeable.

Nevertheless, very likely I should have continued to flutter flimsily along, spending money, but that by now our waning income had almost touched vanishing–point and, although I do not wish to lay stress on the fact, Mr. Langtry also enjoyed the pastime of quiet squandering, so that, as time went on, we began to find ourselves unpleasantly dunned by long–suffering tradesmen. All this made me generally unhappy, for when one lives beyond one's means, with money troubles as constant companions, there can be no compensation for the intolerable worry and anxiety. My anomalous position once realised, I began to lose interest in my daily round of amusement till it became unendurable.

Finally, one night, at a ball given by the Duchess of Westminster at Grosvenor House, I remember feeling that I must forthwith cut adrift from this life, which we could no longer afford to enjoy, and, prostrating myself in admiration before the wonderful portrait of Sarah Siddons, I recalled the fact that the artist had signed his name on the hem of her gown, and had declared himself satisfied to go down to posterity that way. Then from the Siddons portrait I passed on to other great works of art, and became filled with the desire to become a "worker" too. Impulsive as I was in those days, I did not wait for my carriage, but, pushing my way through the throng of footmen clustering round the hall door, I walked, in spite of my white satin slippers, through the wet and muddy streets to my house, happily not far distant, eagerly considering how to remodel my life. But it is not an easy matter to change suddenly from the butterfly to the busy bee. Besides, I had no confidence in my ability to earn money in any profession or even trade, so I was forced to face the fact that my chances of success were remote.

Some of my pleasantest hours were still those spent riding in the Row, and among the acquaintances I met taking their constitutional was Edmund Yates, a novelist of repute, whose best known work is, I think, *Black Sheep*. He was the editor of the *London World*, one of the earliest British society publications. He had undergone various experiences, the displeasure of the Garrick Club — which he incurred in consequence of an acrid article of Thackeray — being one of them, and legal chastisement for taking the liberty of libelling a peer of the realm was another. Perhaps these sufferings explained his bitter attitude toward the world and its inhabitants; at all events, he never missed a chance of rapping hard what he termed contemptuously the "Do–Nothing Brigade."

Yates was, however, always amiable to me, and did his best to incite me to start a career of work, particularly recommending the stage, while exhorting me to take heed of my future in a way that made me reflect. But never having had even amateur experience of acting, and more–over, being strongly averse to the idea of exhibiting myself on the boards, it took a good deal of persuasion on his part to induce me to hint to Henry Irving that I thought of it as a dim possibility. Irving, with his wonderful old–world courtesy, at once offered me the leading part in a drama called, *The Lyons Mail*, which he was about to produce at the Lyceum, enlarging upon the splendid entrance the heroine makes in a stagecoach. For the moment this rather appealed to the picturesque side of my nature, but I was really not in earnest and let the matter drop.

Meantime our financial position grew worse and worse. Creditors became stony–hearted and deaf to our entreaties. At last the crisis came. Bailiffs invaded the little Norfolk Street house, and Mr. Langtry frequently found it convenient to go fishing, leaving me to deal with the unwelcome intruders as best I could.

The same faithful maid, an Italian named Dominique, had been with me all through my astonishing London experiences. This devoted woman took the matter of the bailiffs' sojourn much more keenly to heart than I did, and during this harassing time she never missed an opportunity of cramming my few trinkets and other treasured trifles, and, indeed, anything portable, into the pockets of anyone who came to visit me. In this way some very distinguished friends departed from the beleaguered house with their pockets full, all unconscious that they were evading the law.

In this extremity everyone tried to advise me. I was recommended to embark on all sorts of vocations, professions, and trades. Frank Miles, great on gardening, as usual, enthusiastically besought me to undertake a market–garden of hardy flowers, which was then an undeveloped industry, but Oscar Wilde, who remained steadfastly of the opinion that the stage was the natural solution of my future, threw cold water on the scheme, which he pointed out tragically to the well–meaning Frank would "compel the Lily to tramp the fields in muddy boots." The prosaic presentment of the poetic occupation of flower–growing, added to uncertainty as to the commercial result, caused me to abandon this project.

"Jimmy" Whistler also had a career to suggest. He believed it was not too late for me to become an artist, pretending that he had discovered much latent talent in the caricatures that I had made of him and others while he was painting my portrait. Other friends urged me to try millinery and dressmaking as a means of livelihood, but these occupations appealed to me least of all. Someone even mentioned a cottage in the country!

At this juncture it was certainly a case of "save me from my friends," so it is not surprising that I gave up the unequal contest and fled to my parents in Jersey, leaving the sheriff's dismal emblem, "the carpet flag," hanging from the drawing–room window. Mr. Langtry, always inclined to follow the line of least resistance, still found distraction in fishing *somewhere*!

This cowardly desertion by both of us of our new and clinging friends, the bailiffs, hastened the dismantlement of the poor little red–faced house. The "effects" were sold by auction on the premises. The mock oak, and even the gilded fans, found ready purchasers, for souvenir–hunters were there in great numbers. Everything sold well for the benefit of our tiresome creditors.

And here I may relate a story which in my own mind accounts for some of our misfortunes. Whistler had recently painted the famous "Peacock Room," and thus created a rage for that bird's feathers, and I had in my house a gorgeous stuffed peacock, with outspread tail, mounted as a screen. It was shot for me by the Earl of Warwick, then Lord Brooke, from among the many that thrive and screech at Warwick Castle, and he seems to have been the only person connected with that fatal bird who did not suffer thereby. Perhaps having been reared together saved him.

I had vaguely heard that peacocks were unlucky, but not until too late did I attirbute all my troubles to this one, and when the house was sold up, I was, at all events, thankful to think that I should see the evil thing no more. But it was not to be. One of my best friends, then Lady Lonsdale, hearing of the sale, with great goodness of heart did what she could to rescue my "special pets," and I quote from her letter the outcome of her sympathy:

"I only heard by the merest chance that Norfolk Street was being 'sold–up.' Why didn't you tell me? I was lunching at ____ House, and the Duchess and I drove there at once. Unfortunately, the *black bear* had already been snapped up, but we managed to get the *peacock*, which I will keep carefully for you till you return." (And she did!) "Everything went for immense prices — your little tea–table with your initials on, down to your skates — so I hope your horrid creditors are satisfied."

Therefore, when I returned to London and took some modest rooms they were again perforce decorated by the vindicative bird, which immediately recommmenced dealing me heavy blows. One calamity after another occurred. The most dreadful being the tragic death of my brother Maurice, who had attained a high civil position in India. An enthusiastic sportsman, he had accidentally shot a sacred peacock on one of his forays, after which unfortunate occurrence all luck seemed to desert him.

Some months later, it appears that he was begged by the natives of a certain village in his neighbourhood to rid them of a man–eating tiger, and he pluckily started to hunt it on foot, accompanied by a solitary native servant. He shot at and wounded the beast, but, looking round for his second rifle with which to finish its life, he found that his *shikari* (bearer) had bolted and left him in the lurch. His only chance to escape, therefore, and to get out of the infuriated beast's reach, was to make for a tree, which he climbed. It was a forlorn hope, for alas! the tiger clawed one of his legs. Blood–poisoning set in, of which he died.

This was an awful grief to me, as we had continued to be a most devoted family, and when I recovered a little from the shock of his death, and connected the stuffed peacock in my room with the peacock that had figured in my brother's life, I felt that I could not keep it another minute. But what to do with it was the problem.

Then a brilliant idea struck me. A silly quarrel between myself and Oscar Wilde, on some trivial matter which I have long since forgotten, was fresh in my mind, and I bethought me that a good way to avenge myself would be to make him a generous (?) present of the implacable peacock. So I had the bird of ill–omen placed on a four–wheeler, drove with it to Tite Street, Chelsea, and dumped it down in Oscar's sitting–room in the house he then shared with Frank Miles, the painter.

But that was merely the beginning of a fresh series of disasters, for Miles, thinking it impossible that I could intend to bestow such a valuable gift on Oscar after my recent tiff, and, believing it must, therefore, be meant to embellish his studio, took possession of it, and he, too, became a man of sorrow. His father died soon after, and, though Frank was about to marry a charming girl, the engagement was interrupted by an illness, from which he never recovered.

I should have felt some responsibility for these further tragedies had I not explained to Frank Miles the direful propensities of the bird.

I have not many superstitions, but I certainly hold one about pea-cocks and peacock feathers. Years afterwards, in New York, I was sent for to the bedside of an apparently dying friend, Harry Oelrichs, and, finding a hideous brass and feather travesty of a peacock in the room, I begged the invalid's brother to have it removed, which he did, and, though probably only a coincidence, it is certain that at once the sick man began to mend.

It may be that we create for ourselves evil influences by imagining them to be such; so let that account for the change of fortune that presented itself very soon after the unlucky bird had passed out of my possession.

AS LADY ORMONDE IN "PERIL"
Photo by W. & D. Downey

AS BLANCHE HAYE
Photo by W. & D. Downey

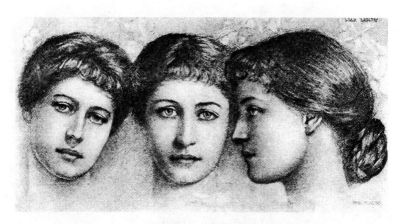

LILLIE LANGTRY
After a Drawing by Frank Miles

AS JULIET
Photo by Lafayette Ltd.

AS PRINCESS GEORGES
Photo by Lafayette Ltd.

AS ROSALIND, FIRST ACT
Photo by Lafayette Ltd.

AT MY WRITING TABLE
Photo by W. & D. Downey

IN THE LANGTRY TOQUE
Photo by W. & D. Downey

IN "THE DEGENERATES"
Photo by Lafayette Ltd.

AS MARIE ANTOINETTE
Photo by Lafayette Ltd.

AS HESTER GRAZEBROOK
IN "AN UNEQUAL MATCH"
Photo by W . & D. Downey

THE LILY AND THE ROSE
Photo by Lafayette Ltd.

AS PAULINE (LADY OF LYONS)
Photo by Lafayette Ltd.

AS ROSALIND
Photo by Lafayette Ltd.

AS ROSALIND, LAST ACT
Photo by W . & D. Downey

AT THE TIME OF MY
MARRIAGE TO
SIR HUGO DE BATHE
Photo by Lafayette Ltd.

A LATE PHOTOGRAPH

Chapter 9

I t seems almost unjust to accuse the tiny house we took in London of being our initial extravagance. It was so small, so modest, so blushing, just one of a row of similar red–brick abodes forming one side of Norfolk Street, Park Lane. We had decided, after our first experience of London lodgings, that we must have a *pied a terre* somewhere in the West End, and I was delighted with the prospect of a home of my own.

When I became engaged to be married to Edward Langtry, he was the complacent proprietor of a stud of hunters, a coach and four (which he tooled fairly well), an Elizabethan house, called Cliffe Lodge, near Southampton, and, besides the schooner–yacht *Red Gauntlet*, mentioned earlier, he had a sixty–ton fishing cutter, equipped with a plethora of piscatorial apparatus, and a small racer, the *Ildegonda*, which had covered itself with cups and glory at the various regattas held along the coast of England.

All these possessions had filled my youthful mind with pleasurable anticipation, which was, however, rudely shattered on the rock of parental investigation when the marriage settlement was being considered. That inevitable meddler, the family lawyer, making it clear to my "Very Reverend" father and my prospective husband that these expensive creations were out of all proportion to his fortune, whereon Edward politely permitted himself to be shorn of most of the aforesaid luxuries before I was allowed to become Lillie Langtry. The Elizabethan house sheltered us for our honeymoon, and then went "by the board" with his other doomed superfluities. Following on these trying disappointments, it is not astonishing that I was impatient to "consolidate" my position this time. So, after one hurried survey, we shackled ourselves with a long lease of Number 17, finding later, to our dismay, that, among other drawbacks, the chimneys smoked and that the public–house next door was a vexatiously prosperous concern.

The furnishing of this hoodwinking little abode was a delightful task, though I fell an easy prey to the so–called "antique dealers." In one's salad–days, no matter how much forewarned, it is only by bitter experience that one learns to look below the surface, and so detect the real from the sham (in people as well as in things). Trusting boldly, therefore, to my superficial knowledge, I secured "amazing bargains" in artificially worm–eater and blackened–oak, wherewith to furnish my dining–room, a poor compliment to the rare old prints which had been contributed by Lord Malmesbury from his exhaustless collection to decorate its terra–cotta walls.

The drawing–room is the only one of the eight or nine others that calls for description, and that I draped with some plum–coloured material, which made it look prematurely funereal. To the rescue of this gloomy room came Whistler unexpectedly one morning, bearing bundles of palm–leaf fans and a tin of gold paint. It seemed strange that the apostle of the demi–tone should advocate garishness, but, feeling that I had missed my expected effect and that he realised it, I listened gladly to his suggestions of gilded trophies to brighten the walls. So we set to work to burnish the fans, but the gold paint rained on us, and splashed us with such animate persistence, that, by the time our work was finished, our eyelashes glittered, and destruction sat on our clothes. Still, the addition of a painted ceiling, dimly representing the firmament, with a pair of birds (prophetically) depicted in full flight thereon, made the drawing–room, at all events, original as regards decoration, though it may have been, and probably was, caviar to many of my friends.

Our newly acquired nest stood on or about the site of the infamous gallows called Tyburn Tree, where, in bygone days, executions raged fast and furious, which fact perhaps accounted for the ghostly happenings in that elfin house. Personally, I can only chronicle the sudden bursting open of firmly closed doors at odd and sometimes embarrassing moments, and of an unaccountably eerie atmosphere; but a butler, sleeping in the basement, shiveringly bemoaned the repeated apparitions of Tyburn victims, who devoted the witching–hours to such rollicking sports as rolling over his bed with their heads in their hands or rearing gibbets at its foot. Finding me steadily indifferent to this terrifying experiences and his haggard morning face — both induced, in my opinion, by the fumes of whisky — he eventually fled from these uproarious nocturnal frolics and our service.

Only months after, when a young housemaid, whose reputation rivalled that of Caesar's wife, related how a man, with long and beauteous curls and the profusion of lace associated with the cavalier, barred her

139

way downstairs one morning in broad daylight, did I feel belated sympathy with the departed butler.

My efforts at entertaining, practised only on intimate friends, were at that time distinctly defective (subsequently, in America, I learned to appreciate the epicurean side of food), but the antique blue glass bowl (the *piece de resistance* on the dining table), with a yellow water–lily floating on the water therein, cribbed from Whistler, and which has since become a popular decoration, caused much frankly expressed derision from my Philistine guests.

An early visitor to this little house of bizarre effects was John Ruskin, then Slade Professor of Art at the University of Oxford. He came one afternoon with Oscar Wilde, who assumed an attitude of such extreme reverence and humility towards the "master" that he could scarcely find breath to introduce him to me. This unusually meek demeanor on Oscar's part aggravated my natural shyness and filled me with exaggerated awe. After a few moments, however, Ruskin's winning voice and charm of manner reassured me, and, taking courage to look at him, I noted that his blue–grey eyes were smiling at me under bushy eyebrows, that his forehead was large and intellectual, that his nose was aquiline, and that the side–whiskers, made familiar by his earlier portraits, had become supplementary to a grey leonine beard.

His hair was rather long, and floppy over his ears; indeed, he was a shaggy–looking individual. He held forth on his pet topic — Greek art –– in a fervently enthusiastic manner, and as vehemently denounced the Japanese style, then at the beginning of its vogue, describing it as the "glorification of ugliness and artificiality," and contrasting the unbalanced form of Japanese art with the fine composition and colour of Chinese art, of which he declared it to be a caricature.

At this moment, James McNeil Whistler was busy bringing a libel suit against the professor on account of the following remark, said to have been uttered by the latter, and published in a newspaper of the time:

"I have seen much and heard much of cockney impudence, but never expected to have a coxcomb ask two hundred guineas for flinging a pot of paint in the public's face."

"James of the white lock" did not content himself on *this* occasion with writing valedictory letters and lengthening the sting of his signatorial butterfly, and brought an action at law against the alleged traducer of his work. The case was hotly contested, and had comic interludes; one of the most amusing of these being the exhibition in court of some of the "nocturnes" and "symphonies" which had called forth the harsh criticism to which Jimmy had taken exception. Whistler's counsel, perplexedly unfamiliar with the American impressionist's work, held one of the famous "arrangements" upside–down for the inspection of the jury. Ruskin's lawyer sarcastically drew their attention to the fact, and the two barristers disputed contumaciously the possible top and bottom of this disturbing "harmony," the critic's defender gaining the day on declaring that he had seen the picture in question hanging in the Grosvenor Gallery, where it was presumably placed by the painter himself.

This altercation practically decided the suit, for it served to convince the jury that the paintings could not be meritorious if even the plaintiff's wise lawyer was unable to make "head or tail" of them, and the verdict was a virtual victory for Ruskin, Whistler being awarded *one farthing* damages. The recipient thereafter wore this expensive coin on his watch–chain. Nevertheless, I wondered why the eminent critic who raved of Turner and wrote reams in praise of his sublime art should have failed to understand and appreciate the delicate beauty of Jimmy Whistler's work,

141

which is infused with so much of the Turneresque feeling.

It was naturally a great delight to meet celebrated makers of history, who all seemed amiably bent on making my acquaintance, including the then Prince Minister, though I admit that my recollection of Benjamin Disraeli, or rather Lord Beaconsfield (for he had been raised to the peerage), is somewhat hazy. On the evening that I saw him first he was sitting at the end of a long room at a big reception at the foreign Office, surrounded by a crowd of "souls," and I was led up and introduced to him. *I* was very shy, and *he* was very busy observing me, so conversation flagged somewhat. Feeling that he ought to say something, I supposed, he remarked quizzically, "What can I do for you?" As it happened to be just before the Ascot Races — a meeting where women all like to wear fresh, beautiful frocks, I answered jokingly, "Four new gowns for Ascot," on which he laughed, patted my hand, and said: "You are a sensible young woman. Many a woman should have asked to have been made a duchess in her own right."

Among the many stories illustrative of Disraeli's dry humour is the following: He bestowed an important living on a poor curate, who had to deliver his first sermon before a most exalted personage. Naturally anxious to make a good impression, he begged Disraeli to tell him how long he should preach, and "Dizzy's" answer is said to have been: "If your sermon lasts three quarters of an hour, you will never be heard of again; if thirty minutes, the exalted personage will snore; if fifteen, you will be favourably considered, *but*, if you preach for five minutes only, you will be made a bishop in three years."

I am under the impression that Lord Beaconsfield was wearing an unusual amount of orders and jewels that night at the Foreign Office, which gave him in my eyes, the look of an Eastern potentate, but, although I met him elsewhere occasionally, the picture I retain of him is a blurred one.

Most of the royalties of Europe came from time to time to London during the season. Among them was King Oscar of Sweden, whose signed photograph I still possess, though I cannot recollect much about him, but this extract from a letter, written to me much later from Stockholm, shows that King Oscar's memory was much better than mine.

"I continue to enjoy my trip, and since the second am the King's guest. I told him I had heard from you, and he particularly begged to be remembered to you and to wish you success in your new profession. He told me he had still got the photo you had given him."

Again, at one of the small dinners given at Marlborough House, I met Crown Prince Frederick of Prussia and our own Princess Royal. But the monarch who came oftenest in those far–off days was Leopold, King of the Belgians. Paris and London were his recreation grounds. He used to enjoy himself in these capitals in the most democratic way, walking about the streets unattended even by an equerry, and paying visits to his acquaintances in London, at all events, at curious and unconventional hours.

For instance, one morning at nine o'clock, the butler, rapping on my bedroom door (I was not yet down), made the startling announcement that His Majesty the King of the Belgians had called, and was waiting in the drawing–room. Very much astonished, I scrambled into my gown, rushed downstairs, and there was His Majesty, wet through, with a dripping umbrella in his hand, having trudged through the pouring rain from his hotel. After making the formal curtsey demanded by etiquette, I sat rather wondering, what explanation he would offer me of his early visit, but, apparently thinking none necessary, he talked somewhat uninterestingly for what seemed to be an interminable period. He wore his usual apparel, a frock–coat suit and its etceteras, but on this occasion it looked ludicrously out of place, considering the weather and the time of day. Next day he called again at exactly the same hour, and this time I sent down a polite excuse.

One afternoon I chanced to meet King Leopold hurrying along the platform of Kings Cross Station almost hidden behind an enormous cardboard box he was carrying, and which, he said, contained a bouquet for Queen Victoria, who was then in Scotland, and to whom he was on his way to pay his respects, and also to make peace, for I heard from someone who knew that she was not over–pleased with him at any time.

The Crown Prince Rudolph of Austria was a callow youth who burst upon the horizon of London one spring. Still in his teens, he was more or less in charge of a tutor, who accompanied him everywhere, and I think the poor man had a difficult and strenuous task. Prince Rudolph was tall, slight, fair–haired, but not good–looking, with deep–set grey eyes and the prominent Hapsburg lip. He seemed very headstrong and impulsive, and was, I thought, a thoroughly spoilt child. Being heir apparent to the Austrian throne, he was extensively entertained, and I think he made the most of his temporary emancipation from the rigid etiquette of the Viennese Court.

One of the first private dances in his honour, at which the Prince of Wales was present, was given by Baron Ferdinand de Rothschild, known to his friends as "Ferdy." The baron had exquisite taste, as indeed have all the Rothschilds, and his house in Piccadilly was artistically decorated in the Louis XVI period. The white ball–room was especially refreshing, at a time when the inspiration of the moment was expressed in a rather ponderous and heavy style of oak and that terrible material called "plush." Of course, I am not speaking of the lovely interiors of homes which retained their decorations of the various Queen Anne, Georgian, and Adam periods, but of the "others." In any case, Baron de Rothschild's ball–room

144

was a searching background for doubtfully clean gowns — a fact our prospective host constantly impressed on those he knew well enough. Indeed, he asked ten or twelve of us to luncheon before this splendid ball, and offered us all new dresses from Doucet for it, which offer, needless to say, was accepted. Doucet duly delivered the frocks, and with mine a petticoat judged necessary for the hang of the gown. Months after, the famous *couturier* sent me the bill for the petticoat (an insignificant one), saying the baron refused to pay it, holding himself responsible for our dresses only. Certainly, at this particular entertainment, credit was done to his white room, all the beauties being present, and looking perfectly gowned. I also tried to live up to the requirements of my surroundings in a pale pink dress of clinging crepe–de–Chine, heavily fringed.

Having been presented to the young prince early in the evening, I danced with him a good deal, and, after promising to be his partner for the cotillon, the royalties went to supper — the Crown Prince taking in the baron's sister. About ten minutes later, Ferdy hastily returned to the ball–room, and took me forcibly down to sit beside Prince Rudolph, who, I heard from the Prince of Wales, had rudely turned his back on Alice Rothschild and was clamouring for my presence After supper he claimed me for the cotillon, making me conspicuous and much embarrassing me by collecting the favours for all the different figures and presenting them to me, to the amazement of my ever–watchful husband. As the evening was warm, and he danced with great zest, the natural consequence was that he got very hot, which caused a friend of mine, whose soubriquet was "Mrs. Sloper," to whisper: "Take care of your dress; there are marks on it. Make him put on his gloves." This I proceeded to do on the first opportunity, calling attention to the finger marks round the waist in support of my request. And what do you think the young man's delicate reply was? *"C'est vous qui suez, madame.* ("It is you who are perspiring, madame.")

During his stay in London this precocious youth and his chaperon came often to our house in Norfolk Street, but one evening, about seven o'clock, he arrived alone, excited in manner and rather untidy, the only explanation he volunteered being that he had left his tutor in an over–turned four–wheeler in Oxford Street. Whether he had had a hand in upsetting the "growler," in order to escape his irksome guardian I do not know, but it seemed to my husband and myself as if this might have been the case, especially as the erratic boy seemed to consider it a huge joke.

It was some time before I renewed by acquaintance with the Crown Prince of Austria. I had been touring in the United States, and the following summer travelled on the Continent with some American friends. Included in our itinerary was Vienna, which I had never visited, and we arrived there one broiling August day to find the city practically deserted. Everyone who could do so had fled from the hot pavements, either to the mountains, to Carlsbad, or to one of the seashore resorts of the Adriatic. Prince Rudolph was in residence at his shooting–box, Meyerling, which was destined to be the scene, later, of such dire tragedy.

Nevertheless, mindful of a promise made to let him know if chance should ever bring me to his country, I sent him a wire announcing the fact. A few hours later, His Imperial Highness answered the telegram in person, still wearing his picturesque Tyrolese *costume de chasse*. He looked sunburned and manly, and a short, pointed, fair beard had vastly improved his appearance. Impulsively seizing both my hands, he exclaimed, in his rather high voice, in which I detected a pathetic note: *"Vous voila a Vienne, chere Madame; vous voila a Vienne enfin."* ("Here you are in Vienna at last, madame.") He certainly seemed genuinely pleased to see me, and I felt touched by his warm welcome, in view of the several years which had elapsed since, as a boy, the prince had visited England. Moreover, I confess to feeling a little flattered when he proceeded to plan entertainments for myself and my companions during our few days stay. Sacher's famous restaurant in the Prater is known to everyone, but there is, in addition to the cafe, a semi–private villa in the grounds, to which Prince Rudolph was in the habit of inviting his intimate friends to informal dinners and delightfully gay suppers. "Rudi" was an excellent host, even "commanding" special performances of vaudeville artists and Viennese orchestras to help enliven these pleasant evenings.

Although the Crown Prince's Palace was dismantled for the summer, he was anxious that I should see it. Wandering, at his invitation, through the apartments shrouded in brown holland, I perceived that the clocks and candelabra on the mantelpieces and other ornaments in the various rooms were encased in glass domes, relics of a hideously inartistic period. Perhaps, however, I should have passed on in silence had I anticipated the consequence of calling his attention to these atrocities, for he instantly replied by smashing them all to atoms with his cane. He was odd, excitable, strange as ever, but there was an added note of sadness that made him gentler and more human and attractive than he had promised to be as a youth.

And now let me digress a moment to relate a little personal anecdote, which leads to another concerning his mother, the Empress of Austria. It was then the fashion to change the colour of the hair to such an extent that it was quite usual to expect any variation of tint, and mine, naturally corn colour, had gradually become almost canary. The change was not generally admired, and, as I was tired of it myself, Prince Rudolph suggested that the Empress' *coiffeur* should employ his skill to find a remedy; so he sent the Court hairdresser bustling to my hotel in the Ringstrasse with a bagful of bottle and brushes, and the man spent several hours — hours which I patiently endured — dying my peroxided hair raven black.

147

How becoming it was, I thought, as I looked at myself in the glass (I had always yearned for black hair), and, as it met with enthusiastic approval on the part of the artist who had achieved the innovation, I felt I had scored yet another success. But, alas! after several washings it became yellow again, with the added glory of heliotrope — zebra–like streaks. The Viennese dye had only worked partially.

I was in despair, and, when I arrived in Paris a week later, I consulted Dondel & Petit, two of the greatest *coiffeurs* and hair–specialists of the day in the city, but, though both were greatly impressed with the novel effect, they declined to take any responsibility, suggesting a wig as the only solution. To my sensitive mind it seemed that everyone in the street turned and looked after my variegated locks. Moreover, I had, that autumn, to face the Argus–eyed American interviewer, but, as my transformed head passed unnoticed by him, I suppose feminine ingenuity had concealed it somehow, though I bought my experience of dyes somewhat dearly.

During the all–day seance to which I referred the Empress' *coiffeur* kept me interested by gossiping about his client. One story I retain, to the effect that Her Majesty was so careful of her abundant hair, that, whenever it was brushed, she had a white cloth laid on the floor, and if one hair was subsequently found on it she was upset for the day. The Empress Elizabeth, beautiful always, was at her best on horseback, and she spent most of her winters fox–hunting either in Leicestershire or Ireland, piloted by that good rider, Bay Middleton. She received so much attention, and was so run after and mobbed when she took her walks abroad, that she laughingly remarked to one of her suite that no poor fox was ever hunted so energetically as she was. Still, I think she liked and appreciated all the adulations she received.

Her Majesty was a great walker, and thus preserved her perfect figure. Arriving in London one autumn, with a new lady–in– waiting (the Countess S.), the two ladies set out at 8 a.m. to walk twice round Hyde Park (about eight miles), and finished the tramp by ascending the dome of St. Paul' Cathedral — all before breakfast! The poor Countess hobbling along, wearing Viennese high–heeled shoes! "Ach!" she wailed to her cousin (Prince Louis Esterhazy) of the Austrian Embassy, after that excruciating experience, "Where can I buy seven–league boots? My Empress will kill me!"

Even with the heir to the throne as an agreeable cicerone, my first impression of Vienna was one of disappointment. Though the Ringstrasse justly ranks with the fine thoroughfares of the world, the greater part of the city consisted of narrow and hilly streets, in which insignificant shops and proud palaces stood cheek by jowl. The beautiful Prater, with its lovely woods to wander in by day and its endless cafes and cabarets which provide good music by night, remains crowned in my memory as the glory of the Imperial city.

Chapter
10

Being young and of optimistic tendency, my nature quickly re
bounded from the shock of misfortune, and I soon ceased
to take our financial tumble greatly to heart, and presently
returned to London, where I took a quiet apartment. Shepherded by my
faithful, white–haired Dominique, who daily gave further proof of her devotion, and appeared to have unlimited resources at her command, I had
not be permitted to feel any acute need of money, although I saw little or
nothing of Mr. Langtry, who now fished perpetually.

Parenthetically, I may say, money has never had an exaggerated value
in my eyes, nor have I counted on it for happiness. I have considered the
ups and downs of life as the hills and vales of experience, and learned
early to accept the unluckiest turns of Dame Fortune's wheel with equa-
nimity, besides it is really surprising to find, in moments of pecuniary difficulty, that one can do without many things which habit had made seem
indispensable, and how little money is needed to keep body and soul
together. Bodice and skirt require much more, and it is true that my ward-

robe was slightly sketchy, because the mourning I was again wearing for my brother Maurice had revived my simple faith in the two–frock religion, and these two frocks were more than a trifle frayed. Still, had I felt so disposed, I could, doubtless, have had many more for the asking, but I did not.

My mind was still quite unsettled with regard to the future, and it is a question what twist my life might have taken, had I not chanced to meet Henrietta Hodson, a quondam actress who had become Mrs. Henry Labouchere, wife of the well–known Radical M.. I should like to print her name in capitals of gratitude, for she determined my future through her sheer pertinacity, and launched me on a career of pleasurable striving after the unattainable.

I had just returned to my humble abode after two or three enjoyable days spent at the Duke of Fife's house at Sheen, where he was entertaining a party for Sandown Races, which are held in the vicinity, and was once more settling down to the mutton–chop of adversity, when the card of Mrs. Henry Labouchere was handed to me.

Without having the least idea of the identity of my visitor, and little dreaming the important role in my life for which Fate had cast her, I gave orders that she should be admitted. Before me stood a woman in the forties, with a rather pugnacious cast of features, a square jaw, short, curly grey hair, a plump figure, a musical voice, and a dominating personality. She plunged at once into the subject of her visit. A rumour that I was studying for the stage was her excuse for coming to ask me to take part in a semi–private amateur entertainment being organised by her for some local charity at the Town Hall, Twickenham, near which suburb her husband had bought himself a house — the historic villa built by the poet Pope, and named for him. "Labby" used it as an occasional refuse from the stuffiness of London and the turmoil of politics.

When Henrietta Hodson's breath failed, and I partially recovered mine, I told her that rumour (for once) had lied; but, quite undaunted, she persisted in her request with so sweet a smile, and so ingratiating a manner, that I finally gave way and agreed to "try." Two days later, therefore, I found myself the guest of the Laboucheres, at their picturesque, turreted villa on the bank of the River Thames, being hurried along the new and thorny path of the actor by my hostess.

Learning words was easy enough, but finding the right inflection was such a constant worry that I began to wonder if it could be my native language I was engaged in speaking, so difficult did it seem to me at first to "get behind" the meaning and phrasing of the "some one else" who had written the little curtain raiser. It was only an affair of twenty minutes, and was designed to give the audience time to distribute themselves in the little hall as noisily as they chose before the renowned amateur actress of the day, Lady Monckton, shone forth in Tom Taylor's drama, called *Plot and Passion*, the main dramatic offering of the evening's programme.

Our little comedy was called "A Fair Encounter," and was a duel of wits between two women, and, as Henrietta Hodson played the other character in the duologue, we rehearsed incessantly, and goaded on by her, I did more hard work in a fortnight than I had believed possible. At the end of it, she pronounced me most promising. I had my doubts, however, for, though Henry Labouchere took only a tepid interest in my undertaking, he occasionally watched us at work, when he invariably made some disparaging remark about my gestures, and, holding his arms and fingers in a wooden manner, he would say, "Why do you do this?" which cruelly wounded my susceptibility.

Still, there was no escape from this one "engagement." The evening came; our little play "opened the ball," and, in the character of Lady Clara, I opened the play. While I stood waiting my entrance, unluckily every criticism of both my host and hostess flitted through my brain, so it is not surprising that, when I found myself on the diminutive stage, my mind became a blank. Alas! not a word of the opening soliloquy could I remember. There I stood, a forced smile on my lips and a bunch of roses in my arms, without the vestige of an idea of what was to happen next. Fortunately, after several promptings from my coach, who was listening anxiously for her cue behind the door, I recovered my wits and my words, and the "encounter" proceeded to a languid finish without further incident.

Still. it was not encouraging to start on my adventure with a lapse of memory, which might have disgraced me for ever in the eyes of Twickenham town, and throughout the playlet, I was filled with such nervous dread lest my memory should again play me tricks, that I felt truly thankful when the curtain fell, and I then and there resolved never again to tempt Fate on the stage. But I "reckoned without my host," or, rather, my hostess, who ordained otherwise, in spite of my lukewarm co–operation.

For some reason, kindly, I am sure, she determined to do her best to make an actress of me, and, within twenty–four hours, I again found myself hard at work, tramping Pope's poetic lawn (for it was summer, and the wise Henrietta loved fresh air) in an endeavour to acquire the stage business and demeanour of Kate Hardcastle, the heroine of Oliver Goldsmith's comedy, *She Stoops to Conquer*, Mrs. Labouchere assuming in turn, with the delight of a retired actress, the roles of young Marlowe, old Hardcastle, the clownish Tony Lumpkin, and any other character or obstacle that I was to meet in the various scenes of the evergreen old comedy. We rehearsed for weeks, until "Labby" sententiously observed that a flock of sheep couldn't have played more havoc with his lawn, and surely I was following my leader with the same blind trust, and, at the same time, following the line of least resistance in doing so.

I was not clever enough to understand Henry Labourchere. When he seemed most simple, he was most complex; when he seemed real, he was sarcastic, and when he seemed cynical, he was really kind. In fact, he was a paradox. But he was constantly amusing. He told anecdotes of his diplomatic days, referred to his failures in financing theatres, propounded the most preposterous radical views, and at times held everything up to ridicule — himself included — for he had the rare quality of introspective humour. Nor was he easy to take at a disadvantage. One of his friends, the Duke of Marlborough, was dining one night at Pope's Villa, and frankly found fault with the cooking. *It was awful — always.* "Labby" twinkled his eyes, and said he made a point of having a bad cook because he didn't want to grow fat. And I know that his joy was to send a footman round the corner to the nearest ham–and–beef shop to get him a sandwich, when he was left along to dine.

When he was editing *Truth*, "Labby" trod on the toes of a good many people, and libel–suits galore resulted. On one occasion he had to attend the Leeds assizes to hear a civil action for slander, in which he was the defendant. Whilst waiting for the case to be called, he wandered toward the criminal court, and, just as he was about to enter, a brawny Yorkshireman, who was coming out, grabbed the lapels of his coat and said, "Say, mister, can you tell me t' coort where 'Labbby' is to be tried?" Recovering from the shock, "Labby" led his unknown and unwelcome friend into the court, and, pointing out a red–haired ruffian on his trial for a shocking crime, whispered, "That's Labby," and quietly disappeared.

A good story is told about Labouchere and Bradlaugh, when M.P.'s for Northampton. On one occasion they were both speaking at the same political meeting. Bradlaugh had the headings of his speech written in bold hand–writing on large sheets of foolscap spread out before him, and Labouchere, who was the first to speak, seeing these headings, thought he would use them, and thereupon began to deal with Bradlaugh's points, one by one, taking them in a round–about order, so as not to arouse his suspicions. As "Labby" dealt with each point, Bradlaugh was seen to cross the heading out with his pencil, until, at last, when Labouchere sat down amidst a storm of applause, Mr. Bradlaugh had not a single point left on which his co–speaker had not spoken. In what manner the latter got out of the difficulty is not told, but how "Labby" must have enjoyed himself.

During my arduous days at Pope Villa Mrs. Labouchere had not vouchsafed the smallest information as to the why and wherefore of all this exercise of brain and body, but she was evidently laying her plans, because, one day, she announced that I was to play Kate Hardcastle at a matinee for the benefit of the Theatrical Fund at the Haymarket Theatre, and that most of the leading dramatic stars in London were to support me. By this time I knew it was useless to protect, and therefore resigned myself to what seemed a brazen experiment.

When I found myself, in due course, on the stage of the old Haymarket for the first rehearsal, surrounded by a bevy of celebrated actors and actresses, I nearly collapsed. Really, I would have given anything to cut and run, but Henrietta was a very positive person, and used to have her own way, and none but myself and "Labby" knew to what lengths she would go to get it. Kyrle Bellew, Lionel Brough, Arthur Pinero, Charles Brookfield, E. Farren, Arthur Cecil and Sophie Larkin, were only a few of the famous artists she had gathered to "support" me, and, in the tavern scene, many more played "thinking" parts. I wonder what they thought about my audacity!

As soon as the public announcement was made of the matinee there was a mixed feeling among my friends and relations, and none of them received the new departure with pleasurable anticipation, the one predominating reason being that the conditions of the theatre were not so well understood than as now. But, on realising that I was determined, or, as I alone knew, Henrietta was, they became eager to see how I should acquit myself in my difficult task, and there was a rush to book seats. When the day arrived, crowds waited for many hours outside the pit and gallery doors for the opening time, buoyed up with sandwiches and other refreshments, while those blessed with extra foresight had come provided also with camp–stools.

And what an audience it was! Packed with the rank and file of London. The Prince and Princess of Wales were in the royal box, and in the opposite one sat the Duchess of Manchester and a large party. My best friends, too, with their attendant swains, were anxious to get as near as possible and crowded into the front rows of the stalls, all more or less tittering and amused, and not at all inclined to take me serious. That, of course, was a trying ordeal, for I had not yet learned that most necessary accomplishment which only comes by practice — the habit of looking into the auditorium without seeing the audience, and I must admit that all the familiar smiling faces in front considerably disconcerted me.

However, I was so intent on pleasing Mrs. Labouchere, who had taken so much trouble in drilling me, that I forgot everything else, and it was, doubtless, this feeling which carried me through that afternoon's performance creditably and without stage–fright. It seems to me now that it was not an easy undertaking for one who had no previous experience of the stage to get through a part like that of Kate Hardcastle and hold the audience. Happily, the afternoon passed without a hitch; countless bouquets were thrown to me, and everything seemed like a dream when it was all over.

At that time, a small, shrivelled figure pervaded every London drawing–room. His name was Abraham Hayward. He had a great reputation as a *raconteur* though to my mind he was too appreciative of his own jokes, and giggled and wriggled in a tiresome manner as he retailed the latest gossip, and I am afraid it was an excessively gossiping age. I don't remember if he wrote memoirs, but he was exactly the type to be successful in chronicling the doings of others.

He was old, but active, and flitted through the Victorian *salons* with a wide–open eye and keen ear. Though self– made, he was an extremely cultured man, wrote essays, reviews, etc., and filled an important place in the literary world for forty years. *The Times* engaged him specially to write the criticism which I print here, and which gives a better account of the performance than I could.

"The company who, with the aid of a social celebrity, performed *She Stoops to Conquer* at the Haymarket Theatre yesterday afternoon were engaged in an undertaking bolder and more hazardous than they perchance anticipated.

"Danger and difficulty enhance the pleasure and merit of success. When we say that yesterday's representation was eminently successful, we are paying the highest compliment to the performers who principally contributed to the result. Foremost among them was Mrs. Langtry, who, it would be affectation to conceal, was the grand attraction of the piece – – the attraction which brought together one of the most distinguished audiences that have assembled in a theatre. The house overflowed with rank, fashion, and celebrity, including the Prince and Princess of Wales. The proceeds of the representation, it will be remembered, were to go in aid of the funds of an excellent institution (The royal General Theatrical Fund). High–raised as the general expectations might have been, they were not disappointed. Even those who came only to look will admit they had their money's worth. Exquisite purity of complexion (remarkable in this lady) unaided by art is apt to become paleness on the stage; the brightest of eyes are not seen to advantage across the footlights, but the finely shaped head, the classic profile, the winning smile, the musical laugh, the grace of the figure — 'a full, flowing roundness inclining to length'––these are the gifts which the public in a theatre can appreciate as well as the privileged admirers in a drawing–room, and the enthusiastic applause which greeted Mrs. Langtry on her entrance must be regarded as the willing, eager homage to the far–famed beauty, as well as a cordial welcome to the *debutante*.

"The audience evidently came prepared to make every possible allowance, but none whatever was required so far as she was concerned. The oldest playgoers, who had seen half a dozen Miss Hardcastles were astonished at the ease with which she glided into the part, the accuracy of the conception, and the felicity of the execution throughout. She was good in all, but the test scene is the one in which she plays the barmaid, and here she assumed the pert tone and the required degree of flippancy without once approximating to vulgarity. I saw, although young Marlowe did not see, the high–bred as well as the high–spirited girl under the disguise when she repels his attempts to kiss her with: 'Pray, sir, keep your distance. One would think you wanted to know one's age as they do horses, by mark of mouth.' The touches of sentiment, admirably given, were marked by the same approximate tone as the mocking irony with which she overwhelms her lover when the mystery is cleared up, and what enabled her to give the full effect to every telling point, was her voice, with which, clear and silvery, and aided by a singularly distinct articulation, she reached, without an effort, every corner of the house.

"As it was understood that her success or failure in this performance was to decide whether she would or would not adopt the stage as a profession, it was confidently assumed that the die was cast, and speculations are already afloat as to the next part she would play. We should give our voice without hesitation for 'Lady Teazle,' for which it strikes us she possess all the leading qualifications, and it is a part which only a lady born and bred can play well."

Mr. and Mrs. Bancroft, who had lent the Haymarket for the benefit, had seen me rehearsing, and, about a fortnight before I appeared, had engaged me at a very high salary to make my professional debut in the coming autumn under their dignified management in what was then the foremost theatre of London. To say that I was enamoured of the profession I was entering would be untrue. I had never been stage–struck, and after all the adulation and social eclat that had fallen to my lot since my arrival in England, there was nothing strange in it for me from the publicity point of view. Indeed, to appear on the stage in the same play, speaking the same words, wearing the same gowns at the same time every evening, seemed a very dull and monotonous existence, after the varied rounds of festivities which had, till now, been the only business of my life. I had loomed so largely in the public eye that there was no novelty in facing the crowded audience, in which I knew most of the occupants of the stalls and boxes, and all in the cheaper parts knew me. Presumably the latter had helped to swell the curious throngs which had made my movements so embarrassing at times.

Thus the excitement of the debutante was denied me, and only the hard work remained. The dreary rehearsals, hour after hour, day after day, in a cold and darkened theatre, were often unnecessarily drawn out, it seemed to me, by endless altercations about things that did not much matter and discussions irrelevant to the subject in hand. (These critical remarks, of course, do no apply to the Bancrofts, who were very practical and business– like.) One advantage of never having felt the glamour of the stage was that I suffered no pang of disillusionment, and, though the Bancrofts were excessively kind to me, I did not feel very happy at the start.

My sentiments with regard to the theatre necessarily diametrically differed from those of the usual embryo actress, who, however stage–struck (in the right sense), cannot but feel added zest in the stimulus of emerging from private life, and even obscurity, to become famous on the boards and a figure in the artistic world. These young aspirants have much to look forward to and little to leave behind in their lives, and though, according to Court etiquette in England, actresses are excluded from Court, as are tradespeople, if they obtain celebrity in their calling it opens the door to many pleasant houses, where they are lionised to their heart's content.

Life seems so narrow behind the scenes, and there seemed to be so many trifling but exasperating rules and regulations, and these, combined with harder work than I had ever thought myself strong enough for, made me often devoutly wish that I was sitting comfortably in the auditorium looking on, rather than taking part in the play, and, indeed, set me deploring the urgent need of money that had obliged me to abandon my previous mode of life, which, now that it was over, seemed so desirable and afforded me many pleasant recollections.

To make matters worse, Henrietta sat in a corner of the stage almost nightly in a highly critical frame of mind, which added to my natural self–consciousness. Still, it showed that her interest in me continued, and, after about three months, she decided that a tour of the English provinces should be the next move. So the Bancrofts very kindly released me, and gave me, on parting, a beautiful silver tankard as a souvenir of my engagement.

I had almost forgotten to say that the part I played at the Haymarket was Blanche Haye, the heroine in Tom Robinson's comedy *Ours*, a play dealing with the Crimean War. Arthur Pinero (whose first work *The Squire*, was being played at St. James' at that moment), Charles Brookfield, Arthur Cecil, and other distinguished actors, besides the Bancrofts, were in the cast. Nor must I forget handsome Harry Conway, the hero, who would go to the war (in the play) in spite of all Blanche Haye's entreaties, and naturally his decision caused me to topple backward in a faint over the knees of an ample lady sitting in readiness to break my fall. I must say I thought the play silly, and old–fashioned; so did the Duchess of Edinburgh, who one night sat in the royal box shaking with suppressed laughter at the absurdity of the Russian scene.

Everyone now began to take a keen interest in my work, and all were most encouraging and sympathetic. When I went on the stage I knew I had burned my ships behind me, for an artist's life necessarily cuts one off a great deal from the events of society — one's hours, meals, work, and rest being all apart from other people's. But my little 5 o'clock dinner was often enlivened by the presence of one or other of my friends, anxious to hear how I was progressing and how I liked my profession.

Among them came the young dramatist named Justin Huntly McCarthy, then at the beginning of a highly successful career, but, fearing his visits bored me, he made the curious demand that he should at least be allowed to open and shut my brougham–door on my departure to and return from the theatre of a night, promising not even to utter a word. It seemed a harmless request, and I granted it, but after a week it got on my nerves to such an extent that I became obsessed with the desire to evade this servile attention, and I was finally obliged to beg him to desist, and to assist at my evening meal occasionally instead.

One of the most gratifying features of my *debut* was the concern in my new departure displayed by that gifted being, W. E. Gladstone. Although we had met casually at Millais's studio, I had not known him further. But now he came often to see me, and would drop in — he was Prime Minister at the time — to find me eating my dinner before going to the theatre.

How wonderful it seemed that this great and universally sought–after man should give me and my work even a passing thought. But he did more. His comprehensive mind and sweet nature grasped the difficult task that lay before me, the widely different orbit in which my life would henceforth move, and he knew how adrift I felt. And out of his vast knowledge of the public, he realised how much he could help me — so that salmon advised the minnow. Never shall I forget the wisdom of Gladstone and the uplifting effects of his visits. Sometimes he read aloud his favourite passages from Shakespeare. Then, again, he would bring me books. He was truly religious, believing, he told me, "with the simple faith of a child." And one could not be in his company without feeling that goodness emanated from him.

Once, during my engagement at the Haymarket, I gave a Sunday party, to which I asked, among other great personages, the Prime Minister. He replied with a long, broad–minded letter excusing himself from a Sunday entertainment, but making it clear that he did not in any way censure me for giving it, as it was my only evening for recreation, while it was his only evening for rest.

Gladstone was credited with having an immense vocabulary of English and a stupendous memory. Indeed, I have heard that, after reading a column of *The Times* through once, he could perform the seemingly impossible feat of repeating it verbatim, and I can hardly conceive how he could otherwise have stored such a vast amount of universal knowledge in his brain.

Among his many excellent admonitions, I remember, and shall always remember, this sound piece of advice. He said: "In your professional career, you will receive attacks, personal and critical, just and unjust. Bear them, never reply, and, above all, never rush into print to explain or defend yourself." And I never have.

Chapter
11

Throughout my frivolous career I had taken constant interest in the drama, was an assiduous playgoer, and knew many of the shining lights of the theatrical profession. Henry Irving was to be seen at so many functions that he seemed a link between the fashionable and artistic worlds, in both of which he was a popular and beloved figure. Whenever I wanted to spend an evening at the Lyceum Theatre it was his pleasure to send me a box, and to his masterly representation of *The Merchant of Venice* I went over and over again, always finding fresh beauty in Ellen Terry's impersonation, and fresh thrills in Irving's performance. I have never seen any Shakespearean productions to approach those of Irving, which are for ever stamped on my memory. The scenery, of course, was artistic, but it was in the lighting, in the Rembrandtesque effects, the chiaroscuro, that Irving excelled.

After the financial crash referred to in an earlier chapter, I appealed to the great and enchanting Nell to give me her views. She came and spent a precious hour of her time, outlining the different aspects of the vocation

I was being so persistently advised to follow. The difficulties and disappointments that I might encounter, and what she termed the "rough side,"
seemed to her almost insurmountable for one who had been so petted and
spoiled and idle as myself.

On the whole, she was discouraging. Yet, a few months later, when I
appeared as Kate Hardcastle, Rosalind, and in other roles, and was on
the eve of departure for the States, I went to the first night of *Much Ado
About Nothing* at the Lyceum, and, at the supper given afterwards on the
stage, Beatrice (Ellen Terry) confided to me that she had had me in mind
for Hero, and that Henry had intended to offer me the part, though she
thought things had turned out far better for me. I don't know. It would
have been delightful to have commenced my stage life in that atmosphere,
and in such a sympathetic part. So, for the second time, I missed my
opportunity of appearing under Irving's management at the Lyceum.

Another well–known and popular member of the profession whom I
met was a Polish actress, Helena Modjeska, who had arrived, fresh from
her triumphs in the States, to make an equally sensational success in London. Her first English appearance, as I remember, was at a matinee in a
small out–of–the–way theatre called the Court, where she played in an
emasculated and rather badly written version of *La Dame aux Camelias*,
called, for some unknown reason, *Heartsease*. She came unheralded,
and yet, in spite of the lack of preliminary puffing and her strong foreign
accent (always a handicap in a great city), she made an instantaneous
impression. In appearance she was ideally suited to the character of
Marguerite Gautier. Extremely slender, she looked as though a breath
would blow her away.

I have seen innumerable Marguerites, most of them splendidly healthy
and solid, and it set me wondering why they should elect to essay a part in
which physique counts so largely. The three super–excellent imperson-

ations of Dumas's frail heroine that stand out in my memory are those of Sarah Bernhardt, Duse, and Modjeska — all different in conception, and yet all satisfying in result.

Modjeska's was, I think, the most womanly and tender, but the most passionless of the three, and therefore missing, in some degree, the intention of the author. Personally, the only role in which I thought she failed was that of Juliet. There her appearance was against her. She looked rather mature, wore a long flaxen wig, and affected some youthful mannerisms which did not seem altogether spontaneous. One piece of business in the balcony scene, where she coyly veiled her face with strands of hair of the aforementioned wig, seemed decidedly strained.

Later on, when I seceded from the Haymarket, Modjeska appeared, under the Bancroft management, as Odette, in Sardou's play of that name. I frequently met her, both in London, and afterwards in America, and found her a simple, lovable, flower–like woman, entirely free from "airs and graces." Her leading man was Johnston Forbes–Robertson, at that time following the dual calling of actor and painter with equal enthusiasm and success. Her made a romantic Romeo, playing and looking the part to perfection.

The world–worship of Shakespeare has tempted managers to produce his works in all countries and in all languages, and I certainly prefer to hear a foreign actor or actress act in an inferior translation in his or her tongue than to listen to our poet's beautiful words marred by a strange accent. How would an American or English artist, however great, be received in Paris as an exponent in the French language of Moliere? I do not think that the proverb of the shoemaker sticking to his last and the actor to his native language is sufficiently followed.

The preparations for my provincial tour proceeded at a gallop. The die was cast, and my nose was kept to the grindstone. Indeed, I was becoming more interested in the stage and my work generally. A repertoire had to be got together, and, among other roles, I was to essay Rosalind — Shakespeare's versatile heroine. Now, whatever I lacked of the technique of my profession, I had been encouraged by my father's example to be a serious student of the great poet, and I applied myself with increased zest to the study of his delicious character. Besides, to be my own manager, my own mistress, and free from unaccustomed control, changed my point of view entirely.

Without dwelling at length on what turned out to be the prelude of larger undertakings, I may say that I was splendidly received in the ten leading cities I visited, my reception varying according to the inhabitants' different notions of hospitable welcome. Perhaps my venture was considered a plucky one at a time when the path of the interloping amateur absolutely bristled, with difficulties. Anyhow, Manchester, the "critical city," accepted me far above my valuation, and acclaimed me deliriously.

The Press was more than lenient; the audiences were more than enthusiastic, and I speedily became what many subsequent visits have proved I still have the joy of remaining — a "Manchester favourite." After the last performance of the week in question, the exuberance of my new friends found vent in taking the horses from my carriage and substituting themselves to draw the heavy vehicle from the stage–door to my hotel. As a steep incline intervened between the theatre and my hostelry, I was conveyed thither more rapidly than safely, and though, at the moment, the anxiety outweighed the honour, I felt very proud the next day.

A week of hectic excitement at Edinburgh culminated on "Student's Night," when the University attended *en masse*, and objected to any portion of the play proceeding without my personal assistance on the stage, whether I had anything to say or not, raising clamorous shouts for my immediate return while I was temporarily absent.

The Scotch capital gave me a dignified farewell, quite in keeping with its traditions. A torchlight procession of students, this time on their best behaviour, escorted my carriage to the Caledonian Station, and, surrounding my saloon, called for smiles and speeches until the train carried me away to the city of Glasgow, where, at the Theatre Royal, I passed a very pleasant and successful week, and was made much of by the coterie of painters and *litterateurs* established there, among the former being John Lavery, who painted a rapid sketch of me as Bacchante, which I saw on my last visit to the city.

The students here tried to honour me in the same way as in Manchester, but I meanly escaped by the front entrance of the theatre, and left them, harnessed and waiting, at the stage–door, as I considered one experience of this kind of locomotion ample in a short and crowded life.

Dublin provided unusually gay and boisterous audiences, and in Mr. Langtry's birth–place Belfast my creature comforts were thoughtfully looked after, I suppose by some of his tenants, who lowered pheasants, hares, and other delicacies, from the gallery to the stage to testify their approval of my artistic efforts, and insisted on my receiving them at all sorts of dramatic moments.

Nevertheless, in spite of this somewhat embarrassing and novel way of showing their appreciation, I must say that one of the prettiest tributes I ever received came from the same city, in the shape of a flock of fluttering doves, tied with blue ribbons to a floral cage, and presented to me by Belfast University. The other towns were warm but more conventional in their greetings.

During this tour Mrs. Labouchere, glowing with pride and satisfaction at my success, turned towards new fields to conquer, and a cable to the United States brought Henry E. Abbey post– haste from New York. The leading American impresario of his time was a dark–eyed man with black hair and moustache, an attractive smile, and handsome, though a little flabby of figure, perhaps, to an English eye.

Mrs. Labouchere's early struggles had made her a shrewd woman of business, and, after being closeted with Abbey for an hour or two, she emerged smiling and victorious, having obtained as high a percentage as he had paid to Sarah Bernhardt the previous season. Triumphant, but still not quite content, she urged me to use my powers of persuasion to extract "just five more," which was easy, for Henry E. Abbey was a *"grand seigneur"* in his dealings, and no haggler. Thus a contract was signed for my American appearance in the coming autumn, about a year after my stage *debut*. A few hurried weeks in London enabled me to collect the necessary wardrobe and support for the transatlantic engagement.

I confess that I was not wildly enthusiastic over the prospect, for the States, at that time, seemed to me to be about as far off as Mars, and nearly as inaccessible. I had travelled very little, and England, to my limited vision, seemed a large slice of the world after Jersey. Moreover, my many friends and relations were within easy reach, and to leave them for unknown lands gave me a feeling of utter depression. But, as I have said before, Mrs. Labouchere was a woman of great determination, and she closed her eyes resolutely to my evident disinclination to migrate.

How the States surprised and delighted me, and how I grew so fond of America that I made it my second home, everyone now knows, and I cannot be too grateful to Henriette Hodson for bringing about my first visit. I must say, however, that she had her reasons for wishing to visit the New World, and that my tour gave her a good excuse. She became gayer and gayer as the time approached, and set about her preparations in the practical manner peculiar to her. She had often told me "Labby" had no sentiment, and that it was by providing for his comfort that she held him. Now she was bent on showing him *le revers de la medaille*.

She dismissed the cook and most of the servants, muffled all the rooms in brown holland, and cut the buttons off his shirts, etc., before she left. "Labby" saw all, and looked on with a smile, quietly remarking that she would be back soon, as she was sure to quarrel with me.

When the time came to say good–bye to England, I, on the other hand, felt increasingly mournful. A crowd of acquaintances saw me off at Euston; my saloon–carriage was heaped with flowers, and everything was done to cheer me up. Nevertheless, after the train had started, I settled back in my seat, feeling very forlorn, and indulged in a good cry. Arrived at Liverpool, I still hoped to the last minute that something would prevent this undesired voyage — even a broken limb would have been welcome –– but nothing intervened to thwart Fate, and I went on board the *Arizona* feeling perfectly miserable. The ship belonged to the Guion Line, and was then considered one of the "greyhounds of the sea."

After we got on board I lost sight of Mrs. Labouchere and my maid, and drifted about until I found what was, I thought, my cabin. Thankful to escape the curious gaze of my fellow passengers, I entered it, and promptly tucked myself up in bed, and, when Henrietta eventually made her appearance, I announced my intention of remaining there for the entire voyage. But my plans seemed likely to be defeated by a yellow, cadaverous–looking man, who presented himself at the cabin–door and claimed the room was the one he had booked. This caused a commotion. Officials were sent for, his ticket was examined, and it was clearly established that my unwelcome caller was right in his claim. However, possession being nine points of the law, I refused to budge. In vain he argued. Henrietta stood, firm as a rock, in the doorway, and declined even to consider his plea. The man declared he was a bad sailor, and that the cabin reserved for me on the ship, though twice the size, was adjacent to the pantry and (as he was already beginning to abhor food) unsuited to a seasick subject.

One by one, the purser, the passenger agent, Mr. Guion (proprietor of the line), and finally the captain himself, appeared upon the scene, the latter offering his private cabin to each of the belligerents in turn, only to be contemptuously refused by both. The ship started, and the fuss continued until, luckily, the wind and the sea ended the situation by driving my wretched antagonist to seek any haven at hand, and, we saw no more of him (nor did anyone) for the rest of the voyage.

This was a turbulent beginning to what proved a very pleasant trip. I soon found my cabin monotonous, emerged therefrom in time for dinner, sat next to Captain Brooks, and found at his table, among other agreeable Americans, one named "Willie" Cutting, a prominent New Yorker, who was destined to be our host on the evening of arrival in New York.

The remainder of the journey was uneventful. Charles Wyndham and his company were on board, but we encountered strong gales, and the *Arizona*, being of very small dimensions, made the big seas really seem mountains high and he and his support were under the weather for most of the voyage. One night the water swished about the corridors, and I think we were all more or less frightened. I waded along the passage ankle–deep until I came upon a steward cleaning shoes at the foot of the gang-way. On asking him in a terrified whisper, "Is the ship going down?" he replied, "D'ye think if the ship was in danger I'd be here brushing boots?" This seemed such a sensible process of reasoning that I returned, with complete confidence, to my berth. The next morning the captain told me that he had spent most of the night "arming" ladies, in various states of dress and undress, back from the deck to their cabins.

There were rats on the *Arizona*, long–coated and tame. Poor Mrs. Labouchere, who was a victim of *mal de mer*, remained in bed nearly the whole of the voyage, and one morning, on opening her eyes, she was horrified to find a fat, genial rodent sitting on her chest. Alas, I knew that fellow! He used to sit and listen while I read to the invalid, and, with unwelcome familiarity, would indicate his need of water by rattling the chain in the wash–basin.

By the time we neared New York I had forgotten my homesickness entirely, and was very keenly looking forward to my first glimpse of the New World. After a voyage lasting over sixteen days, we reached quarantine at daybreak, and, before I was fully dressed, I heard the furious braying of a particularly brazen band. I hurried on deck, and there found a tug alongside with Henry E. Abbey, and his partner Schoeffel, marshalling a perfect army of reporters, while Oscar Wilde, torn from his slumbers at an unearthly hour, still had the spirit to wave a bunch of lilies in welcome.

Abbey and his boat–load scrambled on board, and the troop of newspaper men, having been duly presented to me, all started in concert bombing me with questions, some rather naive, and others rather audacious. It was all very strange to me. Interviewing was then an unknown art outside the States, and therefore such question as "What do you think of America?" seemed surprisingly premature, considering that a morning haze still obscured the beautiful harbour; but when the sun presently shone, and the outline of the bay became visible, I understood their eagerness for my opinion, for I had never seen so noble or picturesque a port.

The first thing that struck me on landing was the sense of hurry around me. I felt that the crowd running to the cars and hurrying and jostling each other in the streets was literally exemplifying the adage that "Time is Money." We were packed into a huge landau, and jolted over rough pavements to the Albemarle Hotel, which overlooked Madison Square, and, for the first time, I found myself in a luxurious hotel. The atmosphere was clear and exhilarating, the sky blue, the sun warm, and, altogether, my first glance at New York was a pleasant surprise.

Henry Abbey lent us his shay (it was a curious high–backed vehicle), and very soon we were on our way up Fifth Avenue to Central Park. Many people in carriages, perhaps recognising me from my photographs, turned and followed, and I was mildly mobbed. The trees were just taking on their autumnal tints, the sumach, the elm, and the scarlet oak, making the park look extra lovely.

On returning to the hotel, I found fresh relays of reporters waiting, and the interviewing continued into the evening. Being favourably impressed, I praised everything. One report asked me what I thought of the paving on the Avenue, which really was very bad then, and, while I was considering how I should answer, the rest of the group shouted encouragingly, "Abuse it, Mrs. Langtry, it will be popular."

We escaped in time to dine at Delmonico's, to which we had eagerly looked forward, and the *chic*, well–dressed women I saw there made me feel quite dowdy, for at that time the English taste in dress was heavy. Mr. Paran Stevens and others of my acquaintance were at the tables, and invitations were showered on me, but, having promised, before leaving England, not to forsake Henrietta Hodson, who was not included, I refused them all on the plea of work.

On returning from rehearsal the following afternoon I found two pianos blocking the entire staircase of the hotel, while four men scuffled and squabbled round them. Seeing me, they made a simultaneous rush, all beseeching me to say it was their particular make of piano I required. Bewildered, I replied that I had no need of any piano except at the theatre. "No!" shouted one of them, but we mean you to have one. Everything that Langtry touches is gold!" And they started wrangling again, and finally both pianos were lodged in my apartment to pacify them.

My opening night at Abbey's Park Theatre had been arranged to follow within a few days of my arrival, and the intervening time was occupied with rehearsals. The boxes and stalls for the *premiere* were auctioned by an amateur auctioneer, W. Oliver of the New York Stock Exchange, and reached the goodly sum of twenty thousand dollars.

I left the theatre and returned to the hotel about five o'clock on the important day with the comfortable feeling that all was in complete readiness. Perhaps half an hour later, Pierre Lorillard, whom I had known in England, rush unannounced into our parlour, excitedly exclaiming, "I am afraid the Park Theatre is on fire!" Sure enough it was, and from my window I could see the building, on which all my hopes were centred, with flames bursting through the roof. A great crowd filled Broadway, their attention divided between me and the blazing pile, the light from which illuminated the whole of Madison Square. The only thing that seemed likely to escape the flames were a large board on iron standards high above the roof, with my name — "Mrs. Langtry" — upon it. I stood intently watching that sign, with a fixed feeling that my fate depended upon its escape from destruction. "If it stands, I shall succeed!" I cried, "And," as it toppled, "if it burns, I will succeed without it!" *But it stood*!!!

The building was gutted, and the whole of the elaborate scenery and all the costumes, with the exception of mine, were destroyed, and, saddest of all, two lives were lost.

The next day the papers declared the burning of the Park Theatre was the biggest and costliest advertisement ever designed to welcome a star to America's shores. Mr. Abbey bore this tremendous blow with characteristic pluck, and, before twenty– four hours had elapsed, had arranged with Lester Wallack that I should appear at his theatre a week later.

Mrs. Labouchere elected that I should make my first bow to America as Hester Grazebrook, in a comedy–drama called *An Unequal Match*, by Tom Taylor. It seemed rather a strange choice, but Mrs. Labouchere ruled, and so it had to be. I made my entrance as a milkmaid, carrying pails on my arms, and, after a love scene conducted on a wheelbarrow amid rural surroundings, became the illiterate wife of a baronet. The next act was devoted to the solecisms of the country girl in her new position, her blunders causing Sir Harry to fall an easy prey to the adventuress of the piece. In the third act I become a polished and witty woman of the world, and, following the pair to Ems, recovered my husband's love and discomfited my rival. It was a queer artificial play, but perhaps Mrs. Labouchere believed in giving the public the unexpected. The evening was memorable, the audience enthusiastic, and the floral tributes showered on me were a revelation.

Chapter
12

The unexpected has occurred so persistently in my life that I willingly accept the theory that there is a destiny that shapes our ends. When I left Liverpool with wild lamentations it did not seem possible that I could ever become reconciled to, or be happy in, any country out of Europe, and yet, after a few months I began to appreciate the theatrical opportunities offered by the New World, and I decided to follow my luck and make the States my theatrical goal. To do this it was necessary to obtain a release from Henry Abbey, with whom I had signed a contract to appear at the London Lyceum during Henry Irving's coming tour in America. I can truthfully say, however, that it was not altogether the idea of continued success that held me. I had thoroughly enjoyed my initial tour; the immensity of the continent was fascinating; the excitement of being whirled over vast tracts of magnificent country from one great city to another, the novelty and comfort of railway travelling, and, above all, the warm-heartedness of the American welcome made a strong appeal, and so it came to pass that, without losing my love for the

Union Jack, I coupled with it a great affection for the Stars and Stripes.

Soon after my arrival in New York, Mrs. Labouchere had somewhat peevishly returned to England, fulfilling "Labby's" prophecy, and happily leaving me to my own devices and free to formulate my own plans for the future.

To Dion Boucicault, the famous Irish playwright and actor, who had long made the States his home, I now turned for advice, and he agreed with me that, purely from the actor's point of view, America is the promised land. Possibly I have the bump of habitation abnormally developed, for it is certain whenever I like a place I feel an immense desire to acquire a house there; so it is not surprising that I lost no time in securing a house in Twenty–Third Street, New York, for my headquarters, and, happily, my mother, though advanced in years, was prevailed upon to cross the Atlantic to be with me.

On my first tour I produced *As You Like It, The Honeymoon*, and *She Stoops to Conquer*, while the following season I was double fortunate in securing a successful English adaption, called *Peril*, by Clement Scott, of Sardou's *Nos Intimes*, and, engaging Charles Coghlan as my leading man, a position he held, with short intervals, for thirteen years. During this time, with his valuable assistance, I added numerous plays to my repertoire, modern costume and Shakespearean. Among the more successful were *Macbeth, The Hunchback, The School for Scandal, Lady Clancarty* and *Enemies* (a comedy–drama written by Coghlan), all of which were well received. Perhaps the most popular of my modern plays was *As in a Looking–Glass* in which, by the way, that winning personality, Maurice Barrymore, created the part of the wicked Jack Fortinbra, and Robert Hilliard played the gullible Lord Dolly.

These two actors got on, more or less, well in private life, but a triangular quarrel occurred over some trivial cause between the above and what Americans designate a club–man, which gave rise to a great deal of newspaper gossip. Now when the American reporter is engaged in the joyful task of "writing–up" personal and private affairs, nothing daunts him, so, grasping this golden opportunity, he interviewed even my theatrical dresser, from whom he learned that one of the two actors was in the habit of kissing my shoes every evening on his way to the stage. He thereupon published such columns of nonsense that it gave rise to a topical song, with the refrain, "He kissed the popular actress' shoes, but it wouldn't agree with me."

I have already said how much I enjoyed the American method of travelling, so when I met Colonel Mann, inventor of the Mann boudoir railway–carriage — at the time a rival of the Pullman coach — and he proposed to design and build a luxurious car "for my very own," I fell an easy victim to the pleasing suggestion.

I think the colonel thoroughly enjoyed planing that car. Being very hard at work rehearsing a new play, I let him have his head, and, beyond an occasional letter with reference to colour or material, he did not disturb me with details, so that, when the finished car and the bill for it burst on my view almost simultaneously, I am not sure whether joy at the possession of such a beautiful perambulating home or horror at my extravagance in ordering it was uppermost in my mind.

The railway–car, which I christened "Lalee" — Indian for "Flirt" — was seventy–five feet long, and really bore a family resemblance to Cleopatra's barge minus the purple sails and plus wheels. Its exterior was gorgeously blue (my favourite colour), and on either side were emblazoned wreaths of golden lilies encircling the name. The roof was white, and there was an unusual quantity of decorative brass, wrought into conventional designs of lilies. The platforms, which were of polished teak, brought (Colonel Mann told me) specially from India, were very massive.

The car's outward appearance was most attractive, and, though striking, was not so garish as the description might indicate.

Of the interior, the observation room calls for no special description, but the designer had certainly devised a wonderful sleeping–room and bath. The former, upholstered in Nile green silk brocade, was entirely padded, ceiling, walls, dressing table, etc., with the object of resisting shock in case of collision — a naive idea which, I am thankful to say, was never put to the test. The bath and its fittings were of silver, and the curtains of both rooms, of rose–coloured silk, were trimmed with a profusion of Brussels lace. The saloon was large, and upholstered in cream and green brocade, made specially for the "Lalee" in Lyons, and I was agreeably surprised to find a piano installed therein. There were two guest–rooms, a maid's room, complete even to a sewing machine, a pantry, a kitchen, and sleeping quarters for the staff. Underneath were enormous ice– chests capable of housing a whole stag, as I discovered later when I brought one back from my California ranch. For extra safety, Colonel Mann had furnished the "Lalee" with thirteen floors and eleven ceilings, which comforting precautions, together with the huge refrigerators, made the car so heavy that I was more than once officially warned to avoid semi–tottering bridges.

After having been a bliss to me through numerous tours, the "Lalee" was doomed to a sudden and tragic end, for it was totally destroyed by the fire during my temporary absence one season.

Perhaps I may mention here an interview with a cowboy, which I thought typical of these Western products. While waiting at a small station for an extra engine, there came a timid ring of the door–bell, and my coloured porter, Ben, announced that there was a lad in leathers demanding admission. He slouched in and stood twirling his sombrero, abashed for the moment at his temerity. Then he took heart to tell me that he loved

178

a girl who was living in one of the more distant of the wooden shanties which composed the tiny town, that she possessed my picture, had read about me in the papers, and added that it would make them both very happy if I could be induced to wave my handkerchief in the direction of her little home, so that he might tell her later that I had done so. To gladden two people at so small a cost was a chance not to be missed, and he departed apparently satisfied. A little later, however, he reappeared at the window of my car.

"Say," he said, "could you give me a bit of ribbon or something to remember you by? Here's my name and address, and, if you ever need me, I will go the end of the earth to fight for you." Wasn't that Western girl lucky to be adored by so gallant a fellow?

Another quaint incident, which is not without its amusing side, occurred during the first extended trip of the "Lalee." One afternoon, two men were observed standing on the back platform of the car, having evidently jumped thereon as the train was leaving a little Western town. They had their tickets, and there was no question of an attempt to get a free ride, so my porter invited them to walk through the "Lalee" to the public carriages. They were about to accept, when the official cautioned them to go quietly as the car was a private one and occupied by a lady. At this piece of information the men stolidly declined to cross the threshold, declaring that they had been living for years in the mountains without seeing a woman, and had no desire to renew their acquaintance with the opposite sex. Becoming interested, I went to the end window of the observation room, but the men immediately "ducked," so that I failed to get a good look at them. In vain did Ben try to break their determination. They stood to their guns, and did not budge until the train drew up at a lonely wayside station, when they dropped off and entered the smoker ahead, thus, it is to be hoped, securing immunity from what they evidently regarded as the "feminine peril."

The glory of the autumn colouring in America is indescribable. The apple orchards of New York State, through which we passed *en route* to Buffalo, are especially graven on my memory. Mounds of fresh–gathered fruit, some golden, some crimson, lay about the trees, many of which still carried their colourful burden. Another potent remembrance of this and subsequent tours is the turn of the leaf in Canada, so flaming and complete in its chromatic scale from lemon to scarlet as to appear almost unreal.

During the five consecutive years that I played in America, I fancy that I grew more familiar with the country than were most Americans, for I can hardly put my finger on any town sufficiently important to be marked on the map in which I have not played more than once.

Certain marvels, such as Niagara, were too awesome to be appreciated at once, but perhaps the first glimpse of the Yosemite Valley from the top of the hill was the most soul– stirring of all of them. The Mariposa Grove of big trees filled me with an almost childish astonishment, for, until I actually saw these Wellingtonias, I confess that I had regarded their existence as a chimera of our American cousins' imagination, but, after having exhausted a bobbin of thread in encircling the circumference of the Grizzly Giant of the group, and having been given ocular proof that a hole cut through a living tree could shelter our cumbersome coach and the six horses, I felt that they were very real indeed. On a medium–sized tree I nailed a silver tablet bearing my name.

Singularly lucky in meeting with no accidents, I still had some narrow escapes. While going south the couplings gave way unperceived, and the "Lalee" was left standing for two hours on a single line in a magnolia forest, but, until an engine returned in burning haste to fetch us. the occupants of the car had been sleeping in blissful ignorance of its jeopardy.

On one or two occasions we jolted off the line, one of these mishaps

180

occurring near a small Texas town. There was necessarily a considerable delay, and the cowboys lounging around the station improvised a rodeo or exhibition of prowess for my entertainment. Among other items, a raw broncho was lassooed, and a substantial present was to be bestowed by me on whoever should succeed in mounting it and riding it up to the inverted barrel on which I was placed. Louis Calvert, who was in my company that season, made a courageous but futile effort to climb upon the tricky beast, which eventually submitted to a seasoned *vaquero*, after a score of badly bruised aspirants had been worsted.

And now let me say a few words regarding my distinguished co–worker, Charles Coghlan. It is, I believe, generally conceded by reviewers of the drama that he was one of the foremost and most intellectual players of his day. I think he told me that he had first studied acting in Paris, and had even played small parts at the Theatre Francais, where he had developed an artistic restraint which later caused him to become the apostle of "reserved force" on the British Stage. For this quality he was praised to the skies by that band of fine critics headed by Clement Scott, and including Moy Thomas, Joseph Knight, and other educators of the theatrical taste of London playgoers at the time.

Coghlan was an exceedingly "brainy" actor, but an equally temperamental one, giving at times a great performance, and at others a purely mechanical one. Inferior artists passed him in the race for fame, and became stars and managers, for he seemed deficient in certain characteristics that help to make a star. Perhaps he lacked magnetism, for, although audiences appreciated his scholarly and eminently natural playing, I do not think he established that electrical contact with them which is so vital for a public favourite.

When he joined me he must have been about forty. An Irishman by birth and disposition, he had lived much on the Continent, and spoke several foreign languages fluently, besides being unusually proficient in his own. He was also author of several successful plays among them *Lady Barter* and *A Quiet Rubber*. The latter was included in Sir John Hare's repertoire to the last. Rehearsals and preparation seemed more congenial to him than the actual performance, for he hated and railed against the actor's make–up, deemed necessary before facing the footlights, urging that, though it was natural for a woman to resort to art to display herself to advantage, it was infinitely degrading to a man. He died and was buried at Galveston, Texas, but his remains were not allowed to rest in peace, for the tidal wave that later demolished that town invaded the cemetery and swept many of the coffins (including that of Charles Coghlan) out to sea, which singular happening to his remains was predicted for him by a crystal–gazer while he was still a young man!

Doubtless every woman that goes on the stage and makes anything of a name for herself receives dozens, possibly hundreds of letters from unknown admirers, of their epistolary attentions or are possessed of an insane desire to become acquainted with those who are more or less in the public eye. I myself have not been neglected in this respect, and though the letters received from my unknown correspondents were usually dropped into the waste– paper basket as soon as the subject of their contents became obvious, I find I have kept two, which came to light recently when going through my correspondence of earlier days. I reproduce them as examples of the difference existing in the point of view of an Englishman and an American. The former evidently believed that my attention might be caught by sentiment, while the latter pinned his faith to my commercial instincts. Let us have the sentimental one first.

"Mrs. Langtry, — I have fallen in love with you. I cannot find any poetic language to express my feelings. I never was any good at making

182

love in the style of the half–penny novelette. I just know that I love you. I don't know why I do, but I *do* (sic). Perhaps you will think this rather impertinent, coming from an utter stranger, but I could not help falling in love with you, dear, could I? I don't think anyone could.

"I am not one of those individuals who run after actresses; indeed, I don't know whether you want to know it or not. As a sort of guarantee, however, I may mention that my father has been a citizen of N—— for over fifty years, and has been on the Commission of the Board for some years. I myself am twenty years of age. So you will understand that, in whatever I say or do, my intentions are strictly honourable.

"Would you meet me at the Central Station on Sunday, 21st inst., at 3 o'clock? Will you come, dearest?

"If you want to communicate with me, if you will put a line in the *Evening Chronicle* in what serves for the personal column (above Lost and Found) tomorrow (Saturday) or any day next week, I will immediately send you my name and address, so that you can write direct. By the by, to enable you to recognise me, I will wear a white flower in my jacket on Sunday. The station is awfully quiet on Sunday afternoons, scarcely anyone about, so there will be no fear of a mistake, if you care to come. Won't you, dear?

"Yours,

"E——J——S——."

The letter from the American, dated from Salt Lake City, in 1893, was more to the point, and certainly the poor man could not be accused of concealing from me either his present circumstances or his future prospects.

"Madam, — To–day a gentleman arrived in this city from Leeds, Yorkshire, England. He eulogised you as being amiable, affable, and one of pleasant disposition, well educated, refined, and cultured, of a very respectable family, high social and financial standing, handsome appearance, irreproachable character, and, last but not least, a thorough Christian lady.

"He informed me that you would remarry if you received a worthy opportunity. He also suggested I write to you, object being matrimony. He likewise requested me not to use or divulge his name. I must confess I know nothing concerning you, but verily believe aforementioned eulogium and information is truth without exaggeration; therefore I write this epistle.

"To you, I presume I am a stranger, unknown and unheard of; consequently I deem it necessary to state who I am and from whom I originated. My deceased father was a paper manufacturer on Esk River. His ancestors and the ancestors of W. E. Gladstone were identical. My deceased mother's name was M—— C——, of Highland Scotch descent.

"My business is a paper manufacturer. In the past I have been connected with the paper–manufacturing industry in this city, but the plant being operated by steam power, I resolved to establish a paper–manufacture industry where a sufficiency of water power and raw material inexhaustible can be obtained, where labour is cheap, and where there is a large field for the consumption of the manufactured product, in a mild and genial climate, and same can be found at San Antonio, Texas.

"I therefore propose to establish a large paper–manufacture industry thereat, employing male and female. As soon as I can dispose of all my property in Utah, I will proceed to Texas, purchase the site, and subsequently proceed East to purchase paper–making machinery.

"If my object to you is acceptable and you propose visiting the United States during the World's Fair, and you have no objection to converse with and see me, I would be pleased if you would name the month you intend being in Chicago and thereby give me an opportunity of seeing you.

"I consider it advisable to describe myself. My height and weight is similar to that of Andrew Carnegie and deceased Jay Gould. Height five feet five, weight one hundred and fifty pounds, age thirty, colour of hair brown, complexion fair, never married, and church member. May I send you a photo? W. E. Gladstone, Lord Rosebery, and the Duke of Marlborough and others have my photo sent from U.S.

> "I am, Madam,
>
> "Yours sincerely,
>
> "W—— H—— G——."

A favourite compliment to, or souvenir of, actresses seems to find expression in calling babies who happen to be of the christening age after them, and there must be a considerable number of Lillie Langtry Smiths, Lillie Langtry Browns, and Lillie Langtry Joneses distributed about the globe. Once, a charming lady, a stranger, visited me in a provincial English town where I was playing. She led by the hand a pretty little flaxen–haired girl of five years and begged me to be her god–mother, saying that she had postponed her christening till I paid a return visit, the baby having come into the world when I was there before.

The greatest suprise of all was to have a *town* named in my honour! This happened my second year in the States, when a Canadian styled Roy Bean, after spending much of his life in northern Mexico, grounded the town in question in southern Texas. The embryo city clearly thrived, for in two or three years it was accorded the privilege of a station on the Southern Pacific, and about that time I received a letter from the founder pressing me to visit it. It was at the moment impossible, and on writing him my regrets, I offered to present an ornamental drinking fountain as a sop; but Roy Bean' quick reply was that it would be quite useless, as the only thing the citizens of Langtry did *not* drink was water.

Time passed, and I came and went and toured, and forgot the circumstances. Then, on a later trip to California by the southern route, the invitation was repeated by the "bigwigs" of the township, who besought me to take advantage of passing through Langtry to bestow half an hour on a reception. The Southern Pacific was willing, and my company and I awaited the new experience all agog, working ourselves up to the high point of interest and anticipation as the train, having crossed the Pecos River, sped nearer and nearer *my* town!

The afternoon sun was blazing down on the parched sandy plain, with its monotonous clothing of sage–brush and low–growing cactus, when the Sunset Express came to a sudden stop. A casual glance from the window of the "Lalee" revealed no reason why we should pause there rather than at any other point of the continuous grey desert, but the three woolly heads of my devoted "staff" made a simultaneous appearance in the doorway of the saloon, announcing, in an excited chorus, the fact that we were actually at Langtry, but, on account of my car being, as usual, placed at the tail end of the long train, we could see no sign of habitation.

I hurriedly alighted, just as a cloud of sand heralded the approach of a numerous throng of citizens ploughing their way along the entire length of the train to give me the "glad hand." That the order of procedure had been thought out and organised was soon evident, for at the head of the ceremonious procession were the officials of the little Texas town, who received me very heartily.

Justice of the Peace Dodd, a quiet, interesting man, introduced himself, and then presented Postmaster Fielding, Stationmaster Smith, and other persons of consequence. Next in order came a number of cowboys, who were also formally introduced. Langtry did not boast a newspaper, and therefore these young men had been gathered in from the ranges by means of mounted messengers. They were all garbed in their finest leathers and most flamboyant shirts, as became the occasion, making a picturesque group, one loosing off his gun as he passed me, in tangible proof of his appreciation of my visit.

Thirty or forty girls, all about fifteen or sixteen, followed, and were announced *en bloc* as "the young ladies of Langtry." And, finally, "our wives" brought up the rear. Justice Dodd then welcomed me in an apt speech, and, after recounting the history of the town from its inception, declared that it would have been the proudest day in the late "King" Bean's life (he had been dead only a few months) if he had lived to meet me, adding, with obvious embarrassment, that his eldest son, aged twenty–one, who had been cast for the leading role in this unique reception, had received a sudden summons to San Francisco on important business. But it was generally whispered that he had taken fright at the prospect of the responsible part he was to play, and was lying in hiding somewhere among the universal sage–brush.

The special concession allowed by the railway authorities being limited to half an hour, I was regretfully unable to see the town proper, which lay across the line and some little distance from the tiny wooded shed with "Langtry" writ large upon it, and which did duty for the station, but happily the Jersey Lily Saloon was near at hand, and we trudged to it through sage–brush and prickly cactus.

I found it a roughly built wooden two–storey house, its entire front being shaded by a piazza, on which a chained monkey gambolled, the latter (installed when the saloon was built) bearing the name of "The Lily" in my honour. The interior of the "Ritz" of Langtry consisted of a long, narrow room, which comprised the entire ground floor, whence a ladder staircase led to a sleeping–loft. One side of the room was given up to a bar, naturally the most important feature of the place — while stoutly made tables and a few benches occupied the vacant space. The tables showed plainly that they had been severely used, for they were slashed as

187

if with bowie–knives, and on each was a well–thumbed deck of playing cards. It was here that Roy Bean, Justice of the Peace, and self–styled "law west of the Pecos River," used to hold his court and administer justice, which, incidentally, sometimes brought "grist to the mill." The stories I was told of his ready wit and audacity made me indeed sorry that he had not lived over my visit.

A tale was related to a Langtryite who had killed a Chinese in a brawl in a neighbouring town, where a large number of the "yellow peril" were employed on some special work, the result being that a deputation of the inhabitants arrived at Langtry crying out for vengeance. Roy Bean received his angry visitors in a conciliatory spirit, did a thriving business at the bar of the "hotel," housed them in the loft for the night, and left promising to consult his book of law. Returning the next morning the J.O.P. took his accustomed seat on the bar–counter with much dignity, and made a speech, discharging the prisoner for the reason that, though he found there was certain a penalty for killing a white man and a modified penalty for killing a black one, he regretted to say, there was not even an allusion to a yellow one in his famous volume.

This resourceful individual also prospered on a system all his own, which allowed for immediate divorce and remarriage, until his methods were frowned on by the Government. A story I recall of his ready jurisdiction was that, on being informed that a traveller was lying dead near by, he went to inspect the corpse. One of the pockets of the dead man sheltered a revolver, and the other contained forty dollars. He judged this case instanter by fining the corpse forty dollars for illegally carrying a revolver and transferring both weapon and money to the commonwealth of Langtry.

We still had a few minutes to see the schoolhouse, which was adjacent to the saloon, but the schoolmistress had sensibly locked the door on this great holiday, so, after pledging myself to send a supply of suitable books from San Francisco, I returned to the train. The cemetery was pointed out to me in the distance, and the significant fact deduced that only fifteen of the citizens buried there had died natural deaths.

One of the officials, a large, red–bearded, exuberant person, confided to a lady of my company that he deplored not having brought me a keg of fresh–made butter, also that he had a great mind to kiss me, only he didn't know how I would take it, and I thankfully add that Miss Leila Repton had the presence of mind to put a damper on his bold design.

On nearing the train, which was becoming rather impatient, I saw the strange sight of a huge cinnamon bear careening across the line, dragging a cowboy at the end of a long chain. The "Lalee" was decorated with a good many cages, for on my journey through the South I had acquired a jumping frog at Charleston, an alligator in Florida, a number of horned toads, and a delightingly tame prairie dog called Bob. Hence, I suppose, the correct inference was drawn that I was fond of animals, and the boys resolved to add the late Roy Bean's pet to my collection. They hoisted the unwilling animal on to the platform, and tethered him to the rail, but happily, before I had time to rid myself of this unwelcome addition without seeming discourteous, he broke away, scattering the crowd and causing some of the *vaqueros* to start shooting wildly at all angles.

It was a short visit, but an unforgettable one. As a substitute for the runaway bear, I was presented later with Roy Bean's revolver, which hangs in a place of honour in my English home, and bear the following inscription: "Presented by W. D. Dodd, of Langtry, Texas, to Mrs. Lillie Langtry in honour of her visit to our town. This pistol was formerly the property of Judge Roy Bean. It aided him in finding some of his famous decisions and keeping order west of the Pecos River. It also kept order in the Jersey Lily Saloon. Kindly accept this as a small token of our regards."

I also carried away a box of resurrection–plants, the gathering of which in the desert sand for sale in the large cities is one of the sources of revenue to Langtry. The dried–up withered little plants preserve the germ of life even if baked in the oven, and after any lapse of time will recover their verdure in twenty–four hours, if placed in a saucer of water; they are pretty too, like diminutive tree–ferns. Later, in England, I gave one to the American painter, John S. Sargent, and his appreciation is certainly a guarantee of the resurrection–plant's ability to live up to its reputation. He wrote the next day:

"Dear Mrs. Langtry, — That resurrection–plant is amazing. It is a green tree to–day. A thousand thanks for such a rarity. I meant to have called to thank you, but am busy sending off pictures.
"Sincerely yours,
"John S. Sargent."

After five interesting theatrical seasons spent in the States, I returned to England to continue my profession, and since then have only occasionally visited America to fill engagements. But however long I may remain absent from the "Land of the Free," the days spent there will remain shrined in my store of happy memories.

Chapter
13

Money came in very freely during my tours in the United States, therefore I looked about in New York and elsewhere for suitable investments, and decided to place a considerable part of my earnings in land, when I should find something I fancied. My second season took me to the Pacific Coast, where I became smitten with the climate and beauty of California, and, as the advice to the young at that time was "Go west, young man," I hoped, with the help of General Barnes, an eminent lawyer of San Francisco, as well as Governor of the Golden State, who personally inspected the property for me, that I had found the exact tract of land which was to increase in value to such an extent as to make me an ultimate millionaire.

Certainly there was no income to be derived from it at the moment and the outgoings would be considerable, but when one is young and successful, and continuing to make money "hand over fist," those little details do not weigh heavily. Moreover, according to General Barnes, a railroad passing through the ranch was in the making and likely soon to be completed, which would, of course, treble the value of this seemingly sound investment.

I may say here that a few hundred yards of abandoned grading was all that I found to establish the fact, and that the present owner of the farms told me lately that work on it has never been resumed, and probably never will be.

Alas! for those railways that always start running in the opposite direction directly one has bought "Real Estate" in American wilds, and those streets that branch unexpectedly away from the "lots" one has acquired in the hope they will presently become the "hub" of the embryo town!

A large amount of dollars was confidingly placed in this ranch of about 6,500 acres, comprising two arable farms with rather good ranch–houses and a vineyard and cottage, all well–stocked and in working order, the whole being, on my acquiring it, called the "Langtry Farms" which name it retains to this day.

The last two weeks of a tiring eight months' tour were passed at San Francisco. There I spent every spare moment in the absorbing occupation of furnishing one of the houses on my yet unseen property in the simple and comfortable manner I thought desirable. The tour finished, and the company disbanded, I felt I had earned my holiday, and set off with a party of friends in my private railway car, "Lalee," to follow the stacks of furniture which had already preceded me in charge of my English butler, Beverly. He was to be relied on, I knew, to make things as ship–shape as possible.

We started at day–break, and after several hours rail, arrived at the border of a stupendous lake, with ferry boats crossing and recrossing it in every direction. Our whole train, with the exception of the engine, was run on board one of the above, and we were ferried across, a proceeding which occupied about an hour. On the other side a little more travel brought us to the railway's end as far as we were concerned. My nearest station, called St. Helena, was a mere village, and my country town was Sacramento, which lay in a beautiful valley about forty miles to the south-east.

The "depot" was crowded inside and out, the whole countryside being massed to receive me, armed with the ubiquitous autograph book and presents of flowers, fruit, and "candy," and offers of hospitality! There, also, among the quantity of queer looking wagons and buggies used in those outlandish parts, was the resourceful Beverly, with two private Wild-West coaches commandeered from my ranch, each with six more or less reliable horses attached, and determined-looking drivers in waiting.

After signing numberless autographs, and entertaining many relays of Californians to an informal reception and tea on my car, we clambered on to the antediluvian stage-coaches which were to convey myself and party, bar accidents, to the "promised land."

It may interest some of my readers to know that its exact position is in Lake County, and that it is formed by a fertile plateau of arable and grass-land in the Howell Mountains. The seventeen miles we had to drive led us, by a corkscrew road, up to the summit and over one of the highest of the group, The way was rough and narrow, and, as the only springs of the two coaches were leather thongs, we felt every stone, but the beauty of the well-wooded gorges, green and cool, with rapid rivers hurrying through them, well repaid us for our thumps and bumps. Then, as we descended the mountain on the farther side, the panorama opened out, and for the first time I caught a bird's-eye view of my property.

The huge plateau appeared a dream of loveliness. Being early July, vast masses of ripe corn waves golden in the light summer breeze, dotted here and there with the enormous centenarian, evergreen oaks. It was, without exaggeration, entrancing. In the distance were the boundary hills of the far side of my land, hazy and blue as the Alps sometimes are, and on which, the mindful Beverly informed me, my numerous cattle ranged. On and down we drove, each turn of the road making us gasp with the new picture, disclosed, till, threading our way through my vineyards and peach orchards laden with fruit, which covered a great part of the near hills, we reached *home*.

Built entirely of wood, the house, which had no pretensions to style but was fairly roomy, stood rather high on piles. It had absolutely no garden, but there were on one side fenced spaces used to corral and punch the cattle and horses after a round–up, and a crowd of nonchalant lounging cowboys, picturesquely clothed in red or khaki flannel shirts and leather bead–embroidered trousers, some on ponies and some on foot, loitered about the front door. They looked askance at *me*, but welcomed Beverly with a broad grin, and, as we were all tired out after our tossing in the "Stages," we went in.

I found the ground floor comprised a large living–room, into which the house–door directly opened, with a dining–room and a kitchen at the rear. A staircase from the former led to a gallery running entirely round it, on to which the doors of the bedrooms opened, no space being wasted in halls and passages.

We found dinner ready, consisting of trout, beef, and quails, all, of course, contributed by the ranch, and prepared by Indian squaws from the neighbouring American–Indian reservation. There were no white servants, male or female, to be found in those wilds. During the fortnight I was there, the squaws came in relays, for, after earning two or three days pay, no power on earth could induce them to work any more till the money was spent, so that there was a continual coming and going of the blanketed, moccasined–footed women. Still, they did fairly well, and when one is up at daybreak, and off immediately after breakfast, dressed in cowboy style, with shirt and breeches, and long moccasins as a protec-

tion from rattlesnakes and so forth, galloping about on a cowpony explor-
ing every corner of the land, one finds hunger a very good sauce.

I had already engaged an overseer, who had managed Haggin's well–
known stud farm, and who, rather unluckily, as it proved later, was an
enthusiast about horses and racing. We soon found some fine old pasture
land which seemed the very thing for the rearing blood–stock, and his wily
suggestion induced me to purchase and import an English stallion named
Friar Tuck, by Hermit, and to allow him to buy me a few brood mares,
whose offpsring he proposed to sell for large sums.

This helped to make the upkeep of my ranch more expensive, as
later, he not only raced the progeny of these animals without success in
California, but entered the mares in some of the biggest produce stakes of
the world, so that, years after, Messrs. Weatherby came down on me for
forfeits for futurity stakes, produce stakes, etc., but he was a good fellow
and meant for the best. I spent a golden time there, making plans for
avenues of eucalyptus and gardens for all purposes, and designs to make
the house a really comfortable one.

The keyword of that ranch was "Liberty," and my cowboys, of every
nationality, including a Chinese, walked in and out of my house in search
of whatever they needed. Redskins from the reservation rode over my
land at will from dawn to sunset, galloping about with rifles slung on their
backs, shooting the game and poaching the trout. Some of the neighbouring
ranches, too, out of the kindness of their hearts, shot my deer (out of
season), and presented me with them in token of welcome. Squatters
annexed cows clearly marked with the brand of the ranch, in fact it was
communism at its best.

Three miles away was a street of wooden shanties called Middleton,
which boasted a general store, a bar, and a barber shop. My brother,
who is of an inquisitive turn of mind, walked over one day and asked if the

barber would shave him.

"Yes," said the barber, "if the —— razor does not break."

The previous day the same wag had gaily observed to a man already sitting lathered in his chair:

"I guess I could —— easily cut your throat.!" Upon which the man ran off, soap and all. But from what I saw of the population of the country round I don't think there was much practice for the *coiffeur* or the barber.

There was a tame faun which wandered around the ranch house, and I several times found it lying on my bed with its forelegs round the cat's neck.

My guests enjoyed the sport very much, making expeditions to the mountains after black bear, which abound there, and keeping the larder full of hares, rabbits, and the partridge–like crested quail which were extremely plentiful. We all took part in the interesting process of corralling the different herds of cattle and the round–up of the horses, so that the live–stock might be seen at close quarters, and the young ones punched with the distinguishing brand. We counted about eighty horses of all sizes, ages, and shapes, pintos, whalers, and a good many mules. My manager was in his glory, and selected and stabled about twenty to use for divers purposes.

When the vineyard had to be considered it seemed impossible that anyone but a Frenchman could copy with it, so a capable man was engaged and brought from Bordeaux to take charge, but, although I am convinced that the Gascon made better wine than any ever brewed in California, a new law putting all liquor into bond for a period of years spoilt the sale of the bottles with the picture of myself on the label, and I suppose now that the country is dry my portrait still adorns the customs.

There was also a sulphur spring on my property, which we intended to develop, and a quicksilver mine which we thought we had discovered, and altogether a fortnight, which was all I could spare from my work, seemed quite insufficient, and I tore myself away, confiding the work to my manager to continue, and already counting the time till I could return as wasted.

The only drawback was the multitude of rattlesnakes that infested all that part of the world, but soon after posting an advertisement on the ranch–house offering a reward of one dollar per head I found long rows of the detestable vipers laid along the front fence, ticketed with the names of the various heroes who had done them to death, so I imagine they were soon considerably diminished. I noticed that many horses bore traces of rattlesnake bites on their fetlocks, but I never heard if it was ever fatal to them.

The lucky escape of a young English girl, a Miss Gray, from death was told me. She was sitting quietly sketching somewhere in the neighbourhood, when she felt a pricking at the back of her neck, but, without paying much heed, continued her painting. Her sister luckily saw the rattlesnake at its deadly work, and, with great presence of mind, beat the life out of it with her stick. Miss Gray's life was saved through wearing a woollen scarf, which absorbed a good deal of the poison, but she was very ill for a long time.

We had another, and in those parts a more unusual, pest to deal with as well, though not such a dangerous one. Black pigs had been allowed to roam about, and had thrived and increased to such an extent that they had become as savage as wild boars, which, with their long tusks, they very much resembled. There must have been hundreds of them, and they wrought such havoc in the corn that the cow–punchers had to be commandeered to deal with them also, which they did by means of a lasso, and for that they got the pig as well as the dollar.

197

It is positively tragic to think that, through a combination of circumstances, I never saw the ranch again. Unavoidably, the two following summers my work took me to London, but I had at least arranged to spend a few months at Langtry Farms with a family party, including my brother and sister–in–law, who came expressly to the States. My brother had already preceded us, and, after falling over a precipice with Beverly in a buggy, on the way from St. Helena to the ranch, without hurting himself, at once set out for some distant mountain to hunt bear, and spend the night unwittingly in the hut of a murderer.

We were just starting to join him when a most unfortunate railway accident occurred. Still bitten with my manager's idea that my ranch would breed superlative stock, I had invested largely in thoroughbred mares, mostly good winners at Monmouth Park, Saratoga, Long Branch, and other race–courses of the East, and had despatched them to the West, along with two pet hacks of mine. The train in which the horses travelled was derailed, and fell down a steep slope. Some of the carriages were reduced to splinters, some caught fire, and nearly all the animals were maimed or killed. There was mercifully no actual loss of human life, though a great many passengers were injured, among them the groom in charge.

I rushed in my car to the scene of the accident, and was glad to find that I could be useful to the overworked doctor by nursing. Most of the victims were suffering from cuts, and soon recovered, though one young girl, on her way to be married, had her face smashed and her looks ruined for life. A big Irishman who had not a scratch was the most difficult of all to deal with. He had taken to his bed, and it required our united persuasions and threats to get him out of it.

This so disheartened me, and of such ill–omen did it seem, that I renounced the visit I had been looking forward so keenly for three years, and we all sailed for England instead. I continued to own the property for

198

a good many years, and at last was glad to sell it for about half the price I gave for it.

It is a singular thing that, although presumably well advised by persons in "prominent" positions in the States and Canada, none of my speculations in land have been advantageous, though, had I followed my New York lawyer's wise advice, and invested it on mortgages in Manhattan Island, I should now be a multi–millionaire, but all my life I have found it easier to make money than to keep it. So perhaps the adage of "A fool and his money are soon parted" fits me, and a good many other people of artistic temperament. Oscar Wilde remarked to me that "Politics and Art" were incompatible — it may be the same with business.

Chapter
14

My decision to return to England was so suddenly taken that I had made no plans, theatrical or other. Having no house to go to, I found myself in a private hotel, recommended by a friend, in the neighbourhood of Piccadilly, one of the many small hostelries that existed in the side streets deviating from that thoroughfare. These little *pensions*, for they were nothing better, were old and worm–eaten, and almost uniformly furnished with chairs and sofas of the sloping, sinuous, uneasy Victorian kind, the windows being curtained with Nottingham lace, and the floors covered with heavy carpets that retained the dust of ages. They were, above all, lamentably deficient in comfort and washing accommodation — a zinc bath with a spoonful of hot water being the best one could hope for, and the cooking was true to type.

Still, there had never been anything different in London, as even the few large railway hotels were bare and elementary, and not to be consid-ered for a lengthy stay; I think even in those imposing edifices bathrooms were few and very far between, and there was the new and much–lauded

Bristol, with its good restaurant, where, however, it was considered rather advanced even to go to lunch.

It seems strange that the English, who certainly understand comfort in their own houses more than any other people in the world, should have allowed America to lead the way in the matter of luxurious hotels, for, although the hotel palaces in the States are now colossal and more numerous, they are not more sumptuous than they already were on my first visit to America so many years before. Even then they would have scorned to offer me, and I would have been ashamed to ask for, anything but a room *with* bath.

The first attempt to encourage the visitor to come to London was the building of the Savoy Hotel by the D'Oyley Carte Company, and the directors showed great foresight in snatching Ritz from the Grand, Monte Carlo, and installing him as manager of the new enterprise. The little quiet, dark Swiss revealed himself as a Napoleon among hotel managers, and, having made the Savoy the *rendezvous* of all who loved luxury and comfort, he set about constructing the many other hotels which bear his name throughout Europe and America.

He told me he drove his father's cows to grass when a boy, and whoever has witnessed this complicated operation will agree that it requires both tact and perseverance — two of the qualities that helped to make Ritz the King of *Restaurateurs*.

To my surprise he telephoned to my house one morning while the Savoy was still in its youth, asking me as a favour to bring a party to dine that evening, and, feeling he had some special reason, I acquiesced. On my arrival I found him at the entrance door of the hotel, the red carpet down, and a superb bouquet in his hand, waiting to conduct me like royalty to my favourite corner. Rather wondering at this extreme homage on the part of Ritz, I followed him through the crowded restaurant to my table, when he told me, in a voice trembling with rage, that a silly lie had come to his ears, to the effect that I had thrown a glass of champagne over the Lady Mayoress' dress (of all people!), and was no longer welcome at the Savoy. So evidently this was his way of refuting the scandalous charge.

After all, it was only a variant of the story that I had put ice down the heir–apparent's back, and was equally untrue. However, one must expect the green–eyed monster to assert himself occasionally.

George Lewis inserted a paragraph in *The Times* offering one hundred pounds reward for the discovery of the author of the spiteful lie, but had no reply.

Once back in London, a variety of work was proposed, and I decided, as it was August, to start with a provincial tour, and come later to town, if possible with something new. Among the authors who submitted plays to me was Sidney Grundy, a Manchester man, a barrister by profession. His real avocation, however, was play–writing, for which he early abandoned the law. His work was, of course, well known to everybody. *The Marriage of Convenience, The Glass of Fashion*, with Herbert Tree, and *Sowing the Wind*, in which Winifred Emery made a great hit, were some that made a particular impression on the public, and had long and successful runs and revivals.

He was a jovial person, in spite of his stature and age; was perhaps rather naive in some ways, though in others firm almost to obstinacy. For some reason he loved to be at loggerheads with the "Fourth Estate," which rather handicapped his plays when the dramatic critics' opportunity came to deal with them, and oddly, it seemed that on the eve of production he invariably had either an interview with the Press or wrote a letter to the newspapers in which he invited controversy in a manner that incited them to dip their pens in acid.

His house, a square, commodious, two–storey building, in Addison

Road, was called Winter Lodge, and, with its carriage drive in front, and croquet lawn and orchard behind, was very peaceful and countrified. There he lived with his wife and daughter, whom he idolised, and he seemed so content with his lot, that, except on business, he rarely ventured farther than his garden, unless to provide himself with an evening paper. He smoked a briar pipe almost continually. He was no bookworm, his given reason being that those who read too much lose originality of thought and expression. The first play I accepted from him was called *Esther Sandraz*, a free adaption of the well–known novel, *La Femme de Glace*, not one of his best by any means, though it ran in London for a while, and with that my old stand–by, *As You Like It*, started my rehearsals.

I must not forget a remarkable play he wrote for me in later years. I had been absorbed in racing for a while, and had temporarily abandoned acting in its favour. But, though I thoroughly enjoyed the successes of my "gees," there was something missing, perhaps the lack of personal effort, and therefore, when the Grundys invited me there to supper one Sunday evening, and the author read me *The Degenerates*, I accepted it there and then, and in a week had completed arrangements for its presentation at the Haymarket in the autumn.

The company I had engaged included Charles Hawtry, Lily Hanbury, George Grossmith, Lottie Venne, Edmund Maurice, and Sidney Grundy's daughter, who made a great success. It was duly produced, raised a storm of adverse criticism in the Press, and, in spite of it, was a success all over the English–speaking world.

This fact calls to mind another play, *Belladonna*, which had much the same handling by the critics, and yet was the hit of the season. Sir George Alexander sent for me to offer me the part. His words were: "Every actress in London except you has written in for the part, but I want you." As I had neither read the novel nor the play, and he was in a hurry for my decision, he handed me the play. He was leaving the next morning for Berlin, and went as far as to say that, unless I played, he would produce a Chinese drama he had. I read it over in a great hurry, first accepting it by telephone at one a.m., and then sending a note refusing it to catch him at the station a few hours after, for which I have been sorry many times.

Coghlan remained in the States after my somewhat hurried homeward flight, so I had to look round for a new leading man. A friend of mine, Lady Augustus Fane, at that moment very keen on acting, heard of my quest, and wrote suggesting an undergraduate just through his Oxford career, who she said had shown great talent in the O.U.D.S., and had played parts elsewhere with her to her satisfaction.

This young man was Arthur Bourchier! Well! I engaged him, and found all she told me to be true, and certainly he was a delightful comrade to boot, and, one way and another, he managed to infuse a good deal of variety into a round of the rather dull cities so often visited by me before.

The tour over, I proposed to play in town, where I had rented the St. James's Theatre for two years. The season was to open with *As You Like It*, with A.B., who had already made a hit in the provinces, in the part of Jacques, myself, of course, as Rosalind, and Charles Sugden the Touchstone. To lessen my work I had engaged Louis Wingfield, who had the name of being the best scenic director of Shakespearean plays at the moment, to arrange a new and original setting.

Thus, feeling quite safe, I went to spend a fortnight of relaxation in my favourite Paris. While there I met, as usual, hosts of acquaintances, American, English, and others, among them being an old friend — Prince Charles Kinsky, an Austrian — who came to a lunch given for me at Voisin's, and, as he sat opposite to me, I observed with my usual frankness that his face was extremely blotchy.

"Yes," he said, "I feel very ill, and only got up from my bed because I heard I was to meet you, and I intend to go back there at once."

The next day he sent a message to my hotel to say it was measles. And he hoped he had not infected any of the party, but, as I had escaped it as a child, and later had nursed my friend Lady de Grey (then Lady Lonsdale) through an attack, I thought I was immune.

When I got back to town Wingfield had not only arranged the scenery, but he had re–arranged the play in a manner so audacious that the company, headed by Arthur B., had struck work, and, the first night being advertised, I had to put in a tremendous lot of time to replace the scenes in the sequence familiar to Shakespeare and myself.

The dress rehearsal having gone off without a hitch, I went home the night before the opening feeling rather ill, but very satisfied. Next morning, the day which is always such a momentous one for artists, I felt so feverish that my doctor was called in, who declared it was impossible for me to play, with my high temperature, but, as that kind of warning had often been disregarded by me before, I determined to defy his advice once again. My brother came to escort me to the theatre about five, and, seeing my condition, became very worried.

"I am quite well," I said, "and I shall play."

"Look at yourself in the glass," he said, and I did, and saw a swollen face, with horrible blotches similar to those that had disfigured Charles Kinsky.

Then the awful truth flashed across my mind — *measles*! And I knew the hopelessness of persisting. So a letter was despatched to Marlborough House to T.R.H. who were to have been present, and notices were hastily posted at the theatre, and there was nothing for it but to resign myself to the infantile complaint. It was all the more bitter because salaries had to be paid for a whole month before I could play.

An actress is often asked which is her favourite character, and I have never hesitated to reply: "Rosalind," so that, having attempted the part within six months of my appearance on the stage in London, and having it in my repertoire, and continuing to give the character incessant thought and study, I was well rewarded by the warm reception of *As You Like It* by both Press and public when at last I was able to appear at the St. James's' after my illness.

I have presumed to add a short analysis as I interpreted her. It is by the wish of one of our leading dramatic critics, who approved of my performance.

ROSALIND

The role of Rosalind is so feminine and, in certain scenes, so subtly womanish, that it is difficult to imagine the boy actor of the Elizabethan period being able to give full significance to the moods of this marvellous creation. Shakespeare intended *As You Like It* to be pure and unalloyed comedy, and the choosing of an open air setting from beginning to end of the play adds considerably to the joyous note. Rosalind has not a really melancholy mood. Even in the first act, though separated from her banished father, she is fairly content with her lot. Certainly she quails for a second under the unexpected wrath of the usurping duke, but she realises the next second that he is unjust both to her and, what is worse, to his absent brother, and she turns on him with a proud, fiery, reproachful speech.

When banished, it is the thought of leaving her beloved Celia that weighs with her, for Celia, in her lovely speech to her father, in which she describes their life from childhood, makes it clear that they have been hitherto inseparable. But the moment the latter declares her intention "to go along" with her, Rosalind's high spirits reassert themselves, and never really desert her throughout the comedy. Of her meeting with Orlando I feel there is not much to be said. It is as slight as the first meeting of Romeo and Juliet, and, although Orlando feels the pang of sudden love, I do not think Rosalind takes the occasion as seriously.

When she appears at Ganymede in the forest, she certainly has no idea of seeing him there; it is her father she is seeking, and, if Orlando has not acquired the curious mania of hanging verses on trees, Rosalind might have thought no more of the young wrestler. But her fancy is caught by these tributes of praise, which she never doubts are intended for her, and, although she pretends ignorance of the writer, even Celia is not taken in. Now we come to the first of the Ganymede–Orlando scenes. When Rosalind sees him she says: "What shall I do with my doublet and hose?" which, I think, is usually made of too much importance, for, as she has no notion of revealing herself, it is the very disguise she would have chosen. On the contrary, she emphasises the mannish side of her versatile character, and bewilders her lover with her wide knowledge all through this delightful dialogue. But I do not think she could have carried the scene off so airily had she been half as much in love with him as she knew him to be with her. Between this and the second forest scene time had elapsed; she has seen her father, has no doubt had daily meetings at their cot and elsewhere with Orlando, and is now as deeply in love as it is in Rosalind's nature to be.

This later scene is the antithesis of the former one, where she simulates "the saucy lackey" with gusto. Here, though still disguised, she is indeed the coquette, the woman revelling in the whimsical courtship and lingering over the mock marriage, often on the verge of revealing herself and just recovering her self– control in time. How characteristic of a woman in love is her peevishness at his dilatoriness in keeping his tryst, and the whole gamut of moods of the love–sick woman which she plays on the unsuspecting Orlando. But is he really unsuspecting by now? I have never analysed his character, I thought it better not. I realised it would be difficult, almost impossible, to play those forest scenes unless Rosalind is convinced she is unrecognised, but I must say the alacrity with which he is ready to rush into marriage with a girl he has only spoken five words to filled me with misgivings. Anyhow, the play, after that scene, is over, and the only thng to whip it up at the end is the much–liked epilogue.

The St. James's was to prove an unlucky theatre to me, for, before the season was over, I was laid low with pleurisy, and Arthur Bourchier took the theatre off my hands for awhile, and made his first bow there as manager. I am not sure his recollections of that period are altogether satisfactory.

Antony and Cleopatra, at the Princes', Oxford Street, was my next venture, for, though St. James's was still on my hands, the stage was too limited for the spectacular effects which I felt necessary to the play. I cannot conceive that particular Shakespearean tragedy being successful against a green baize curtain. Small wonder it is, therefore, that, saddled with the rent of the two theatres, both closed, the losses incurred by my illness, and the expenses of the coming production, with its architectural scenes, purple galleys, Roman chariots and milk– white steeds, and so forth, I found myself, unexpectedly, on the eve of opening, short of two or three hundred pounds to pay the carpenters and working staff. What was to be done? It would take too much time to cable to my American bank for funds — the London one was dry.

Suddenly I thought of the Rothschilds. Happy thought! Down went a messenger post–haste to Newcourt, their headquarters in the City, with a note to Alfred Rothschild, whom I knew the best, explaining the unfortu- nate circumstances and pleading a temporary loan. Now so absorbed had I been in my rehearsals that I was unaware that the house of Rothschild was at that moment in a fever of anxiety, shared indeed by all the London banks, over some unwise transaction entered into by the firm of Baring Brothers, in which "trillions" were involved, and which was known as the "Baring Crisis." As I had unwittingly used the word "crisis" in my description of the financial condition at the Princes', Alfred Rothschild told me later that he read aloud my communication, which reached them in the midst of a rather solemn lunch, thereby causing general and much–needed hilarity.

The carpenters' clamors having been silenced with the Rothschild money, the play was presented to the public on the appointed night, but, though I was very anxious to play Cleopatra, the whole play when staged resolved itself into a number of scenes more or less disjointed, which flitted from Alexandria to Rome and elsewhere in rather a bewildering way for the audience. I don't know whether any of the great actresses of the past essayed Cleopatra, but it is never mentioned among their triumphs. We all know that Cleopatra was a great coquette and subjugator of men, but the love scenes in *Antony and Cleopatra* are very short, and contain a great deal of bickering, so that the moods of the Egyptian Queen, unlike those of Rosalind, were so foreign to my nature that I found them very difficult to portray.

Coghlan's Antony was a good performance; still, I think without the scenic effects we now employed the play would not have been so acceptable. Herbert Tree, rushing from the Haymarket at the close of his performance, arrived in time for Cleopatra's death, and was very enthusiastic, but I am sure that was the scene I played and stage–managed the best.

During the rehearsals I sat next to Lord Hartington at a dinner– party one evening, and he helped me very much with suggestions, being brimful of Egyptian and Greek love.

On one occasion when I was playing in *Antony and Cleopatra* at the

Princes' Theatre, Mr. and Mrs. Gladstone (one night) occupied the royal box. The next evening, during the performance, the stage door–keeper came to my sitting–room, giggling, to tell me that an old man representing himself to be Mr. Gladstone had called, but he felt sure there was some mistake, as he was not in evening dress! Naturally he was immediately shown in, and proved to be the genuine article, with his arms full of Shakespearean commentaries to prove that I was mistaken in the interpretation of a phrase.

The tragedy ran for some months, until a series of pea–soup fogs weakened the attendance, and, as the expenses amounted almost to the capacity of the theatre, I was rather glad to end the run. Afterwards I tried one or two plays for which the stage was too large, and which suffered from untoward happenings on the first night owing to too hasty production and other unexpected causes. The two plays produced were *Lady Barter*, by Coghlan, and *Linda Gray*, a crude melodrama by an unknown author. The first was an adaptation from *Le Demi–Monde*, and the first two acts went so well that the Prince of Wales came from the royal box to compliment Coghlan and myself at the end of the second act. Alas! H.R.H.'s praise so stimulated the author that he forgot his words in the third and final act, and to complete the unfortunate occurrence, Lewis Wallet, the lover who had to finish the play in a despairing attitude, chose to bury his head on a table laden with small silver objects, which he scattered all over the stage and orchestra.

All worth recording of the first night of *Linda Gray* was that the chimney in the royal room smoked H.R.H. and Prince Christian out of it, and that they spent most of the evening on the stage, very busy hearing us our lines, of which we were none of us too sure, also that Bernard Gould (Bernard Partridge) wore an opulent false moustache, which dropped off in the love scene.

After a short run, my tenancy of the huge, draughty barn of a theatre luckily came to a close.

In moments of financial panic other women besides myself appealed to the good–natured Rothschilds for temporary help. Alfred was, I think, the most popular of the family. He was a little, gentle–voiced, delicate man, a bachelor, living in a treasure house in Seamore Place, where he sometimes gave receptions, but more often restricted himself to luncheons and small dinner– parties. At these latter he rather liked to invite one woman only, and perhaps three or four men, and to the lone woman after dinner he invariably and with great secrecy, gave a *bibelot* of no great value.

Having compared notes with some other of his women guests who had received similar presents, I determined to tease him. So when one evening he whispered the usual remark, "What shall I give you, beautiful lady?" I picked up a priceless enamelled bediamonded Louis Seize snuff–box, the gem of a collection lying on a table, and said calmly, "Oh, this will do." He had a weak heart, and for a moment I really thought I had stopped it. When he got his breath he promised me something much prettier, and out came one of the well–known gift–boxes. All his time when at the office seemed to be employed in writing cheques, at least I always found him so engaged. He never stopped, but went on signing and talking and adding to the heap already before him on the table, until I felt it must be a dream of Tantalus.

In Alfred Rothschild's set were two distinct and vivid personalities in the diplomatic world of London at that time — Monsieur X and the Marquis de Soveral. Monsieur X, who was in the Russian Embassy, and Don Luiz Soveral, who was First Attache in the Portuguese Legation, seemed to be unusually imbued with their importance and share in the direction of their respective countries' diplomacy.

The former was a pale creature, with dust–coloured hair, washed–out eyes and a sensual mouth; not a beauty certainly, yet he seemed confident that with the fair sex he was practically invincible. Of course one met him constantly and everywhere, so that he must have had a social success.

He was a large eater, and a greedy one, and this reminds me of an anecdote concerning a German Baron, likewise representing his country in London at about that period. I knew he had an unusual appetite, but the most incredible story ran that, at a well–known restaurant, he had eaten a whole ham for his supper one night after the opera. Let us presume his dinner was a sketchy one.

While on this subject of abnormal appetites, a strange bearded man, carrying a gun, and accompanied by two or three spaniels, who used to come to the Deanery in my childhood to see my elder brothers, and incidentally to empty the larder for his supper, explained to no one of them that he considered a goose an awkward bird, too much for one and yet not enough for two.

Now I came to what the Americans call "a different proposition," to wit, Luiz Soveral. There is no doubt that *he* was clever, tactful, and possessed the qualities needed for diplomacy of a high order. The then Ambassador of Portugal being old put a great deal of responsibility on his capable shoulders, and his country must have appreciated his work, for he later left the Legation in Portland Place to become premier of his strip of a country.

He had large, dark, expressive eyes, good features, and a mat skin, while his heavy black Mephistophelian eyebrows and Kaiserish moustache gave him a fire–eating appearance, yet there was no one more suave. His shaven chin and cheeks were of such a blue hue that he was given the sobriquet of the "Blue Monkey"; nevertheless, in spite of this rather bizarre combination, he was a decidedly handsome foreigner. Combining great charm of manner with a pleasant voice, he talked a great deal and exceedingly well on most subjects of the moment, and no dinner could be dull at which he was a guest. Besides, he was just enough of a gossip and *raconteur* to please the womenkind, though I don't think he was a favourite with Englishmen. After all, they had not much in common, for he cared for no kind of sport, and none of the games of chance one associates with the Latin races, but he was gay and witty, and captivated a great many of the fair sex.

Once, when in Paris, the Marquis de Soveral took me to see a bull–fight, which the French authorities had permitted on condition that neither bull nor horses were hurt. This particular one was conducted as the royal Portuguese *corridas*, and was far more picturesque than the ordinary Spanish variety. Of course, there were the usual matador and picadors, but on this occasion the latter rode good horses clad in suits of mail to make them immune from the terrible horns that repeatedly tried to gore them, but the novelty and great interest was to see how the two young Portuguese noblemen would acquit themselves. These it seems are always included in the bull– fights attended by royalty, and are chosen from sixteen grandees of the land. They arrived in the arena wearing costumes of the seventeenth century, and drawn by twelve white horses in a coach of the same period. Their game seemed to consist in showing their prowess in attacking the bull without allowing him to come in contact with the superb Arabs they rode, and which, they told me, were priceless. I must say these sagacious animals seemed to understand and enjoy the sport dashing between the bull and the side of the arena, as it seemed to me, having hair–breadth escapes. We had lunch with the two brilliant young *caballeros* before the show, and whenever the Marquis de —— – did anything especially daring he advanced to the box, and, bowing low, said in a loud voice: *"Madame, je vous offre le taureau,"* upon which Soveral told me to bow also, as I was being paid a great compliment usually reserved for royalty. The young Portuguese, who appeared to have taken a great fancy to me at lunch, as far as I could gather without understanding what he said, repeated the offer of the bull so often that it became most embarrassing, especially as the vast arena cheered lustily, evidently taking me, as we sat in the Portuguese Embassy box, for someone very special. Towards the end of the *corrida*, a woman entered the arena, the first in the world to do so, the announcement ran, but, after one or two timid advances, she retreated to a far corner, and sat still on her horse, sur-rounded with picadors, etc. I must say I think she was very plucky to compete at all, especially as all the bulls were very fine, savage animals. The beautiful pageant, shorn of all its horrors, delighted me. The end of each bout was daringly undertaken by a celebrated matador, who made the gesture of giving the *coup de grace* without doing so. Then all the matadors leapt from the arena as a trumpet sounded, and the great doors, opening, admitted a quantity of oxen with cowbells tinkling, who lured the bull out of the ring in their midst.

There was Prince Louis Esterhazy, who was for many years Military Attache to the Austrian Embassy. He was an old fop with the frame of a slim boy; he was a fine horseman, and had ridden military steeplechases in Austria, and had broken his nose at the game, but, in spite of this detri-ment to his beauty, he looked extremely well in his Austrian uniforms, of which he seemed to have as many as his Emperor.

I watched Queen Victoria's State funeral procession pass, in all its sombre pomp, from a window of the Berkeley Hotel. The Kaiser, on a black charger, riding between the Prince of Wales and the Duke of Connaught, looked remarkably well, but when General Prince Louis Esterhazy rode by on a restless thoroughbred hack, which he controlled with great ease, we all thought him the most resplendent figure in the *cortege*. On that occasion he wore the white and gold uniform of the Austrian Hussars, one of the several regiments which he had commanded, and many decorations and medals adorned it.

I thought Prince Louis a discontented, disgruntled person, always standing on his dignity and looking for slights from high quarters, and really he deserved some of them. For instance, the Prince of Wales had a horse called "Florizel," by St. Simon, who had won some good races, but turned whistler, and, without the slightest reason, Esterhazy thought he was expected to buy it for the Austrian State Stud. He made the mistake of explaining to all and sundry that he really could not buy a "roarer" to please H.R.H. Before long this indiscreet prattle reached the latter's ears, and made him very angry, and he told me to tell Esterhazy what he thought of his conduct. I conveyed the message as delicately as possible, but the episode occasioned a mutual frigidity for some time.

All this time I was living in Pont Street, in a house I had newly bought, my furniture, horses, and carriages having arrived from America. Always hard at work at the theatre, I took for granted that my house was being conducted on the usual lines, but I had some rude awakenings. A butler was my factotum, and seemed more or less what a butler should be. My *chef* was a young Frenchman, who had come over to learn English.

All went smoothly (on the surface), until one evening when I had a supper–party after the theatre, during which the butler swaying under the combined influence of champagne and women *Americaine*, contrived to upset the contents of a dish into the lap of my new blue Worth gown. There was nothing to be done but to excuse myself, and to change from top to toe. Whenever a gown suited me extra well Worth used to say, "'Ave 'alf a dozen in different colours," so that when I returned in ten minutes in the facsimile in pink it created some amusement.

The next day the jovial butler was evacuated, and Louis, the *chef*, reigned in his stead, and a splendid butler he made, and no wonder, for *mon petit cuisinier*, as he likes still to call himself, was Louis Barrerya, now the opulent proprietor of four great Parisian restaurants; respectively, the famous Cafe de Paris, Armenonville, Fouquet's on the Champs Elysees, and the beautiful Pre Catalan, which, in the olden days, was a farm, with well–groomed cows roaming the paddocks, where we used to drive to drink fresh milk! Indeed, it was drinking iced milk there one hot afternoon that caused the sudden death of the clever actress, Adelaide Neilson, at the age of thirty–five, and whose performance of Juliet stands out in my memory as incomparable. King Edward, I think on his last visit to Paris, delighted Louis by recognising him as having waited on him at my house, and shaking hands with him.

It is one of my pleasure when in Paris to motor out to the Bois with him and his wife to lunch at the Pre Catalan, my favourite of his four big establishments. There we sit in a spacious private salon, with a balcony overlooking the restaurant, eat the best of everything, and, with the band playing below especially for my benefit, we talk over the past, and what a memory he has! He recollects a luckless admirer with a revolver, who occupied a room in the hotel opposite, thoroughly resolved to kill one and all who should enter through the front door, which he commanded from his window, and the manner in which the male portion of my guests were conducted over a plank laid from the area railings through the dining–room window, happily hidden from his view.

He reminded me, too, of an escapade of a young officer in the Guards, which might have ended tragically for him. I was lying dangerously ill at my house, and this headstrong young man determined to see me for a few months, in spite of the fact that he was on Guard at St. James's. He managed, however, to change into mufti, and absented himself, thinking all was quiet., As ill–luck would have it, Queen Victoria suddenly elected to come to town that afternoon. Lord E. C. — in the same regiment — was one of the first to hear of Her Majesty's intended visit. He had his suspicions about his brother officer, and, flinging on his uniform, dashed to St. James's Place, just in time to turn out the guard as he passed, and thus save the situation. Louis Barrerya has happy memories of the time he passed in what he calls *"La Maison du bon Dieu!"*

Then there was Lord D——, who disguised himself as a cabby in order to have the pleasure of driving me in his private hansom after the theatre one evening, and who, instead of taking me home, drove furiously about the West End. I wondered whether I was in the clutches of a madman, and tried to calm him through the trap, but, though he answered me very politely, he pursued his tactics, till at last I persuaded him to pull up at No. 1 Belgrave Square (Reuben Sasson's house). The latter, who never went to bed, opened the door himself, and I hopped out, and told him of my fears. But, after peering at the cabby, and making him talk, we discovered the fraud, and ended the evening eating bacon and eggs cooked by Mr. Sassoon himself in a little private kitchen he had installed leading from his den.

Rather bitten with the delights of the Casino at Monte Carlo, I provided myself with a roulette wheel and cloth, with which to while away an hour or two when I gave a supper after the theatre. Our play was limited to shillings, so it was not dangerous to our pockets, but one night, when about a dozen of us were gathered around the table, the door–bell rang repeatedly, and Louis rushed in exclaiming, "It is the police." Consternation sat on our faces. Sir George Arthur, preserving his presence of mind, grabbed the money lying on the table and hid with it behind the curtain, others disappeared under the table, and I started a stammering exposition of the mildness of the stakes to the two bobbies, who suddenly tore off their false beards and disclosed the laughing faces of Claude Lowther and Robert Peel.

The former, when younger, was very fond of travesties of this kind, and on one drizzling afternoon persuaded me to drive to Clarkson's, who disguised us respectively as a match–boy and a flower–seller. Leaving my carriage standing at Clarkson's — for even the footman failed to recognise us as we trotted along the Strand — Claude every now and then beseeching me "to shuffle, not walk," we thought Pall Mall would be a nice quiet place to dispose of our wares, and an old gentleman emerging from the Carlton Club was my first client. He bought some violets, then looked suspicious, threw a pound into the basket, and said, "I'll take the lot, come and have a drink," which invitation came as an unwelcome surprise from such a quarter, and as I looked across the street to beckon Claude I saw him held up by a policeman — a real one this time — it seemed that he had been pursuing pretty girls with his matches, trying to force them to buy, and he was let off on condition that he "move on," and I was accused of interfering with old gentlemen. We then went to Bond Street, where Claude enticed his barber, Gilbert of Truefitt's, to square two policemen on point duty, but it was no longer amusing now that we were under police protection, so we hailed a cab and drove back to Clarkson's to be ourselves again.

Everyone knows how Claude Lowther has devoted years of restoring Hurstmonceau Castle, and his good–nature in throwing it open to the public. One Sunday, Herbert Tree, who was spending the week– end there, suggested passing himself off as Claude. He graciously received the tourists, and, to Mr. Lowther's horror, had them make themselves at home in the gardens, and eat as much fruit as they liked, pointing out a heavily laden peach tree as their first objective. Claude bided his time, and, later on, introduced himself to them as Herbert Tree. "I am very glad to meet you," he said, "and I should like to see you all at His Majesty's," and forthwith began scribbling free passes to every part of the theatre.

But Claude Lowther was at his best with his chief accomplice, Norman Forbes. The following story is not a bad one. They were walking in the Park one Sunday, and found a Socialist meeting in progress. "We must stop this somehow," said Claude, "I am President of the Anti–Socialist Society." So he walked among the crowd, nudging them, and pointed out Norman, who was waiting for him as Zucchi (it was just after Zucchi's forty days fast).

Norman was mobbed, and placed on a chair to recount his experiences, but, warming to his subject, he made such audacious assertions in broken English that a voice in the crowd shouted "Liar!" There was a momentary pause, then Lowther rushed into the breach, restored the mob's confidence in Zucchi, and the interrupter was chased from the Park by the indignant people, thus effectively breaking up the meeting.

Chapter
15

When I went on the stage my "casket of gems" consisted of a row of small pearls and two or three insignificant rings. Henrietta Labouchere was positively shocked. "What!" she exclaimed. "You, the sensation of three London seasons, have got no jewellery!" And I read contempt in her eyes. Certainly if jewels are well set they add *eclat* to the wearer, especially at those Court functions and galas where women have to form part of a glittering whole. But I have always thought that so many carats of diamonds perched on a woman's head or wound around her throat may make their owner look ostentatious and vulgar if worn on the wrong occasion, and yet the temptation to some is too great to be resisted. Neither did I admire the style of setting in those Victorian days, for it was exceedingly ponderous. Here and there I saw something artistic that pleased me, on Mrs. Oppenheim, for instance, I observed a delicately mounted diamond necklace of Empire design, on which I complimented her. And she laughingly replied, "It is to hide the first wrinkle," adding good–naturedly, "You won't require one for some years."

Pearls, of course, are not only lovely, but discreet, but, excepting the royalties' fine strings, I saw very few worn at that period, and it sets one wondering whence the vast quantities that adorn everybody the last few years have been obtained. The Ilchester black pearls were uncommon, with their mysterious sheen, and no doubt unique and priceless, but I thought unbecoming to their very handsome wearer, and Lady Wharncliffe's antique Persian turquoises (immense plaques inscribed with love legends), were most alluring. But of all gems, my birthstone, the opal — I was born in October — appeals most to me. Its extraordinary variety of moods, like a chameleon under the influence of its surroundings, sullen in dull weather and scintillating with colours in the rays of the sun, fills me with never tiring interest. No wonder Ella Wheeler Wilcox dedicated a poem to its birth. I curtsey to this high priestess of taste.

In spite of its beauty, however, there is a very strong prejudice against it, being unquestionably associated in some minds with misfortune. We all have our individual superstitions, of course — there are those who believe that turquoises, which Persians believe are made from the bones of people who died of love, change their exquisite blue to green when worn by the heartless; some ascribe an evil influence to amethysts; some say that pearls mean tears, and some attribute all the good or evil which happens to them to a particular piece of jewellery. What interesting stories are connected with those famous stones which are among the world's greatest treasures; the ruse by which Nadir Shah obtained the Koh–i–noor; how the great Orloff diamond was stolen from the eye–socket of an idol; the tales of ill–luck which are said to follow the Hope blue diamond. One's imagination is fired by the description of the one hundred and eight rubies which adorned the "Peacock Throne," but the pearl which was cut in halves to adorn the ears of a statue of Venus in the Pantheon, and that of the same value swallowed by Cleopatra, seem to emphasize the adage of "casting pearls before swine." To come to later times, the story is illuminating of a well–known peer who, having lost a great deal of money racing, thought he saw an easy way to settle his debts. He mustered the family diamonds, and carried them off to one of the most respectable Bond Street jewellers. After a good deal of hemming and hawing, he nervously asked to man to take out the diamonds and replace them with paste.

"I need the money," he said, "and her ladyship will never know."

The jeweller's eyes twinkled.

"I am very sorry, my lord, but I have already done so at her ladyship's request."

The ignominy of possessing no jewels having been pointed out to me by Henrietta Labouchere, under whose masterful influence I still was, I paid an early visit to Tiffany's store in New York, which I was told was famous for originality of setting. And here I commenced a collection which ultimately grew into almost an important one. Although I was never inordinately fond of jewellery, I found it useful in enhancing my appearance, particularly on the stage, and I came at last to enjoy the possession of gew–gaws. So when one morning I discovered that they had all disappeared — for stolen they were — it came as a great shock. The robbery was most mysterious, and so cleverly planned that, with all the seemingly direct clues, Scotland Yard was unable to make any arrests.

My jewels were invariably kept in a large tin box about two and a half feet long by two feet high. This was portable and fire–proof, and accompanied me on all my tours. When I was travelling it was always confided to the care of the office of the hotel at which I happened to be staying. When in London it was deposited at the Sloane Street branch of the Union Bank for convenience and safety. When I wanted any important pieces I used to send my butler with an order to the bank to bring the case temporarily to my house, 21 Pont Street, which was only a few doors off, when I would select what I wanted and return the rest; thus I felt them in safer keeping than in my own "chub."

One morning, wishing to get some special jewels out to wear at the opera that night, I sent the usual written order to my butler to fetch the box. I was reading, and did not notice how time had elapsed until, suddenly looking at the clock, I found that I had been waiting almost two hours.

At that moment my butler mounted to my boudoir with the midday post, and, upon my asking for the jewels, he assured me that the order had only just then come into his hands.

When he brought me the box a few minutes later, I took from it what I wanted, and returned the rest. At that time everything was all right.

Not long after that, I went for a trip to Ostend, Baden, and through the Black Forest, and I left my jewels (with the exception of a few favourite ones which I never was without) in the bank, locked in the tin box which was afterwards to cause so much trouble. I was away about six weeks, and then merely passed through London on my way to join a yacht at Cowes for a trip along the south coast. So, unfortunately, I went yachting in ignorance that my jewels had already been stolen a fortnight at that time, and it was only when I returned in the autumn that I discovered the theft.

Shortly after my return home, one morning, as soon as the bank was open, I sent my butler as usual to fetch the box. In about twenty minutes he returned with an ashen face, and told me that it had been delivered to me on the 18th August.

"How can that be?" I asked in astonishment. "I was away on the Continent on that date!" But the frightened man could only add that the bank representative was downstairs, with the order to prove his words. In a moment the clerk stood at my bedroom door — a thin, red–haired creature, whose naturally white face was several shades whiter than usual —and appeared horrified at the happening. He held out the order for my inspection, and even across the room I saw that, although the writing resembled mine, the signature was obviously forged from one which, years before, I had given to the proprietors of Pear's soap.

A clerk afterwards described the man who had taken the case away as florid, stout, and of sporting appearance. Why it should have been delivered to a stranger of this description Heaven only knows. It was a piece of the most reprehensible carelessness on someone's part.

The stolen jewels comprised the following pieces: a large tiara, almost a crown, of diamonds and fine large pearls; a *riviere* of immense sapphires and diamonds in a Tiffany setting; a tiara, necklace, and bracelets, *en suite*, of rubies and diamonds; a turquoise and diamond tiara, necklace, and bracelets; a *parure* of large emeralds and diamonds, which had formed part of the Empress Eugenie's collection; a brooch in which was the largest ruby in the world; a pendant with a magnificent pigeon–blood ruby, a stomacher of black and pink pearls, set in diamonds, and many miscellaneous brooches, bracelets, rings, etc., altogether of the least computed value of forty thousand pounds at that time.

Stunned at the discovery, I felt at first incapable of thought. Unfortunately my jewels were not insured, so the loss fell entirely on me. Then, as my brain began to work again, I argued that it would be almost impossible to get away undetected with such a large amount of well–known stones, and that, without wasting a moment, I must see my lawyer, and consult him as to the steps to be taken. George Lewis (for it was to him that I rushed as early as I thought he would be at his office) was at that time of an age that is habitually called, *in a man*, the prime of life. A solicitor, as his father had been before him, he specialised in cases dealing with the seamy side of existence, and came into the limelight through his clever handling of the Bravo case. Later, it became customary for the fashion-able world to appeal to him in their social slips, wives who wanted di-vorces, husbands who did not, people who had compromised themselves one way or another, all flocked to his little office parlour in Ely Place, where often, over a cup of tea, he gave them shrewd advice, helped them over stiles, suppressed scandal, mediated between and calmed down many ruffled couples, and made a name for himself as a lawyer who could do anything for anybody.

Having told him all I knew of the disaster, I placed the matter in his hands, and together we drove to notify the police at Scotland Yard, which was all that could be done for the moment. But, when I declared my intention of catching the train to Manchester, where I was running two horses that very day, George Lewis' face was a study of horror and dis-may. He evidently thought that for advertising purposes the theft should be treated as a family bereavement, and even my logical explanation that, because I had had the misfortune to lose my jewels, it was all the more important that I should back my two potential winners failed to shake his conviction that it was almost indelicate for me to be seen in public.

I went down with a party of friends, who, when I told them of my loss, seemed strangely unsympathetic, and almost immediately changed the subject, until we reached Crewe Junction, where the newsboys were cry-ing out, "Great Robbery of Mrs. Langtry's Jewels!" and then they con-doled with me most genuinely. It seems that I had announced the fact so calmly that they could not believe it was true, and thought I was trying to be funny, and indeed it was some time before I fully realised the fact myself.

As time went on, I had various interviews with Inspector Moore and others of Scotland Yard, and during one of these Moore produced the forged order, together with the one I had given my butler, which, it will be remembered, was so long in reaching his hands. On placing one upon the other, with a strong light behind, the two looked identical, with the exception of the signature.

A few weeks later I received an extraordinary letter, signed only with initials, from a man who described himself as a London solicitor, assuring me that I should never recover the jewels through the police, and I was beginning to fear the same. He said they were, at the time of this writing, in a safe deposit vault in London, and the party he was acting for would return them to me on payment of five thousand pounds. So, clutching at a straw, I went to the head of Scotland Yard, and announced my intention of getting back my property by fulfilling their requirements. He tried his best to dissuade me, even suggesting that, if I were fortunate enough to get my jewels back in such an irregular manner, I might be *un*fortunate enough to be locked up for compounding a felony.

No sympathy for the scheme was shown at the bank either, and for a few days I let the matter rest. Then I advertised in the Agony Column offering to negotiate, and waited feverishly for the reply. It was to the effect that the jewels were now in France, and must be paid for in Dieppe. The five thousand pounds to ransom them was rather grudgingly advanced by the Union Bank, and two of my friends (Lord Shrewsbury and J. Smyth Pigott) started off with the money, full of hope, only to be disappointed, for, on arrival there, an individual met them and tried to lure them into the country, saying that "fifteen detectives had come over in the boat." Perhaps the whole affair was a hoax, or a bluff to distract the attention of the police, or perhaps they hoped to knock my emissaries on the head and get another five thousand pounds out of me. I received another letter from Dieppe a little later, written this time by a ticket–of–leave man, of which I should have taken no notice had I not been going to Paris anyhow. That being the case, I gave the writer an appointment at my hotel there, though without much hope of a favourable result. It gave me a curiously creepy feeling to be shut up in my *salon* at the Ritz with this convict, discussing the theft of my jewels and the possibility of getting them back. However, nothing more opposed to my preconceived notion of a burglar bristling with house–breaking implements could be imagined. Here was a mild–mannered little man of most deferential attitude, who really seemed to take a genuine interest in my misfortune. But the interview was, as I soon perceived, to be a futile one, for he evidently knew no more than I did about the whereabouts of the articles, but he knew his subject when he generalised on the habits of thieves. One he told me of, who lived in a suburb of London, was a highly respected churchwarden, or something of the sort. His was the master mind that planned the robberies, though he took care not to implicate himself, or, as the little burglar put it, "soil his hands," in spite of the many "hauls" he had made. But all this did not help me in the least, and I wondered why he was so anxious to see me, unless it was to find out if I had any left.

All this time a lawsuit was pending, which I was bringing against the Union Bank for negligence. They, on the other hand, contended that they had merely accepted a tin box for custody, without a list of its contents. The amount I was suing them for was forty thousand pounds. My counsel, chosen by Lewis, were to be Sir Robert Reid (afterwards Lord Loreburn) and H. H. Asquith (since Prime Minister), and the bank was to employ Sir Edward Carson. The morning fixed for the hearing found me in the court–house, sheltering in a waiting–room till the case was called when Sir Robert Reid came to me to suggest a compromise. George Lewis had not arrived, he said, and it must be settled *at once*. The opponents offered ten thousand pounds. Would I accept? I asked *his* opinion, and he was favourable to it, and went off to conclude the bargain. About ten minutes later George Lewis bustled in, and I told him what had been decided.

"Not enough," he cried breathlessly. "I can get twenty–five thousand pounds at least," and rushed after Sir Robert, but too late — everything was signed. So it seems that if my counsel had not been in such a hurry, or if George Lewis had been earlier, I should be fifteen thousand pounds richer, and indeed I have good reason to believe I could have secured the whole amount demanded, for I was told on the best authority some years after that the bank dared not make this case a test one in view of the many chests of priceless treasures lying in the vaults of the various banks unclaimed for years, and that I ought to have stood to my guns. However, I had to be satisfied with ten thousand pounds. My jewels were never traced, for the thieves had too long a start, and time to get them broken up and out of England. This great loss gave me an absolute distance for jewellery, and, though I have a few things left, I seldom care to wear them.

Shortly after the lawsuit I went on tour, appearing in Clyde Fitch's play, *Gossip*, and a gag which I could not resist in the circumstances was noticed by the dramatic critic at Birmingham, who alluded to it as follows,

"Mrs. Langtry made a good point last night at Birmingham. She is, as Mrs. Barry, in the play *Gossip*, supposed to be offering her husband, who has failed in business, all her jewels to save him. She enters laden with jewel cases, which she hands to her spouse, who inquires: 'What is all this?' to which Mrs. Langtry, in her character, replied: 'My jewellery, *or what is left of it.*' But the next line is better still. The husband says, 'What on earth shall I do with it?' And the answer was, 'Sell it, pawn it, I don't care, but don't send it to the bank.'"

Chapter
16

While I was playing *Mrs. Deering's Divorce*, at a melancholy little theatre in the Strand called Terry's, in the month of January, two years after the regrettable Boer War, an impresario was shown into my dressing–room. There was a dense fog at the time, and everything inside and out looked very dreary. The object of this visit was to propose a theatrical tour in South Africa and the Transvaal, and he could not have chosen a more propitious moment, for, when he expatriated on the delightful sunny climate over there, and told me of the magnificent theatre, as fine as His Majesty's, almost finished at Johannesburg, waiting for *Someone* to open, I felt I must go. Moreover, my spirits rose at the thought of passing the next winter under a cloudless sky, in a part of Africa hitherto unknown to me. And so it came to pass that, the following autumn, I set sail for Durban in the *Walmer Castle*, with my company, scenery, and properties, viz., with everything to be seen and heard on the stage.

My repertoire of plays consisted of *The Degenerates, Mrs. Deering's*

Divorce, The Walls of Jericho, and, of course, *As You Like It*, which has been inseparable from me during my theatrical career, and which managers have always insisted on including.

Although not known London names, with the exception of Charles Sugden, I was well supported. Tom Kingston, good–looking and an excellent actor, was my leading man. A great favorite in Australia, from whence he had just returned after a long stay, I am sure, had he had the opportunity, he would have "made good" in town, but, to my regret, he died a few years later.

The impresario, his name was Smith, turned out to be a very amiable and easy man to get on with. He had an interest in the theatres of South Africa, and was, I believe, a partner of Williamson, the well–known Australian theatrical manager.

We struggled into the crowded boat–train on a raw, miserable November morning, and, on our arrival at Southampton, went at once on board.

My brother came to see me off, and we found lunch ready and waiting, but the saloon was so overcrowded that it became a problem to find a place, and I looked with some concern at its occupants, who I presumed were to be my fellow–passengers. However, after lunch two–thirds of the most doubtful–looking cleared out miraculously, and I discovered that the company was in the habit of giving a free meal to all and sundry on these occasions.

The absolute difference of type of the travellers from the Americans in whose company I had so often crossed the Atlantic struck me. The men, in whom the Jewish cast of features greatly predominated, were, I surmised, interested in the mines of the Transvaal. Not many women were travelling towards the continent that trip, and I was afraid I was doomed to a dull voyage. The next morning, Sunday, was very cold, and, of course,

out of the twenty–seven boxes I had with me, I found that the one absolutely indispensable cabin trunk, containing my warm things, had by mis-
chance been confided to the hold. We were then in the Bay of Biscay.
What was to be done? I beseeched the purser to obtain it for me, but he
had no authority. The chief officer was appealed to, but he would not
hear of his men opening the hold on a Sunday, and he held out no hope of
my getting it before we reached Madeira, when, of course, the necessity
for such clothing would be past!

Finally, the baggage officer was induced to listen to my plaintive explanation (through my cabin door) that I should have to stop in bed until
we reached a milder climate, and he gallantly declared that by hook or by
crook he would secure my trunk, and it hove in sight about midday. After
all, there blew such a gale in the bay that I might just as well have remained
in my cabin, for all I saw of my companions during that part of the voyage.

The only stop between Southampton and Cape Town was made at
Madeira, and, at the sight of that sunbathed, picturesque island, I scrambled
into the first boat leaving the vessel to go ashore, so that I might see as
much as possible of it.

The town is very hilly, and paved with great round projecting cobble-
stones, and I suppose that is why the sledge–like bullock– carts drawn by
oxen are the usual means of conveyance, wheels and springs being worse
than useless owing to the roughness of the pavement.

The usual trip for visitors of passing vessels is to go to the top of the
mountain. This almost perpendicular ascent we made in a train, on either
side of which were vineyards and plantations of sugar–cane and bananas,
which, with bignonias and other sub– tropical climbers, covering the pa-
tios in luxurious profusion, gave this island an extremely fertile aspect.

At the summit was a large hotel, where we breakfasted on fresh fish,
and afterwards, indulged in a pastime, I should think especially provided

for tourists, of which one trial was sufficient, in my case at all events. Outside the restaurant were stationed rows of toboggans, each one with two swarthy Portuguese in waiting to manoeuvre it. Inside each was a seat into which two could just squeeze. My secretary, Mrs. Goldsmith, and I, in search of a novel experience, seized this opportunity and, with a native behind and one in front steadying the toboggan with guiding ropes, it began a mad dance down the narrow cobbled hill with a deep ditch on either side; the fun evidently consisted in racing, and ours seemed bent on winning at any price.

Such a jolting I never endured; sometimes we plunged headlong down a particularly steep part; then our Portuguese changed their tactics, and for a few minutes we would go sideways like a crab. Then steam was got up again, and all went merrily until we landed in the gutter, whence, amid a lot of shouting and tugging at the cords, we were hoisted up on the level again, in fact we endured every sensation of danger short of being actually thrown out. However, our guides eventually landed us safe, and we entered the small town bruised, but triumphant.

There were many shops filled with exquisite drawn–thread work and embroidery of Madeira and Teneriffe; others displayed basket work fashioned into lounges, chairs, tables, etc. When I returned to the *Walmer Castle*, the deck was littered with the same class of work, but we found more amusement in watching the native boys, who crowded round our vessel in small boats, and eagerly dived for coins, which they brought up to the surface in their gleaming teeth.

The heat was intense. The officers donned their white uniforms, and looked more fascinating than ever, and we followed suit by putting on our summer costumes, and not until I left Madeira again on my return voyage did I ever want even a serge gown.

An Entertainment Committee was organised, to which we all subscribed, and then began a round of gaiety. The band played twice a day, in the morning, and again in the evening after dinner on the brilliantly lighted deck. Three nights a week there were dances, and for two or three days we were all busily engaged in preparing for the great entertainment of the trip, which was a Fancy Dress Ball, with prizes for the best costume, all to be made on board. We were marched down the deck, the second class passengers judging the first, and the first the second.

Some of the disguises were most cleverly contrived, and would have done credit to their designers anywhere, and, as they had to be made out of material found on the vessel, one can conceive the difficulty. One man appeared as a ship's ventilator, and a pretty girl came as the *Walmer Castle*, all the details being carefully carried out. There were sports also in the afternoon, with the usual egg and spoon, sack races, etc., and, what was new to me, a potato race for women, who, provided with baskets, had to pick up as many of those strewn on the deck as possible between two blasts of a horn.

There were also three or four concerts during the voyage. Of course, owing to the heat, all these functions took place on the broad deck as we approached the tropic zone.

One night we staged a breach of promise case — I was the plaintiff. I forget who was the defendant. Lionel Phillips was the prosecuting counsel, and Major Mullins, the judge. A jury was empanelled, and we amused a large audience for an hour or more with this trial, which, of course, ended in the ignominious ejection of the defendant, who was found to be contemplating bigamy — the plaintiff consoling herself with one of the jury–men.

From Madeira to Cape Town the weather was almost perfect, as I am told it generally is in these latitudes. So smoothly did the vessel glide along that the very worst sailor could not have been inconvenienced. It was the most restful voyage I ever experienced. The monotony of the turquoise sky and sapphire, almost violet, sea, was only relieved by occasional flights of flying–fish, or the gyrations of the porpoise, or the spout of the whale.

When I came to know the passengers, I found some of the pioneers of South Africa aboard. Among them Lionel Phillips, who, sitting beside me on the deck one night, gave me the details of his thrilling experience in the Jameson Raid. As everyone knows, the raid failed, and they were seized by the Boers and sentenced to death. The captured men were imprisoned in one large room, and, after a little serious talk, they lay silently thinking of their fate, for they had not the slightest doubt but that they would be shot at daybreak. I asked Lionel Phillips what *he* felt, and he said at first he felt a little frightened, but that, after reasoning it out, he came to the conclusion that, as one could not escape death, it was of little importance whether it occurred at daybreak or in twenty years to come, and when Kruger relented, and they were reprieved, his thought was joy at not having to leave his wife.

Sir Godfrey Lagden was another passenger who entertained me with stories of his career, and incidentally I learned from him the terrible thunder–storms I might expect on the *veld*. He had had several horses killed by lightning, and his own life was saved by getting out of the saddle and sheltering beside the animals.

There were at least two or three very audacious card–sharpers taking the trip, and they had the immense impertinence, after scraping acquaintance with me, to suggest that I should add to my profits by giving suppers when playing in Johannesburg, at which they would manipulate the cards. Never having been approached on such a subject before, I felt I should be as criminal as they if I kept silent, but, on consulting with the fellow passenger whom I thought the most capable of advising me, he merely remarked that I was not responsible for the morals of the passengers, and the matter ended, excepting that I warned the card–playing members of my company.

It is amusing to add that, before these swindlers revealed their nefarious business to me, I sat down to poker on deck with two of these and the wife of one of them. I may say I noticed that if any player had a good hand she always topped it, and afterwards swindler number one, who had been the chief victim, warned me against the married couple, with whom he said he would never play again. So it would appear that the biter is sometimes bit.

The weather became torrid as we approached the equator. Sand from the Sahara, blown forty miles, made everything on the ship gritty. The pretty little flying–fish leapt out of the water on to the deck, and once or twice even through the port. It was rather disappointing not to make Neptune's acquaintance crossing the line. I expected sports of the traditional description, but they had been abandoned for some time, so the only indication we got of our change of latitude was the appearance of the Southern Cross in the heavens.

In the fortnight exactly we got to Table Bay and Cape Town, not at all tired of each other, but rather fonder, and very sorry to separate.

Some immense strawberries, brought to me on board by an old friend of my family, helped me to realise that the seasons were reversed, and that it was getting on to midsummer in these parts. But our journey was not yet over. We were bound for Durban, Natal, where the tour was to start. There was another week to get through, but only a handful of passengers besides ourselves were completing the voyage, so there was no excitement, no dances — just rest.

My impresario was part owner of the theatre I was to visit in Durban, and he had told me to be prepared for some sort of a reception, and to remain on the ship on my arrival. As the few other passengers cleared the gangway, the Mayor of the town came on board with a huge basket of flowers, and made me a suitable speech. He was followed by the President and Stewards of the Natal Jockey Club, all bent on receiving me warmly, the latter naturally appreciating my love of horses.

After some conversation, we turned to go ashore, and, to my amazement, I found myself the recipient of cheers from the whole crew, massed along the shore–side of the vessel, and in front of me at the landing–stage I saw tiers of seats and an immense crowd assembled to receive me. Embarrassed, and very much touched at this right royal welcome — for it was nothing less — I was conducted to a landau in waiting, and I believe one of the very few in Durban, and drove to the Marine Hotel at the end of the pier.

Outside the landing–shed I caught my first sight of the means of locomotion most generally used by the inhabitants, the ricksha. There was an unbroken line of these odd little vehicles down the long pier, with their attendant Kaffirs and Zulus crouching with their faces hidden. Thinking it a strange and uncomfortable position, I asked if it was habitual, and was told by Mr. Smith that this was a pose taken to show their respect for the "Great White Chieftain."

There was a great deal of rehearsing to get through before opening in three days, and the following morning I found a ricksha of my very own waiting outside, with a solemn looking, hulking Zulu as "pony" named Jim. The theatre wardrobe–mistress had made him a loin–cloth of my racing colours, turquoise and fawn, and with huge pampas grasses, dyed to match, standing upright on his head, scarlet hibiscus flowers over each ear, and calabashes of snuff and so forth hanging everywhere, he was a "glowing" sight.

For the fortnight I played in the town it was my sole mode of conveyance, and the dignified way in which my Zulu trotted me to and from the theatre was a distinct reproach to the capering Kaffirs, whose exuberance in the shafts of their rickshas occasionally resulted in the discomfort of their patrons. All the waiters at the hotel were Indians, clad in their native garb. Soft–footed, patient, and anxious to please, they seemed ideal servants.

In addition to much private hospitality, I was tendered a public luncheon, and a race–meeting was organised in my honour. The race–cards were printed in my colours. I was presented with many racing trophies, and I watched most of the racing from the steward's stand — the only woman who had ever invaded the sacred precincts. But the intense heat was trying to a degree in the theatre, and, when I had to wear the leather boots and woollens of Rosalind as Ganymede, I almost collapsed in my dressing–room after the long forest scenes.

A local dresser assisted my own, and entertained me occasionally with the doings of those who had passed before. One story of George Edwardes' musical comedy girls jumping on chairs to escape cockroaches seemed exaggerated, but, when I saw the Natal variety smiling at me one evening over the screen in my dressing–room, I was not surprised.

When my engagement there ended Jim seemed so cut up at leaving me that I thought it would soften his grief if I gave him a souvenir as well as the prosaic tip. I therefore took the giant Zulu to a Curio shop and bade him choose a string of beads or something native that he would add to the extensive collection already adorning his person. But he turned his back on these gew–gaws and seized the most valuable bundle of white ostrich feathers in the shop. The indignant proprietor snatched them from him and substituted a cheap feather boa. The negro received the humbler present with mitigated joy, but promptly wound it round his woolly head in company with the cattle horns, dyed pampas and calabashes. They have quaint ways of expressing their affection, and a friend of mine who spent some time in Africa received a letter from a negro as follows: —

"Hope you are well. You are my father and my mother. My only help is the Lord Jesus and you. Please forgive precedence."

From Durban we travelled through the war area to Johannesburg, playing at Pietermaritzburg and another town for three days each *en route* for the London of South Africa. There we enjoyed five weeks of the same hospitality as Durban had shown me, and played to crowded houses. But what delighted me most was to find my comrade of the Stage, the lovely Lily Hanbury, settled in a pleasant house with her husband, Herbert Guedalla, who was there on legal business. We passed our time together as far as possible, and she was so hospitable that I had not to depend on the chicken and legs of mutton served at the hotel, which needed sawing asunder, nor the butter that came from Australia, nor the fish that had been round the world, but, as the food was excellent, as well as Sir Abe Bailey's and Sir Lionel Phillips', who amongst others entertained me, I knew that fresh and good things were to be had.

Christmas I passed with the Guedallas, and I wonder if I shall ever again eat roast turkey and flaming Christmas pudding under such torrid conditions. A large party sat round their hospitable table, with the temperature at I don't know what.

Our next stop was Pretoria, which I found distinct in character from the other towns of the Union I had visited. Beautifully situated, with the Ugaliesberg Mountains as a background, it gained added charm at the end of a journey across the vast *veld*, reminiscent of a grey, undulating sea.

My journey from Johannesburg started in piping heat, and ended in one of those violent thunder–storms described to me by Sir Godrey Lagden, and, though not the first I had experienced during my tour (for while on the Rand I had several times seen lightning dancing over the ironstone rocks in a dangerous mood), this one dwarfed them all, and I did not relish my drive to the hotel in an open carriage in the thick of it.

Such an hotel as it was! A mean–looking wooden building with a stoep running round it, and as comfortless inside as it promised to be at the first glance. Two rather determined attempts having been made in Johannesburg to snatch the bag containing the few jewels remaining to me, I decided to express them home, and go without for the remainder of the tour, since they became an anxiety, not only to myself, but to everyone around me.

The theatre was as unattractive as were the rather meagre audiences, for the population was largely composed of Boers, who did not flock to see English companies, just then at all events, and I think a long–bearded Boer, who nightly occupied the stage– box, and sent me fruit in washing–baskets, was probably my only Dutch admirer.

My first thought was to visit the late President Kruger's home, which lies at a certain distance from the centre, but, when I mounted the stoep, guarded by its two stone lions of world–wide renown, and rang the bell, I was met with a severe rebuff. To my politely expressed desire to be allowed to see the interior, the "lady" who answered the door slammed it in my face, amid imprecations from the caretaker's whole family, who suddenly swarmed from every door and window, and whose shrill Dutch screams of *"Verdommte Englanderin,"* mingled with threats of calling the police, caused me to retreat hastily to my waiting cab. However, I scored in the end, for, having made the acquaintance of Paul Kruger's grandson, one Jacobson, I later, in his company, made a triumphal progress through the unpretentious white–washed house, much to the imperfectly–

swallowed disgust of the blear–eyed custodian.

Save for the aforementioned genial family, it was uninhabited. A door on the left of the narrow hall opened into the principal sitting–room, the centre of which was taken up by a towering catafalque draped in black and smothered in wreaths, some composed of natural flowers, now dried and withered, together with a good many artificial tributes that had better stood the test of time, but were thick with dust. The Kaiser's colossal wreath occupied the most prominent position on one of the walls of the room, all of which were crowded with funeral offerings, altogether making a very sepulchral *ensemble*. What I saw of the rest of the little house was quite ordinary.

Another point of interest in the town, to which my attention was called, was the wall over which Winston Churchill made his escape after being taken prisoner in the war. I snapshotted it, and sent him a copy.

Had it not been for a very unusual Zoological Gardens I don't know how I could have passed my time. It had been planned, and was still presided over, by a Dr. Gunning, who had well stocked it in a comparatively short time with wild beasts, and had sensibly given them, as far as possible, a miniature reproduction of their natural homes to live in, so that they not only looked in better health and spirits than in most zoos, but one could form an idea of their habits in their wild state. One feature was a long walk fringed on either side with a collection of brilliantly coloured macaws and parrots, very happy on their perches in the open air. The Gunnings were delightful to me, and the only pleasant hours I passed in Pretoria were in their house.

Glad enough when the engagement there was over, we travelled to Cape Town via Bloemfontein and across the Karoo, accompanied by the dearest little meercat, kindly given me by Dr. Gunning, which I called "Pretoria," and which in two days had become as tame as a dog, and quite as companionable. By the time we reached the Mount Nelson Hotel at Cape Town, the pretty little African squirrel had realised that she had nothing to fear, and she became quite saucy, playing hide–and–seek about the passages of the hotel, and sitting on my shoulder in a friendly manner. One day, finding a newly–landed hotel arrival's door open, she galloped round and round the room, terrifying the occupant.

She really was the spirit of mischief, tearing the muslin blinds into strips so that she could look out more easily, eating my white shoes, on or off my feet, and burrowing into the springs of the easy chairs to make herself a comfortable resting place, so that only the merest tip of her curled tail could be seen. At sunset exactly she ceased her capers, and crept into the darkest corner to sleep, when even the sound of cracking nuts could not dislodge her. Dr. Jim, always afraid I should be dull in a strange country, offered me a night–ape as a "pendant," which begins its wild flying antics at that hour, but I declined with thanks. When I left the hotel a bill was presented for "reparations," which practically amounted to re-furnishing the sitting–room, so "Miss Pretoria" was an expensive toy.

I arrived in Cape Town on a Sunday afternoon, and my first visitor was Sir Starr Jameson, at that time Premier of the Union of South Africa. The same evening I dined with him at "Groote Schuur," his guests being Rudyard and Mrs. Kipling, Sir Godfrey Lagden, and others. Cecil Rhodes, alas! did not live to occupy this charming house, on the building of which he had bestowed so much thought, and when he died he bequeathed "Groote Schuur" to the nation, to be used as an official residence by the Premiers, and there Dr. Jim and his household were installed.

It was a capacious house, built in pure Cape Colonial style, approached by a long avenue of pines, with the familiar wide stoep running its whole length, and it presented a home–like and comfortable appearance. I arrived for dinner, just as the sun was setting behind Table Mountain, and found the party assembled on the bougainvillea–covered verandah. After the usual introductions, Mr. Kipling hurried me off to a spot a short distance from the house, to see and sit in Cecil Rhodes' favorite seat before night–fall, with the huge mountain frowning over it so closely that it seemed in a few yards more I could touch it.

I fell to wondering at the colossal brain which could think under such crushing conditions.

The dining–room was, like all of the reception–rooms, long and low, and entirely panelled with some dark wood, and the dining– table profusely decorated with branches of the beautiful violet bougainvillea, everything else being luxurious and harmonious. After dinner, bridge was the order of the evening, but, tired after my journey, I retreated rather early to my hotel.

Dr. Jim did his best to make my stay agreeable, and, though very busy himself all day, he thought out and planned entertainments for me, some of them of an original kind.

Cecil Rhodes had evidently a *penchant* for wild beasts, for in the park were buildings and cages which made of it a miniature zoo, and one of Dr.Jim's strange notions of the way for me to spend a "happy day," was to pay a visit to the interior of the lion's den, from which he especially promised me I should emerge safely. Another was to drive over the rough tracks to the top of Table Mountain in a Cape cart! Neither of these suggestions, telephoned by him to my hotel in the early morning, met with my approval, but he certainly succeeded in making my two weeks pass very pleasantly, and it was the only town during my South African tour that I regretted leaving.

Sir Abe Bailey had a very attractive house at Muizenberg, the near–by bathing–place, also built by Cecil Rhodes. Its drawing– room was entirely lined with grey marble, which, in a colder climate, sounds a decidedly chilly scheme of decoration, but it seemed to fit in. The great rolling waves dashed against and broke over the semi–circular wall that bounded the garden of this uniquely–placed house.

The flora of the Cape was extremely fascinating to an amateur gardener like myself, the mountain being carpeted in parts with spreading masses of the large, wax–like, flowered heather, pink, red, yellow, and white, that only endure under glass in England, and look meagre and unhappy at that. Twice a week in Adderley Street, women sit in rows beside baskets of the freshly gathered blossoms, to be bought in armfuls for a few pence. But Cape Colony is a veritable garden of all kinds of floral treasures, and, of course, the various amarylli, belladonnas, nerines, etc., are indigenous, and arum lilies grow in the fields.

I had a few spare evenings waiting for the home–bound boat, and spent them going to the various places of amusement. There was a mighty wrestler called Apollo at one of the music–halls, and a wrestle between him and a distinguished amateur was advertised for one evening, so I thought it would be interesting to see it. My surprise may be imagined when a youthful, slim, and hitherto unsuspected member of my company walked boldly on to the stage to oppose him. Apollo looked down on him from his great height, smiled, and shook hands, and proceeded to play with him and toss him as a cat does a mouse, but, being fortunately in an amiable mood, he literally let him down gently. Still, I saw watching this only son of his absent mother with my heart in my mouth, expecting worst. The boy, who had just inherited a large property in the shires, had come out under an assumed name, mostly to see South Africa, and his mother had begged me to keep an eye on him.

Before my visit to South Africa I was told I should feel the "call" to return, but, though I enjoyed my six months tour, and reaped a fair harvest of gain, I have never had the idea of revisiting it.

Chapter
17

The Imperial Theatre was the victim of circumstances. Unfortunately, it was born at the same time as the Westminster Aquarium, of which it was an adjunct, and its early life was overshadowed by the proximity of its more important twin brother. The latter's name was really a misnomer, for the fish swimming wearily in their dusky tanks were practically ignored by the crowds, who thronged the vast building to hear topical songs and brass bands, and to see thrilling acrobatic feats.

Among the most popular of the latter was the nerve–racking "Zaza" performance, in which a graceful woman of that name, clad in a black *maillot*, was fired from a deafening cannon near the roof into a huge net over–hanging the audience.

Naturally, with these sensational doings close by, the legitimate drama would have been flouted at the Imperial, and I only remember negro minstrel troupes and other overflow performers from the main building "holding the boards" there from time to time. Later on, as the Aquarium declined in thrills, and consequently in favour, Miss Marie Litton, an actress of great qualities, valiantly rented the neglected playhouse, and dignified it with a season of Shakespearean and old comedy matinees.

How the manager fared financially I do not know, but the theatre became a very pleasant afternoon *rendezvous*.

The principal member of her company was Kyrle Bellew, a *jeune premier* of renown, who was especially successful in romantic roles, to which his physique also seemed markedly adapted. His diction, inherited from his famous father, was academic, and his voice musical. His figure was slim, his back was singularly undulating, his face was purely Florentine, lit up by very bright, expressive eyes, and he was admittedly the best lover on the English stage. What wonder that women set him up as a theatrical hero? What wonder that a coterie of idle women, of whom I was one, and Lady Lonsdale (later Lady de Grey) was another, met practically every afternoon to admire "Curly" from the front, and to have tea after the matinee in the green–room with Miss Litton and our idol. Here we met as a rule Lord Alington, a wealthy patron of theatrical venture, Oscar Wilde, Whistler, and a few others, and passed a pleasant half–hour in these, to us, unusual surroundings.

It was the first time I had gone behind the scenes of a theatre, and I felt immensely important and privileged. How far was I from imagining that I should ever tread those or any other boards in a professional capacity! Or that Kyrle Bellew would play young Marlowe to my Kate Hardcastle on my initial appearance at the Haymarket Theatre? Yet things shaped themselves so.

Time elapsed, and so did Marie Litton's tenancy, and the theatre was again given over to darkness and silence for a long while. Mrs. Labouchere, always dashing in her methods, being desirous that I should make my debut in London as Rosalind before appearing in *As You Like It* in the States on my first American tour, hit upon the deserted Imperial for the purpose, and during the fortnight I played there it was crowded to the doors. Excepting for the speculation of Miss Eleanor Calhoun, who elected to follow in my footsteps in the same theatre, and in the same play for the same length of time, immediately following my tenancy, I do not think it sheltered a theatrical company again until twenty years later.

It was then that, having accepted a play from Pierre Berton (Sara Bernhardt's leading man), he, with considerable shrewdness and knowledge of the inconstancy of actors where production of a piece is concerned, drew up a cast–iron contract bristling with forfeits in case of non–fulfilment within a time limit. Thus something had to be settled without delay, and I sent my manager from Belfast, where I was playing, to London to hunt for a home for the Berton play. An unkind fate lured him to look over the Imperial, by that time in very bad repair, but, optimist that he was, he hurried back with a radiant face to say that he had found a great property.

Two thousand pounds spent would make it up to date, and three thousand a year was the small rent asked for a long lease. The optimistic manager further pointed out that wise theatrical proprietors easily found foolish people to sublet their theatres to, and, with my triumphant fortnight there still in my mind, I persuaded myself that it seemed an undertaking with a fair chance of success and not very much monetary risk.

I took the poor unfortunate playhouse, and, at the first interview with my architect, Mr. Verity, when we discussed the indispensable changes required to modernise it, to improve the line of sight, and to decorate it ever so simply, we found it would run into at least ten times the money calculated. Still, I sanctioned the outlay, full of hope, and the first work which was to improve the line of sight was begun.

For this purpose it was necessary to lower the stage, but the dismay of all was profound when, after laboriously picking up an unusually thick cement foundation, the Thames began to lead in, and this inquisitive neighbour had to be restrained. This was the first untoward happening, and there were many more, with which I will not tire my readers.

Still, these *contretemps* only temporarily discouraged me, and I fell more and more in love with bricks and mortar, and marble and gold, so that when the beautiful theatre was completed I had spent nearly fifty thousand pounds on its conversion. The marble of different colouring which lined the walls was all especially quarried in Italy, and the colour–scheme of the furnishings, curtains, banners, etc., was that of nature's spring garb — purple, green, and gold. By dint of working night and day, I was able to open in time to comply with P. Berton's redoubtable con-tract, though the first–nighters had to scramble through a good deal of dust in the unfurnished corridors. The play that was really the cause of all this expenditure and trouble was called *The Royal Necklace*, and dealt with the episode in which the unfortunate Marie Antoinette, Cardinal Rohan, and Madame de la Motte were concerned, but it was certainly not worth while. Spectacular, and beautifully mounted and costumed, it yet had the inexcusable fault of dullness, and only ran a few months. Then Harry B. Irving and Lewis Waller rented the house from me in succession, and when I took possession again I tried a second season with a play of Paul Kester, called *Mlle. Mars*, a comedy concerning Napoleon I and a pert comedienne of the First Empire. Charles Buchel just then was providing very artistic posters for His Majesty's, and I appealed to Herbert Tree to think one out for me, which he did. An attractive figure of Mlle. Mars filled the entire foreground, while in the far distance was a back view of a diminutive Napoleon. *I* thought the poster an admirable one, but it was not so much appreciated by my Napoleon (Lewis Waller). The play was successful, and seemed to please both Press and public. However, we all failed to popularise the theatre, and at last I realised that Westminster, although only three minutes from Charing Cross, was, and still is, out of the playgoers' beat. The theatrical fluid starts at Piccadilly Circus and, gathering force, flows in a steady stream along the Strand. Only then did I understand a gloomy prediction by Herbert Tree when I was enthusiastically propounding my plans:

"You are going to lose your money, and I am sorry."

A sympathetic comment, which I took the wrong way at the time.

When casting about in my mind for a play that might please, I thought of a comedy called *Captain Brassbound's Conversion*, by Bernard Shaw, and I print a portion of the delightfully characteristic letter I received from him in answer to my enquiry.

"I wish *Captain Brassbound and his Conversion* were at the bottom of the sea, or that you were a less pertinacious woman.

"I am at present distracted by house–hunting, as I have to turn out of this on the 21st and find new country quarters. My London rooms are being spring–cleaned. When they are habitable again I will let you know, and you can come to see me. You will have to come to lunch, as that is the only way in which you can make sure of me. I will then try to talk you out of this folly, since I can't write you out of it.

"In any case nothing can be done until the autumn. People will not go to the theatre in the warm weather; and the experience of the Jubilee year — which was disastrous to the theatres — does not promise well for Coronation year. You had better let your theatre for the summer months to some idiot — there will be no difficulty in finding one — and reserve the possibility of *Lady Cicely* for September of October. Even if the play had the most brilliant success, its run would be cut short in six weeks or so if you put it on in May."

One memorable night I must not forget to chronicle. I had, in conjunction with Hartley Manners, written a play called *The Crosways*, which I was to tour in the States, and, on the eve of my departure, the King, on hearing of our literary effort, commanded a performance. So the theatre was reopened for a single night. The King and Queen occupied the royal box, while the stalls and boxes were filled by their Majesties' friends, the pit and gallery tickets being offered by me to the Queen, who caused them to be distributed among the humbler members of the household servants, and I was told it was amusing to see them wait to take their cue to applaud from the royalties. The play was a success, and I was summoned to the royal room to be congratulated.

To cut the story short, the property, including the Aquarium, had now passed into the hands of the Wesleyans, and, as they were quite as anxious to get rid of this incongruous building in their midst as I was to abandon it, my lawyer succeeded in freeing me from the monstrous white elephant which was gradually eating up my capital. Soon after, the theatre was pulled down, and transferred lock, stock, and barrel to the East End of London, where it is still used as a cinema–house. In fact, the history of the restored Imperial Theatre can be likened to the well–known epitaph on a baby's tombstone:

If I was so soon done for,
I wonder why I was begun for.

Chapter
18

My acquaintance with racing began when I was still of tender age. Once a year Jersey gave itself up to complete levity and enjoyment, when the entire population of my native Isle precipitated themselves on to Gorey Common, where for two days in the month of July the Jersey Race–Meeting took place. These days were regarded as a public holiday, and disappointment was the lot of those who expected any kind of work, domestic or other, to be carried on during this annual festival.

"The Races" were considered an adequate excuse for any kind of shirking, and, from the Governor of the Island down to the oldest inhabitant, all considered it a duty to place the seal of approval on the national sport by putting in an appearance on the sandy course, and it was a tradition also among most of my countrymen to finish the evenings in revelry.

The classic race of the meeting was "The Queen's Cup," for which only Jersey–bred horses were eligible, but the lack of lime in the Island's soil which is responsible for the diminutive stature of our lovely fawn–like cattle is also a factor in producing such under–sized horses, that it is not worth while to breed them, so the competitors were few for the event. Larger fields turned out for the rest of the card, English or French–bred horses being brought over specially to compete. At that time the Channel Islands meetings were not run under the rules of the English Jockey Club, therefore the horses taking part were debarred from further racing on English courses, and as, in addition, the stakes were small, the animals engaged were necessarily of very poor class. Still, the occasion was seized upon as a fitting pretext for a vast picnic.

The Governor and his staff arrived in state. Our own family barouche was paraded, and, with as many of my brothers as could be crammed into the carriage besides my mother and myself, we set off to broil in almost tropical heat. The course was right on the sea, and the blazing sun, combined with the salt air, beat down on us for hours, leaving its mark so definitely that for a week afterwards we smarted, and bathed in buttermilk. It was *de rigueur* for ladies to remain in their carriages or cabs, and, looking back, I really believe it must also have been *de rigueur* not to watch the racing. The lunch seemed by many to be considered the principal event, and continued as long as there was any food to be consumed.

Quantities of gloves were betted, which I always seemed to win, though I had not the remotest idea whether I had backed the winner or not.

When I was about fourteen and my brother Reginald a year younger, we went halves in a weedy English mare that had run at the Gorey Annual Meeting without distinction. Flirt was put up to auction in the Jersey cattle market, where she was knocked down to Reggie's bid of thirty shillings! He brought her home, and stealthily installed her in a disused out–house, and we fed her as far as possible from the family stable bin. Her poor legs were in a sad condition, but with blistering and patience we got her fairly sound. I hacked her about the roads to divert suspicion, while my brother gave her her real preparatory work, and we managed to land a selling plate of thirty pounds with her the first time of asking — Reggie, of course, being "up."

The dean, always rather unobservant, actually knew nothing of the proceedings until he read of our triumph in the local paper, and then it was too late to interfere, so he contented himself with a remonstrance to my mother, who had been most friendly to our venture.

We two had always had an adoration for any quadruped that could be ridden or driven, from the moke up. When we were respectively eight and nine years old, we determined to make ourselves an equipment out of an old rumble, which was discovered in the corner of the coach house. The carpenter fitted it up somehow to please us, and to it we harnessed the lawn–mowing donkey, while, in order to lend dignity to the "turn–out," a farm hand's little boy was engaged at a penny a week as groom, and sat with crossed arms in solemn state, nearly smothered in an old hat of my father's, with its distinguished ecclesiastical shape, and a discarded scarlet uniform coat belonging to one of my soldier brothers. It is a pity that there were no photographers at that moment to snap this unique conveyance, which caused so much mirth in the parish.

I suppose I clung to my admiration for the donkey, for some time ago a sketch by a London artist on vacation in Jersey found its way to the London *Graphic*, showing that I still enjoyed struggling with the obstinate animal, even after my first season in London. He depicted a model donkey gaily trotting along, whereas, *in reality*, he good–naturedly spent an hour vainly trying to persuade the stubborn little beast to budge!

My next racehorse was a present from an eccentric young bachelor, with vast estates in Scotland, a large breeding stud, a racing– stable, and more money than he knew what to do with.

Lillie Langtry

My life had been consecrated to the theatre for so many years that any extraneous interest seemed superfluous, and when this offering was made abruptly to me one day at lunch at my house it was at first hastily refused, till one of my guests, of racing predilection, persuaded me to change my mind.

My new possession was a two–year–old chestnut colt called Milford, and, although a gift horse, one could look in *his* mouth with impunity. It was some time in March, and he had come through a trial so triumphantly that only now that I have developed my early love for racing can I realise his breeder's unselfishness in parting with him. The animal continued to be trained in the donor's stable, and I forget all about him until Messrs. Weatherby wrote requesting me to register my colours, as the colt, with his engagements, had been transferred to me, and was due to run in an important race in a week or so. I happened to be wearing a fawn and blue cloak at the moment, and quickly resolved on that combination.

As I was playing nightly at the Criterion in *The Fringe of Society*, and had visions of the gallery boys shouting to me on the stage for tips, if it became known that I owned a racehorse, I adopted the assumed name of Mr. Jersey, which, nevertheless, failed to hide my identity.

Milford made his maiden effort in a big two–year–old race at Kempton Park, and won very easily, in spite of the loudly expressed wish of a sporting marchioness that he would drop dead first. Of course, this was repeated to me the same evening, it having travelled with the proverbial speed of disagreeable news. He proceeded from one success to another, and the Coventry stakes at Ascot, and July stakes at Newmarket, were among the plums he gathered for me in his victorious first season on the turf, and he retired to his winter quarters unbeaten, having earned for me over eight thousand pounds in stakes. Up till now I had never even set eyes on this flyer, much less seen him run, but the next year Mr. A. died, his stable was dispersed, and I had to make other arrangements about housing him.

Sam Pickering's stable at Kentford being recommended to me, I sent him there, took a tiny house in the village, with the disproportionate name of Regal Lodge, as my racing–box, and then the fun began. I bought Lady Rosebery at the sale of Mr. Abington's stud, intending her for the paddocks, but before she retired she won the Lanark Cup, the Jockey Club Cup at Newmarket, and ran second for the Cesarewitch — a race for which I always have had a particular liking from the outset of my racing career. Milford unaccountably did not maintain his two–year–old form, but with Nobleman, and one or two platers, I had a satisfactory season, and realised more and more the fascination of the national sport of England.

My venture was looked at rather askance in those remote days, when "Mr. Manton" was the only woman owner of any importance, but, as my zeal was rewarded with continued success, the prejudice gradually wore out.

Happily Regal Lodge was situated on the edge of the farm of the most astute racing man of his day, and my growing interest in the thoroughbred soon made us friends. This was the well–known Captain James Machell.

He was past his prime when we met, having only recently recovered from a sad mental lapse, but by figuratively sitting at his feet I learned much in a comparatively short time.

Every day saw him at Regal Lodge, either to tea or to dinner. Horses and racing filled his mind to obsession, his literature was comprised of sporting papers and, when he was not walking about his farm spudding up thistle or predicting great victories for Ravensbury's progeny, he passed a good deal of his time making imaginary handicaps. He was very methodical, and a little book he carried in his vest pocket and perpetually showed to his friends caused them some amusement. It contained his assets. Everything he owned was set down in detail, but his stud, his farm, his house, his racehorses were all estimated at such a fictitious value that he made himself appear very wealthy indeed. He liked to surround himself with young people, and during race–meetings his Newmarket house was a *rendezvous* for all young owners. He could be bitter for all his charm of manner, and I doubt if he ever forgave an injury. When his intimate friend, Lord Calthorpe, died without leaving him, as he expected, the adjacent farm of Landwades, the captain was very much upset, and, though he promptly rented it from the executors, he continued to resent the deception. I have heard him say to his stud–groom in a biting tone:

"Put this or that mare in the paddocks that ought to have been mine."

One piece of advice he gave me was to keep a good plater in the stable that could be used as a retriever in case of a bad week, as he had made a habit of doing in his younger days, and from what I gathered he had a very discerning manner of using his. Men who are having a bad week usually feel desperately anxious to get out when they think of the black Monday awaiting them, and knowing Machell to be long–headed and a good judge, they often went to him in their trouble.

He usually had a very useful horse entered to be sold for one hundred pounds in a seller in case of need. He would persuade them to buy it for one thousand pounds, which gave him one thousand to back it with himself, and, after a good win for all concerned, would buy the horse in at the subsequent auction for a few hundreds. The only drawback, he regretfully added, was that one could not repeat the dose with the same animal.

I grew more and more keen about racing, and soon had about twenty horses in training. My lot had been moved to Fred Webb's at Exning, when one day I received from Mr. W. A. Allison of the International Horse Agency a printed card, which he was circulating among trainers and owners, with the pedigree and racing career of a chestnut colt by Grand Flaneur out of Seaweed, aptly named Merman. About six months before, I had imported a very speedy mare, Maluma, from the Antipodes, but, unluckily, she had stood the passage through the Red Sea so badly that she was a veritable bag of bones, and literally could not stand when she arrived at Etheldreda House training establishment.

As Merman was another Australian, it required some courage to risk a repetition of this dismal experience. When I strolled into Mr. Allison's office in Pall Mall a few days later, it was certainly not with the idea of purchase, yet he was so certain he was right this time that in half an hour he had persuaded me to become the owner of the horse, later pronounced by Machell and Tod Sloan to be the best long–distance runner of his time in the world. In order to avoid the Red Sea, I decided to bring him round the Cape, which proved a wise move, for, though he had a rough journey, he landed at the docks in the best of health and spirits in a heavy snowstorm. He ran I think twice before he was acclimatized, the second time at Nottingham, ridden by S. Loates. I did not see the race, though I backed him, but he failed to win. Being almost bottom weight in the Lewes handicap, I resolved to run him with our stable apprentice, Sharples, up.

As Merman walked round the paddock prior to the race, Lord W. Beresford came up, and explained to me that Australian horses usually run barefoot in their own country, and he thought it worth trying with my importation. The captain told me that one of my racing qualifications was that I always went to the right source for information. Perhaps I did, anyhow, I took Bill Beresford's advice, sent for the farrier, and there and then had Merman's plates removed, and he won very comfortably. His next outing was the Cesarewitch, which he also annexed, and over that I had my biggest win on the Turf, thirty–nine thousand pounds, while, to make the souvenir even a happier one, my friends backed him, too. The Cesarewitch was the first big handicap I appropriated, and although I controlled my feelings and appeared, I hope, outwardly calm, I was really trembling with excitement.

Brayhead, after winning the Liverpool Cup, was selected to lead Merman in his work, and finally, in a gallop over a mile, the Australian beat him in a canter, giving him three stone, and he looked such a real good thing in the race at 7 st. 2 lbs. that I backed him regardless of Monday, and yet he only won a neck. I had been having rather a lean time, and as the two horses passed the judges' box I feared The Rush had got up. "Second again," I thought sadly, and then I looked and saw No. 7 (Merman's) hoisted on the board. I think I was a little dazed, for I found myself walking in the paddock with the old Duke of Cambridge only after the jockey had weighed in and the horse was in the box. The explanation may be that so many crowded round to congratulate me that more time had elapsed than I imagined.

The Prince of Wales had a very good win (I put his bet on with the stable one), and was very pleased. Fred Webb was sent for, and congratulated and shaken hands with by His Royal Highness. Allison came along with a beaming face and "I told you so," and I had a very happy birthday. I had people staying with me for the meeting, and others to dinner, and my old *chef*— who was a bit of an artist — had a birthday cake already baked, and decorated in coloured sugar with Merman winning a neck from The Rush. How prophetic! I cannot recall all the races he ran in or won, but the Jockey Club Cup, Goodwood Cup, and Ascot Gold Cup, shine at me from my sideboard, all inscribed with the name of my very gallant horse.

I have always regretted not being present to see Merman put the seal on his fame on Ascot Heath, but I was on a visit to my mother in Jersey, and I was so absorbed in landing a shoal of mackerel in St. Aubin's Bay with my old fisherman on the day, that I forgot all about racing momentarily. Late in the afternoon I went into the town of St. Heliers to find my racing– colours flying everywhere, even tied to the whips of the cabbies, while from the office of the local paper rushed the editor shouting like a schoolboy, "You've won." It was certainly a great victory, for, among others, he beat the winner of the Grand Prix, on whom long odds were laid. I had been at a supper at the Carlton, in the room off the lounge, at which King Edward and the present King were the Saturday before, and had told them that Merman had a good chance and they backed him.

Next day my grand horse was in the paddock, fresh and ready to run for and win the Alexander Plate, but Robinson was bluffed out of starting the horse by an owner with a competitor in the race, who threatened to object if he won, on some alleged irregularity of entry, and it *was* only a bluff, for when the horse was led away he said, "Of course I should not have." Had I been present I should have laughed at him, as I knew he was too good a sportsman to do such a thing.

Feeling that he had reached his apotheosis after his Ascot success, I retired him to the stud, in spite of Tod Sloan's protestations that he had never been well ridden before, and that he would never be beaten if I allowed him to steer him in future. Robinson also prophesied more gold cups, but I was obstinate, and so at eight years old he ended his racing career, with legs as sound and clean as the day he was foaled. I was very sorry afterwards, for he did not transmit his excellence to his progeny.

To return to Maluma, this charming mare took a year to recover, but won among other races the Lewes Handicap and the Prince Edward Handicap at Manchester, over both of which wins I profited well. Poor Maluma meet her death at Liverpool. She was leniently handicapped in the Autumn Cup, and, with Tod Sloan as her pilot, appeared a certainty if, in racing parlance, "she stood up," and that is just what she did not do. Coming into the straight with the race well in hand, she slipped, broke her shoulder, blood–poisoning set in, which caused her death, and her jockey, Sloan, was rather badly hurt. It was a striking example of the "slip between the cup and the lip," but though I joke about it now, I was very grieved to lose such a sweet mare. Cheiro, the famous palm–reader, nearly a year before, foretold this accident and the month of its happening.

These useful purchases made me open to consider more animals from down under, and Aurum, who was always considered Trenton's best son, was my next importation. He had some engagements to fill over there, and Mr. Wilson and I were to share the stakes. He had just won the Caulfield guineas, was engaged in the Victoria Derby and the Leger, and, as I was anxious to win a Derby, even if it were an Antipodean one, I agreed to the condition that he should remain there to run for the season. But, alas! there is no certainty in racing for he was interfered with in the Derby, cut his fetlock, and finished second to a horse he had already beaten easily.

However, he pulled off all the other races, including the St. Leger, and was duly shipped to England. Being a gross horse, the inaction of the long voyage had made him very fleshy. Nor am I afraid that there is any question that he arrived at Webb's with a doubtful tendon. Unfortunately, he could never be wound up, though William Robinson, who, later, trained for me, assured me he could both fly and stay, and that even Merman, then at his zenith, could not live with him. It was the more vexatious because Aurum proved almost sterile at the stud, and, beyond his very good daughter, Aurina, who beat Polymelus and others in the Prince Edward Handicap on three legs, sired nothing noteworthy. How my trainer got her to the post was a miracle, for she developed a leg about a week before the race, and broke down immediately after.

Another importation of mine was a New Zealander called Uniform, who won me yet another Lewes Handicap, but did little else, although he was a beautifully moulded horse. I cannot complain of my adventurous purchases of Australians, for I won many thousands over them — Aurum being the only exception, and he had cost me the then considerable sum for a racehorse of five thousand pounds.

I observed that there were two types of trainers at Newmarket: the old school, who coddled their horses, kept them close in their boxes, and heaped clothing on them; and the younger generation, who were beginning to believe in fresh air and natural treatment, and who, I think, showed more commonsense. Of the first mentioned was a certain Martin Gurry, who afforded a lot of amusement by his quaintness and originality of phrase. When one of his owners engaged Percy Bewicke (the crack gentleman rider) for his horse at Goodwood, Gurry, who had never heard of him(?), said in dismay: "Oh, dear! I hope he is not a moustached jockey" — his description of a gentleman jockey. This trainer was church–warden of the Newmarket Church, and after a successful meeting presented a handsome stained–glass window to embellish it, and when asked what inscription he wanted put under it, said, "Oh, simply, 'Gurry to God!'"

He was illiterate, but, to conceal the fact from his fellow trainers when travelling to or from race–meetings, he would always buy a paper and pretend to read it. One day he was busily poring over the shipping advertisements, and on being asked what was the news, replied: "There seems to have been a lot of shipwrecks." He was holding the sheet of *The Times* with the little ships printed thereon upside–down.

An inhabitant of Newmarket told me that she took two undergraduates to Gurry's to go round the stables, and was shown into the drawing–room to wait. The old fellow, coming to fetch them, thought it was etiquette to knock at the door of the room before entering. After various offers of tea and other refreshments had been refused, he said persuasively, "Won't you wash your mouth out with a little brandy?"

The most palatial racing establishment at headquarters is Egerton Lodge, over which Richard March has presided since it was built, and where he was so successful with King Edward's horses, and continues to be with the present King's stud. He had two worried moments that I know of, and on each occasion I was able to be of use. The first of these occurred when a change of abode was suggested to H.R.H. by Mr. Arthur James, who also trained at Egerton. Marsh telephoned to me at the Savoy, where I had a flat, imploring me to do what I could with Mr. James. I sent for the latter, and told him truthfully that I considered it a great responsibility for him to encourage the Prince of Wales to move, for which advice he thanked me, and so that incident ended.

The second was when King Edward, the year following Minoru's victory in the Derby, had thoroughly made up his mind to move, lock, stock, and barrel, to Blackwell's inspite of the united entreaties of his manager and trainer.

I was at Regal Lodge for the July Meeting, when, about 11 o'clock on the Tuesday, Marsh rang up to know if he could see me at once.

Out he came.

The King had written a peremptory letter to Lord Marcus saying the move was to be made, and refusing to further discuss the subject. Marsh was in despair, as he said he had grown up with Egerton, and in leaving it he would leave his life's work. I suggested others. "No use," said Marsh. "They know nothing of racing, and have no influence in that direction. Won't you help once more?" Well, I would try.

In the Jockey Club enclosure I met the royal patron. I broached the subject. As I expected, he shut me up, but suggested a visit to Regal Lodge and gardens next day before racing.

Certain enlargements and changes had been made since he had seen it the previous year, and, after inspecting them, we sat in my boudoir with a *gouter* of peaches and hock before us, and, taking my courage in both hands, I referred to the tabooed subject as sportsman to sportsman.

He said: "The Egerton establishment is too expensive. My racing expenses must be cut down. I shall save hundreds a year at Blackwell's." Though, when it came to the point, it seemed only the upkeep of the gardens and grounds that would be less. Anyhow, after a long talk, he arrived at the conclusion that my arguments were *sound*, and that he would lose more than he would gain by transferring his horses to the heart of Newmarket, thereby losing, not only the advantages of the private gallop in the grounds, which helped to win the Derby for Minoru, but also the privacy of his enjoyable visits to his beautiful stables, for an insignificant saving, and, as soon as he got on the course, he told Marsh to stay where he was.

It was a great pleasure to be met and thanked by him and Lord Marcus, both with happy faces, and the latter's characteristic remark — "You are a brick!" — made the slight service I had rendered them worth while.

Lord Marcus Beresford, who, as everyone knows, managed the King's stables and the Sandringham stud, was certainly one of the most popular of the racing lot, and extremely knowledgeable on racing matters. I was talking to King Edward one day at Newmarket, just before a race in which a horse of his called Persistence was to run, and His Majesty called Lord Marcus up to ask if he had any chance, to which Markie promptly replied:

"Well, sir, if Persistence can do it, he has!"

Then again, another of the King's horses, Perrier, had disappointed badly in the Derby, and finished in the ruck, and later Lord Marcus was trying to cajole some foreigners in search of a stallion into buying him. He took them into the horse's box after, and said, "Now this horse should have won the Derby, he was running, well, *second*, but just at the critical moment six others passed him." The buyers, carried away by Marcus' graphic description, signed *"Oh, quel malheur!"* and, I believe, bought him.

He was very angry with the judge once for not giving him a race he thought he had won. He said he ought to retire, but, if he did, the Jockey Club would no doubt select his successor from a Home for the Blind. Perhaps many people know the following, but it is amusing enough to chance. An assiduous race–goer, nicknamed "Half–crown" King, because that was his limit on a race, was travelling from Manchester in a compartment full of racing pals, including Marcus Beresford. The latter took charge of all the tickets, and when the time came to show them pretended he had lost one. He therefore advised Mr. King to hide under the seat, to avoid being delayed through explanations, which he did, only to hear Marcus, on handing the tickets to the guard, say, "Yes, there *is* one over, but it belongs to a gentleman who prefers travelling under the seat." And out crawled poor "Half–crown" King from his ignominious position, covered with dust.

Seymour Portman was another well–liked racing man. He was an official at Kempton Park, and his tact and amiability were proverbial. He was enormously stout, and I heard that one afternoon he went to tea with a lady, and threw himself into a chair in the drawing–room to wait for her. An agonised yell brought him to his feet, and he found he had literally squashed his hostess's pet toy terrier. It was an awkward predicament, but he solved it by stowing that poor little carcass away in his pocket, where it remained till he got rid of it outside.

As far as I am concerned, the pleasures of the Turf do not merely consist in owning horses and seeing them win. I like the routine of racing.

The fresh air, the picnic lunch, the rural surroundings, all tend to make a race–meeting, to me at all events, a delightful outing. Besides, enjoyment is contagious, and everyone appears to be bent on having a good time. Even if bad days follow each other, and all the favourites fail, the plucky better hopes to retrieve his losses until the last race of the meeting is over, and, supposing he does not, is there not the next week to look forward to, when one either has a "certainty" of one's own, or someone else promises to provide one, to get back the money "temporarily lent" to the bookies on "Black Monday?"

Owners are, as a rule, good–natured, and ready to tell modest betters of their horses' chances, provided they keep it to themselves, but if a man has the reputation of being a "plunger" it is not so easy for him to get information. There was an Oriental who used to frequent the various meetings, and who generally turned up at the stall when any horse of mine was being saddled. Judging him as likely to have a pound or so on a race, I always "put him wise."

One day at the Ritz in Paris he came in while I was talking to his wife, and, pulling out a beautiful pearl necklace from his pocket, said quite casually, "I got it for two millions after all." Upon which she replied, "Well, I really did not need another, I already have more than I can wear." And later I saw him taking open banks at baccarat, and was told he never had less than a thousand on a horse! So I was distinctly wrong in my sizing up, and I have no doubt his money accounted for some strangely short prices I got about my horses.

When travelling, I never miss a chance of seeing famous studs, so in the States I visited Haggin's beautifully situated farm near Los Angeles. The journey was made in a tram, along ways cut through orange–groves laden with fruit, but I thought the stock seemed more plentiful than wonderful.

During an engagement at San Francisco I went with Mr. Richard Tobin (now American Minister to The Hague) and a party to the stud farm which sheltered Ormonde. We went by train, and from the nearest station we had about an hour's drive. A well–turned– out coach was sent to meet us, and Dick Tobin tooled the four spirited horses over extraordinarily rough roads with consummate skill, in spite of the deep and wide cart ruts. The groom I recognised as one who had sat behind me frequently when driving with Lord Lonsdale. He seemed very contented with his change of surroundings.

One of the proudest moments of my life came after lunch, when Mr. Macdonough, the owner of the farm, asked me to be photographed holding the celebrated Ormonde. Perhaps my expression was a little strained, but I was told that he had savaged a groom a fortnight before. It may have been amazement at the temerity of a mere woman that made him stand stock still. His box was a bower of Marechal Niel roses, in full blossom on January 1st. I also saw Ormondale, who proved to be his best son, then a yearling, and tried to buy him, but he was not for sale.

Happening to be in Austria at the high point of my racing enthusiasm, I asked the Emperor's permission to visit the Imperial stud at Kisber. He was so nice about it, for, besides acceding to my request, he lent me his suite of rooms at the palace, there, and gave all sorts of orders for my comfort. Thus, when we arrived (I was accompanied by Prince Kinsky and Prince Louis Esterhazy), we were met at the small station by a victoria and four barren thoroughbred brood mares, driven by a Cheko in a picturesque Hungarian costume. To say they were full of life is a mild way of describing their antics. However, we arrived at our journey's end in safety.

My maid, who followed in a luggage–cart drawn by four other light–hearted mares, was not so fortunate, for she, the trunks, and the four Hungarian soldiers in charge of the conveyance, were all capsized in a ditch, but she eventually turned up neither frightened nor hurt. I may say they utilised the barren mares in this way for all purposes. Arrived at the palace, I found it very scantily furnished; no carpets anywhere, even in the Emperor's room, where a camp bed, a chest of drawers, a jug and basin, and a couple of chairs comprised the furniture. Later on, my maid dragged in a sponge bath, explaining that our chambermaids, as she facetiously called them, were all booted and spurred, and, indeed, the whole stud was in charge of the military.

For meals we went to a small *auberge* in the precincts, with a sanded floor and one long table, at which we sat in company with about twelve Hungarian officers. The food consisted of *goulash*, and other highly seasoned Hungarian dishes, and the dinner was enlivened by strolling Tzigane musicians. Woe betide them, however, if they played a wrong note, for one or other of the officers (who seemed to be endowed with very sensitive ears) would either belabor them, or catching hold of them by the ear, throw them out of the inn.

The morning after my arrival I was up at cock–crow, looking with much interest on a tan ring in front of my window, round which officers were employed in breaking in young stock. After breakfast we drove to see the mares, about a hundred in each of the immense paddocks. We were conducted to the middle, and then mounted Chekos galloped about rounding them up, somewhat after the manner of cowboys. I felt my nerves rather tired when the mares came tearing along from all four corners, stopping suddenly when they were within a yard or so of us. A lot of mutual biting and kicking went on even then, and perhaps I did not inspect them so carefully as I might have done, but I noticed that they were nearly all chestnuts, and seemed to be rather characterless and light of bone.

The final move was to an open railed–in space at the end of the yearling paddock. This time, luckily, we had the rails between us, for with

Chekos behind them cracking whips and shouting, eight wild yearling colts thundered into the small enclosure at a gallop. It was a surprise to me to see thoroughbred stock handled in that way, and I wondered why there were no "casualties." It must have been very cleverly engineered, and not so dangerous to them as it appeared, and it was certainly a thrilling moment. The stallions, of which there were seven or eight housed near the palace, were not a grand lot. I think Kilmarnock was the star.

Presently there came a lull in my racing activities, for, lured by Arthur Collins to play in *The Sins of Society* at Drury Lane, I returned to the Stage, and afterwards toured again in America. All this time I kept my racing going, as well as a stud farm at Gazely, near Kentford, from which I hoped for great results; but apparently my luck did not lie in that direction, and after a few years I gave up attempting to breed blood–stock.

My next trainer was Fred Darling, as I felt, with the facilities at Regal Lodge, I should like again to train privately. His father, Sam Darling, brought him to discuss business with me at Sandown Park one race day, and I must confess when I saw him I felt rather doubtful. He was about twenty–one or so, but, being rather small of build, he looked about sixteen, still, if his father recommended him, I knew he must be clever, and how he proved it, and has now become a foremost trainer, with a Derby to his credit, everyone knows. George Edwards at that time found his stable over–full, and we made several successful deals with him. Vitange, Shylad, Raytoi, Yentoi, were all bred and bought from either George or his brother, Major Edwards, and did good service.

The two first named, though only aspiring to be platers, landed big coups, while Yentoi, bought expressly to win me a second Cesarewitch, fulfilled his mission with the greatest ease, and, had he kept sound, would have gone on to greater things. Then Raytoi, ridden by Jennings, which we fancied immensely, finished third in the next year's Cesarewitch, after being nearly knocked over the rails, and he vindicated our judgment by winning the Rutland Handicap at the next meeting, starting such a hot favourite that it was useless to back him. Soon after, a split pastern ended *his* career.

Two nice mares I owned at that time were Alspice, who broke down when favourite for the Derby Cup, and Maud Mackintosh, a delightful filly who went out every Saturday for some time, and regularly won her race. She was my great pet, and when she fell dead in the paddock at Newmarket after a race, from heart– failure, I went into a corner of the paddock and cried. All the aforementioned accidents happened the same autumn, and within a short time of each other — a sure sign that, after my twenty odd successful years on the Turf, the pendulum was swinging the other way with a vengeance. So I decided to give the game a rest, and Fred Darling went to Germany, to train as successfully on that side as in England.

Other useful horses I owned at different times were Gazetteer, Smilax, Brayhead (who won a Liverpool Cup for me), Vergia (who was homebred), Joe Chamberlain, Calgary, and Bridegroom, who missed winning a second Jubilee by the shortest of heads.

Chapter
19

When war was declared I happened to have an engagement in the States, where I spent three seasons, and there I took part in benefits for the wounded in most of the big cities, sometimes travelling a long way to do so, for that was the only help that I could give. Each summer I made the voyage home more or less *un*comfortably, but in 1917, when the submarine war was at its height, how to get back to England became a problem. The English and American lines were considered out of the question for women, and perhaps I am not cast in a heroic mould, for the idea of a prolonged tussle with a submarine, during which I should have to sit, wrapped in my life–saving indiarubber suit, patiently awaiting the result, did not appeal to me. Furthermore, it might take weeks to cross the Atlantic with a convoy.

Still, home is home, and I was desperately anxious to get there. Certainly plenty of boats of other nationalities were available, but the choice was difficult. Finally the Spanish line was decided upon, and I secured a cabin in a vessel of about ten thousand tons, not in its first youth by any means.

Scheduled to leave New York on September 1st, we actually got off on the eighth, and that through the fortunate circumstance that Baron Moncheur, head of the Belgian mission to the States, was to be a passenger, and used his influence with Washington to obtain the ship's release, a concession which, after America's entry into the war, was apt to be withheld indefinitely. He himself was smuggled on board as the ship weighed anchor, for the Germans were thought capable of sinking even this relic of the Armada to drown him.

There was an army of rats traveling with us, and the very first morning I awoke to find that a hole had been gnawed by them in my friend Mlls. Guillou's skirt, which had been hung on a peg. The major–domo, naturally very surprised (?), had the grace to change the cabins, but with no better result, and during the whole voyage they kept us company, subsequently, however, confining their attention to the peaches I purposely placed within their reach. Other disagreeable cabin mates were cockroaches, centipedes, etc., loathsome things that crawled up and down the wall night and day. Still, weighed in the scale against submarines, they were less dangerous, if almost as unnerving.

The food was curious, and seemed to consist mainly of mixtures of rice, pimentos, and tomatoes. Everything was served haphazard, fish coming quite later in the varied repast. I was the only Britisher abroad, and at one table of eight persons I counted six different nationalities, French, Japanese, Cuban, American, Canadian, and Spanish, dining together.

Until we were near the Azores we were lulled in security, then someone raised a small panic by declaring with authority that all floating mines eventually found their way to and congregated off the coast of Spain, and that numberless vessels had been "sunk without trace."

After this somewhat startling information life–belts were kept handy and the passengers alert. The steerage was crowded with picturesquely garbed Spanish labourers returning home to the Peninsula from Cuba, etc., with their earnings, and a wild lot they were, so much so that we felt that, although all was well in fair weather, it would be a case of each for himself in a predicament. We reached our objective, Vigo, notwithstanding the gloomy prophecies of the passengers, there to find a strike of railway men existing in Spain, and the military in charge of the trains. The horror of the journey to Madrid still lives in my memory, for the soldiers driving, seemed to treat signals with complete disregard, and we once pulled up with a jerk, to find our train nose to nose with another coming the opposite way on the same line of rails.

We were all huddled in a Noah's Ark coach, the like of which I have never seen, benches and seats of different sizes and shapes being strewn about the floor in an aimless fashion. Our only light was one small oil lamp, which gave up the ghost early in the night; no means of washing, and no food except what one could grab in a three–minute wait at the station, with a great risk of being left behind, and, indeed, we shed a good many passengers in this manner. After this thirty–hour crawl (for we progressed at tortoise speed), I remained a week in Madrid, spending all the daylight hours in the Prado gallery, where the Goyas entranced me.

During my short stay in Spain, I was to a certain extent able to gauge the attitude of the average Spaniard during the war, which the following conversation overhead by me may serve to illustrate. A German and a Frenchman were engaged in a heated discussion in a fashionable cafe, where I happened also to be dining, when a Spaniard murmured in a bored voice: "I don't understand why you are quarrelling — you are both foreigners!"

Our journey from Madrid to the frontier was equally terrifying, for our train was really sandwiched between two accidents, one of which had occurred the night before, and the other happened the night after, both causing loss of life, so that I was thankful to reach France and civilisation.

Once safely back in England, I played at the Coliseum for a time, and was on the stage at the moment that a bomb demolished John Bull's office. The crowded audience felt it was uncomfortably close, and the gallery made such a din that not a word of the play could be heard. We went on steadily with our lines, and I was surprised to receive an ovation from the audience at the close. Subsequently, the stage manager, waiting in the wings, seized my hands and thanked me for my *sangfroid*, which he said had averted a panic. But as the stage of the theatre, with its glass roof, was the real danger–spot, the auditorium being protected with sand bags, I do not know why the packed gallery made such a fuss.

This, however, was not my first experience of threatened panic in a theatre. We were playing at Bridgeport, Conn., where the great showman, P. T. Barnum, lived, and he happened to be in the stage box that evening. The play presented was W. S. Gilbert's *Pygmalion and Galatea*, and I had just commenced my scene with Chrysos in the second act when I heard sounds of hurrying footsteps behind me. Thinking it was caused by some clumsy stage hands, I went steadily on with my lines, until several people in the audience rising to their feet caused me to look round, and then I saw that the whole of the back of the scene was one sheet of flame. On top of this discovery the stage manager rang the curtain down. That was the signal for general alarm in front.

The whole house rose to its feet. The women began to scream and the men to shout. My stage manager had made a fatal mistake. A glance showed me what had happened. The great baize curtain that hid the pedestal on which I posed as the living status Galatea had caught fire, but the firemen were already subduing it, and the danger had appeared much greater than it really was. I rushed to the deserted prompt entrance, and rang the curtain up again, thus showing the audience that there was no further cause to fear, and that, in any case, I was between them and the flames, and, pulling Chrysos back on the stage, I went on with my lines. The first sentence happened to be: "Are you very ill?" which seemed so apposite to the audience, coupled with my presence of mind, that they broke into mingled laughter and applause, and sat down quietly to enjoy the rest of the play.

About half an hour after all this excitement, Barnum, who had apparently been sitting quite still in his box, crept on to the stage to ask if the fire was really out!

Certainly I seem to have had an unusual acquaintance with fire, for, besides the Park Theatre conflagration, of which I have already spoken, the Theatre at Oswego, New York State, was burnt down in twenty minutes while I was playing there one bitterly cold night. We were all ejected into the snow, but the crowded audience showed such courage and calmness that there was no loss of life.

One other experience of this sort might be of interest to record. When I was about eleven years old my father brought home, as a novelty, a small spirit stove, which proved so interesting to me that I insisted on cooking some little delicacy over its flame. I wore my hair hanging loose about my shoulders, and in a moment it had caught fire; I ran to my mother in terror, and, in spite of her fright, she succeeded in extinguishing the blaze. My face and neck were horribly burned, but, owing to the wonderful nursing and care I received, not the slightest scar was left.

After my experience at the Coliseum, I retired to Regal Lodge, and spent the last year of the war cultivating vegetables, with the help of the village girls at Kentford, until the Armistice brought us back to life again.

Never shall I forget the village blacksmith running into the stable–yard shouting, "War–r–r–r is over!" in his best Suffolk, and my tempestuous rush to London to join in the celebration. After a world–shaking cataclysm such as we had just been through, ideas and plans which before had seemed of such paramount importance now seemed small and trivial by comparison, and for the time being I found my interest in both acting and racing lapse. I felt weary of the responsibility of owning houses, and was glad enough, when I found eager purchasers to pass mine on to others.

In that condition of mind I came, the following January, to the warmth and cheerfulness of the South of France, and drifted to my favourite Monaco. Here, much to my surprise, the old mania for possessing a home in any land to which I had taken a fancy reasserted itself, and I found myself, who had just been at such pains to get rid of all responsibility, hunting high and low to acquire new ones.

I was accompanied in my strenuous search by an indefatigable house–agent, who, after showing me over all sorts of luxurious but conventional villas, pointed out to me, half–way down the ravine of St. Devote, a bungalow belonging to one of his *croupier* friends, which, on amount of its unique position, I immediately annexed.

Where there is a will there is a way, even in house construction. I scooped wine–cellars out of rocks, kitchens out of rubble– heaps, and , coaxing a side of the ravine from the Monegasque Government, I made of it one of the most picturesque gardens in the principality. My little house, clinging to a rock, is ideally situated betwixt mountain and sea, and it is impossible for one who loves Nature to be other than happy in such surroundings. My hanging gardens I tend myself — as far as they need gardening, for the inaccessible part of the precipitous rocks clothe themselves with lovely alpines, stocks, maindenhair ferns, wild orchids, wallflowers, bluebells, snapdragons, masses of geraniums, and other unbidden but welcome guests, and even cinerarias perch themselves on lofty ledges, and do better there in their wildness. In the cultivated portion irises, mimosas, daturas, cyclamen, primulas, and all the lovely winter blooming flora thrive.

Small successes sometimes please one out of all proportion, and last year, when I was awarded the first prize (a medal) by the Horticultural Society of Nice for the best garden on the Riviera, minded by *"La proprietaire,"* I was a very proud woman.

There are in effect two Monte Carlos. The one of tinsel and garishness, of fortunes made and lost in the close atmosphere of the Casino Rooms or the Sporting Club, and that other Monte Carlo, known only to those who come and make it their home. For among the green profusion of foliage clothing its mountain–side are many lovely villas, owned and occupied by people of all nationalities. Towering on the heights above me is the Persian palace built by Prince Mirza Rizza Khan, where he lives with his family. He is a poet, and collector of *objects d'art*, as well as a great diplomat, and one part of his beautiful house is given over to an extraordinarily fine collection of Persian enamels and antiquities, which he generously allows the public to visit. Close at hand is the Villa Khelim, which belongs to a Turkish General, Sheref Pasha.

A colony of Dutch, as well as English and Americans, have settled in the principality, so that Monaco is living up to its reputation as a *rendez-vous* of the world. Among the villa residents is the Baroness Orczy (Mrs. Montague Barstow in private life), and her delightful Italian garden, with its wealth of flowers and its tinkling fountains, is a fitting accompaniment to her tales of romance and adventure.

At Menton–Garavan, near the Italian frontier, lives that genius, Blasco Ibanez, whose remarkable novel, *The Four Horsemen of the Apocalypse*, is the most widely read book in the world except the Bible, and must be recognised as the greatest pro–ally propaganda written during the war, and indeed we had no stouter champion of our cause than the author in any neutral country. The work has been translated into every language, including Chinese and Japanese.

It is curious to see how these self–made exiles transplant a bit of their own country to the adopted one. The English love their chintzes and yew hedges, the French stick to their brocaded walls and period furniture, and at Fontana Rosa, Blasco Ibanez, with his Moorish cinema–theatre, his rose–hung *parrals*, his fountains, his Valencian tiles, has made of his garden a veritable bit of old Spain.

Artists, above all, love this beautiful shore, and there is the pathetic story of the recent death of Arthur Burrington, the water colourist, who spent so much of his time here. He fell dead at his easel, while painting in the woods, and, as his body could not be moved without the consent of the authorities, the peasants placed candles at his head and feet, and watched over him.

What a wonderful cathedral in which to lie in state, with tall pines as the pillars, the blue Italian sky as the dome, birds as choristers, and the simple people he had known and loved as the principal mourners.

A witty Frenchman thus classified for me the other day the four principal resorts of the Riviera. "Cannes for a cure; Nice to amuse oneself; Monte Carlo to be ruined, and Menton to be buried in" was his comment. But this last seems to me an insult to the "Pearl of France."

There is yet another classification, also by a Frenchman, which likens Cannes, Nice, and Monte Carlo, to the World, the Flesh, and the Devil. Again I take exception to this stigma on Monte Carlo, for here I am, after four consecutive season in my Monte Carlo home, better physically, and quite sound financially.

Not that I object to a mild flutter myself at the Casino or Sporting Club, both within a stone's throw of my villa, and I find it sometimes most amusing to watch others and their systems. One gambler risks his money according to the stars; another by mathematics; a third is guided by time, and excuses her losses by the clocks being fast or slow, lamenting that she goes to bed too late to get up in time to "take the sun." The astrological gambler says when Saturn is in Venus one should play *inverse*, and when the moon turns her face towards Mars one can only wait for a change of mood, and so on.

Naturally, if one plays with fire one is apt to burn oneself, and it is only unreasoning people who imagine that Monte Carlo, with its luxurious gardens and sumptuous Casino, is maintained to enrich visitors. But there *are* occasionally very large sums won and taken away by people who are wise enough to leave before they lose their money, for the pendulum swings invariably from good luck to bad in gambling as in life.

In my own case, as these Memoirs show, I have had a fair share of both. Born in the sign of Libra, the scale has tipped both ways for me.

In these recollections I have striven to give the story of my experiences and career, and it must be born in mind that I have dealt with the late Victorian and Edwardian period, so that they may appear mild to some who are looking for sensation. The fact is that what was considered *risque* and compromising then would pass unnoticed in the present day.

As an example of this, I quote from an American newspaper of twenty years ago:

> "Lily Langtry astounded the guests of the Granada Hotel by smoking a cigarette in the dining–room."

The Marchioness of Ripon, not long before her premature death, remarking on the changed habits of society, summed things up by saying: "In our day women *hid* their *lovers'* photographs, and put their husbands' on the mantelpiece. Nowadays they *display* their lovers' pictures, and bury their husbands' in the bottom of their boxes."

I am so glad that Richard Le Gallienne has undertaken to write a foreword to my book, because he is a Channel Islander, because we have always been warm friends, and, above all, because, being so great, he will be lenient. I cannot say all I think about him, but, indeed, he is the most companionable genius I have ever met, and I think it is hard on the world that he should bury himself in the Adirondacks. The last time we met was at a supper given to me by Belasco, on the eve of my departure from New York, at which he surprised and enchanted me with a charming poem written in my honour, embossed and illuminated on white vellum, and I think, as he has so kindly consented to write the foreword, I cannot do better than to use this poem from the same pen to put finis to "the days I knew."

To Mrs. Langtry on her Departure from America.

I do not bring you flowers,
Or singing birds,
To say farewell,
Nor even words;
Nor to the altar of your eyes
Do I bring signs;
Such antiquated tribute
To the youth
Of the eternal Spring
I do not bring.
And, surely — stars above! —
I bring you not
That miracle called love:
All I can bring —
The one gift worthy you —
Is to bring back again
The wonder and the joy and the delight

278

Lillie Langtry

Of mortal eyes that saw a little while
The loveliness immortal.
I that am poor in all that is not you,
What can I do
Saving bring you back yourself as offering!
Had I but pain
Then would I bring that too —
Alas! there is no pain
For me and you.
So all bring,
As tribute to your feet
Is that most precious thing
The joy you gave,
Indifferently sweet
As some bright star,
That shines alike on all,
And shines for none alone;
Shines but for shinings' sake
In the high heaven afar.
Fair star, too soon to sink
Behind the sea,
My little hoard of star–dust
Here I bring,
As offering:
You unto you — from me.

RICHARD LE GALLIENNE

FINIS

279

EPILOGUE

If an attempt was made to do even a brief biography of all the friends and acquaintances Lillie Langtry made during her lifetime it would take a separate volume in itself to complete the task. But herewith are some brief bios of some of the people that took part in "The Days I Knew," starting with the illustrious lady herself.

LILLIE LANGTRY - Lillie lived her remaining days at her villa in Monaco, tending to her flower garden and sometimes visiting the casino in Monte Carlo, where she reportedly became the first woman to break the bank. She died of influenza on February 12, 1929, at the age of 75. At her bedside was her butler's widow, Mathilda Peat. As she had requested, Lillie was buried in the graveyard of St. Saviour's Church in Jersey, the church where her father had been rector. She was survived by her estranged husband, Sir Hugo de Bathe, whom she had married in 1899, her daughter Jeanne Marie and her grandchildren. In her will, which she had changed just three months before her death, she provided for her daughter and grandchildren and Mrs. Peat. She left personal items to the Jersey Museum but left nothing to Sir Hugo, who did not attend her funeral.

EDWARD VII - Known as Bertie throughout his life, he was the Prince of Wales and then became king of Great Britain in 1901 upon the death of his mother, Queen Victoria. He was 59 at the time. He died in 1910. He and Lillie Langtry remained good friends throughout his life.

Lillie Langtry

EDWARD LANGTRY - His fortunes turned sour after the family business declined and he began to spend more time fishing than he did with Lillie. In 1887 the marriage was dissolved in California. Edward, an alcoholic, died of head injuries in 1897. It is said he still was very much in love with Lillie.

PRINCE LOUIS OF BATTENBERG - Generally accepted as the father of Lillie Langtry's only child, Jeanne Marie, who was born in 1881. Prince Louis assumed the surname Mountbatten in 1917. He died in 1921 at the age of 67.

OSCAR WILDE - One of Lillie's closest friends, Wilde became a successful writer and eminent celebrity during his short but tumultuous life. Following a celebrated trial in 1895, he was convicted of "gross indecency" for his homosexuality and sent to prison for two years. Wilde was only 46 when he died, in 1900.

JUDGE ROY BEAN - Probably the most unlikely historical character to be linked with Lillie Langtry. Bean saw a picture of Mrs. Langtry and immediately became one of her most ardent fans. Legend has it that he changed the name of the town of Vinegarroon in Texas to Langtry in Lillie's honor. Though they never met in person, she did visit Langtry, Texas shortly after Bean's death in 1903.

RICHARD LE GALLIENNE - Poet and writer Le Gallienne was another friend and admirer of Mrs. Langtry's. He wrote the foreword and end piece for her autobiography. He died in 1947 at the age of 81. He was the father of famed actress, Eva Le Gallienne.

WHAT THEY SAID ABOUT LILLIE:

"Lillie Langtry hapens to be, quite simply, the most beautiful woman on earth."

-JOHN EVERETT MILLAIS

"That woman is a real marvel. And she's so pretty she takes away a man's breath."

-THEODORE ROOSEVELT

"She is complete and perfect and in no way could be changed for the bettter."

-JOAQUIN MILLER

"I was surprised to find...that Mrs. Langtry's thinking is as cogent -- and as cogenclty expressed -- as that of any man."

-BENJAMIN DISRAELI

"Lillie is the greatest there ever was."

-DIAMOND JIM BRADY

"I dare any man to tell me a better name for a town than Langtry."

-JUDGE ROY BEAN

"I resent Mrs. Langtry. She has no right to be intelligent, daring and independent as well as lovely. It is a frightening combination of attributes."

-GEORGE BERNARD SHAW

"What I find astonishing about Mrs. Langtry is that she has a genuine talent on the stage."

-MARK TWAIN

"There shines in Lillie Langtry a purity of spirit. Therein lies the essence of human poetry."

-WALT WHITMAN

"You are the loveliest thing that ever was."

-JAMES McNEILL WHISTLER

"She had dewy violet eyes, a complexion like a peach. How can words convey the vitality, the glow, the amazing charm that made this fascinating woman the centre of any group she entertained?"

-COUNTESS OF WARWICK

"Lillie is a superb actress."

-SARAH BERNHARDT

"I would rather have discovered Mrs. Langtry than to have discovered America. She is the most beautiful woman in the world."

-OSCAR WILDE

"She still had a fine figure and a noble carriage, and if you were walking behind her you might have taken her for a young woman. She told me she was sixty-six."

-W. SOMERSET MAUGHAM

READ MORE ABOUT LILLIE LANGTRY

There are several books available to learn more about Lillie Langtry. Among them are:

"Lillie Langtry - Manners, Masks and Morals" by Laura Beatty (1999)

The author attempts to lift the masks and reveal the real Lillie.

"The Jersey Lily" by Pierre Sichel (1958)

A novel which, in addition to recounting the Langtry story, presents a detailed background of Victorian and Edwardian life.

"Because I Loved Him" by Noel B. Gerson (1971)

A biography whose title is taken from what Lillie told Somerset Maugham about Freddie Gebhardt, who became the most celebrated man in two hemispheres "Because I loved him," said Lillie.

"Lillie" by David Butler (1978)

A novel about Lillie Langtry written by one of the major writers of the Masterpiece Theater series, "Lillie."

"The Diary of Lillie Langtry" by Donna L. Harper (1995)

A unique novel with stories of the people who Lillie met and might have met in her travels.

"The Prince and the Lillie" by James Brough (1975)

A definitive biography of Lillie Langtry and the Prince of Wales. The book upon which the Masterpiece Theater series, "Lillie," was based.

"Lillie Langtry - Her Life in Words and Pictures" by Jeremy Birkett and John Richardson (1979)

Profusely illustrated book of Langtry pictures.

And *"The Jersey Lillie"* by Sonia Hillsdon, *"The Astonishing Mrs. Langtry,"* by Horace H. Booth, *"The Life and Loves of Lillie Langtry,"* by Margaret Plimpton, *"The King In Love,"* by Theo Aronson, *"The King's Mistress,"* by Alan Hardy and *"The Gilded Lillie,"* by Ernest Dudley.

Other books of interest:

"Uncle of Europe" by Gordon Brook Shepherd.

The author tracked down a wealth of unpublished letters, some to Lillie Langtry, in this biography of Edward VII.

Books on Judge Roy Bean which mention the Langtry, Texas story include *"Roy Bean, Law West of the Pecos"* by C. L. Sonnichsen, *"Vinegarroon"* by Ruel McDaniel and *"Judge Roy Bean Country"* by Jack Skiles.

The 13-episode Masterpiece Theater television series entitled *"Lillie,"* released in 1978, with Francesca Annis as Lillie, Dennis Lill as the Prince of Wales, Anton Rodgers as Edward Langtry and Peter Egan as Oscar Wilde, is available on videotape and DVD.

Lillie made one motion picture: *"His Neighbor's Wife,"* in 1913, when she was 60.

Lillie Langtry

Printed in the United States of America
Design: Trans Media Images
Typesetting: Fujimori Graphics
Set in New Times Roman

LaVergne, TN USA
28 December 2010

210369LV00006B/22/A